Italo Calvino
Metamorphoses of Fantasy

Studies in Speculative Fiction, No. 13

Robert Scholes, Series Editor

Alumni / Alumnae Professor of English and
Chairman, Department of English
Brown University

Other Titles in This Series

Italo Calvino
Metamorphoses of Fantasy

by
Albert Howard Carter, III

U·M·I Research Press

Ann Arbor, Michigan

Produced and distributed by
UMI Research Press
an imprint of
University Microfilms, Inc.
Ann Arbor, Michigan 48106

Library of Congress Cataloging in Publication Data

Carter, Albert Howard, 1943-
   Italo Calvino: metamorphoses of fantasy.

   (Studies in speculative fiction ; no. 13)
   Revision of thesis (Ph.D.)—University of Iowa, 1971.
   Bibliography: p.
   Includes index.
   1. Calvino, Italo—Criticism and interpretation.
2. Fantasy in literature. I. Title. II. Series.
PQ4809.A45Z684 1987   853'.914   86-24957
ISBN 0-8357-1780-1 (alk. paper)

To family literati:
Nancy, Rebecca, Marjorie, Avise

Contents

Acknowledgments

I would like to thank various persons and institutions for help and support. I thank Richard R. Hallin, former provost of Eckerd College and Lloyd W. Chapin, the current dean of faculty, for grants for research and typing. I also thank David W. Henderson and Carol B. Parker of the Eckerd College library for assistance with interlibrary loans. I thank the staffs of the Biblioteca Nazionale in Florence, the Library of Congress, and the libraries of the following universities and colleges: Claremont Graduate School, Cornell, Georgetown, St. John's (Minnesota), South Florida, Wells, and Vassar. I also thank my former secretary Jean Cobb Schultz and my current secretary Shirley E. Davis for their help. I am grateful as well to my student assistants over the years: Janet H. Boggs, Sheila Jackson, Suzanne Howland, Colleen Adomaitis, Cyndi Clymer, Martha Klincewicz, Teri Coy, and Terry Wikoff.

For help in completing the manuscript, I would like to thank the office of Edmund D. Pellegrino, M.D., director of the Kennedy Institute of Ethics, with whom I was teaching during the summer of 1986, Marti Patchell, his assistant, and David Miller. I also thank Professor Roberto Severino, Department of Italian, Georgetown University, for reading the typescript. I would also like to thank William Weaver, not for any particular service to me, but for his accurate and sensitive translations of Calvino's works over many years, a valuable service to all English-speaking readers of Calvino.

For support without which this book might not have been completed, I thank Albert B. Friedman and James F. Childress, with whom I did NEH Summer Seminars, Meghan Ducey, Hubertien Williams, Linda Scott, James H. Matthews, Harry W. Ellis, Bernhard Kendler, Denise Der Garabedian, Peter Meinke, my students (who seem to like Calvino), Wilmina Rowland Smith, Harvey and Dorothy Corson, and my immediate family, to whom this book is dedicated.

1

Introduction

When Italo Calvino died of a stroke in September of 1985 at the age of 61, Italy mourned the loss of her most prominent and respected living author. Ordinary readers knew his *Italian Folktales,* scholars had studied his works, and more than one critic has suggested that Calvino would be receiving the Nobel Prize one year or another. The death was sudden, unforeseen, surprising — qualities that often characterize Calvino's fiction. In his last book published in his lifetime, *Mr. Palomar,* the title character, ironically enough, expires in the last sentence. But Calvino was not Palomar and, when he died, he was still writing actively, preparing the Norton lectures for Harvard later that fall. Thus some further work may still be expected to appear posthumously. Throughout his corpus, Calvino was an ambitious, ever-growing craftsman; like Flaubert and Joyce, he never wrote the same book twice.

I first read Italo Calvino in 1968 while in graduate school. I was pleased and amazed: each book was different in subject and technique; each explored new narrative dilemmas. I wrote my dissertation, "Fantasy in Italo Calvino" (University of Iowa, 1971), discussing the corpus through *t zero.* I spent a year in Florence, Italy, supported by a Presbyterian graduate fellowship, and interviewed Calvino at his home in Paris in November of 1971. As the years went by, Calvino's books kept coming and I kept up. (Although he and I exchanged some letters, I have never felt that this study was "authorized" or uncritically favorable.) My discussion of "Last Comes the Crow" appeared in *Italian Quarterly* in the spring of 1981.[1]

My approach to Calvino has been through the rhetorical success of the texts in establishing fantasies for the readers to follow. While his fantasy has brought him the most notoriety, all of his work, whether obviously fantastic or not, can be approached by his skill in leading the consciousness of characters and readers through various speculations. By choosing fantasy as a focus, I have meant to have a heuristic device, a way of asking questions, not a procrustean frame to prejudge the work. Nor do I believe that Calvino felt that fantasy was a technique that he would consciously work variations on, book after book, although he was well aware of his flight to fantasy after working in realistic modes. I believe Calvino's greatest contribution lies in his ability to use the generally contrafactual realm of hypothesis, speculation, imagination, as a way to explore what is possible in literature. For this generally nonrealistic realm I use the word fantasy, without meaning to restrict Calvino's work (or my inquiry) to a subgenre that often has fairly strict conventions and its own historical evolution. I would agree with Rosemary Jackson that "Fantasy, then, has not disappeared, as Todorov's theory would claim, but it has assumed different forms." She continues, "With Kafka and Calvino, 'truth' remains an evasive, impossible object, as it had been for Mary Shelley, Maturin, and Hogg."[2] Thus Calvino is not a science fiction writer in the tradition of Jules Verne, nor a surrealist, following André Breton. When I visited him, it was clear that he felt inspiration from a wide variety of sources, literary, graphic, cinematographic, and intellectual.

In the Greek word "phantasia," we have an emphasis on seeing, on "making visible," which suggests the importance of imagery in establishing alternative visions. I wish to explore how the alternative visions are made visible and plausible through literary elements so that we can explore intensified human desires and the limits of human thought. My emphasis will be on the fantastic dimensions of a narrative itself as a textual construct, for example, the fantasies of the literary characters as models for the readers, and I will keep in mind also the parallel fantasies of readers, which we can only speculate about briefly, and the original fantasies of the author, which are so distant as to be impossible to recover. The author's original musings are not the same as the final product, because of the interaction with the literary medium, especially for a highly self-conscious writer such as Calvino.

The collective meanings of "fantasy" in the *Oxford English Dictionary* raise some problems in evaluation of fantasy through the centuries: is it fraudulent? is it misleading? is it freeing? is it true? These questions persist in Calvino's work, especially in the later fictions, notably *Mr. Palomar*.

Calvino himself wrote briefly on fantasy when he edited a two-volume set of fantastic tales from nineteenth-century Europe and America, *Racconti fantastici dell' ottocento*.[3] (For our purposes here it is not important to try to separate fantasy from the fantastic.) The first volume has twelve tales of what he called "the visionary fantastic" ("Il fantastico visionario"; Eichendorff, E. T. A. Hoffman, de Nerval, Mérimée), while the second has fourteen pieces of "the daily fantastic" ("Il fantastico quotidiano"; Poe, Dickens, de Maupassant, Bierce; see chapter 7 of this study). In his introduction, Calvino wrote that the fantastic literature of the last century could claim a certain modernism in meaning, "as if a welling up of the unconscious, of the repressed, of the forgotten, of the dispelled from our rational attention" (my translation: "come l'insorgere dell'inconscio, del represso, del dimenticato, dell'allontanato dalla nostra attenzione razionale," p. 5). The fantastic, he wrote, shows that the world is complex beyond our ordinary understanding of it, yielding an oscillation between the two worlds. In touching on Tzvetan Todorov's theory, Calvino points out that the Italian sense of fantasy is wider than the French: Todorov divides the fantastic (which can, at some level, be explained) from the marvelous (which cannot be explained). Calvino would join the two realms in his sense of fantasy, and so would I.

I have not developed an elaborate theory, partially because of dissatisfaction with such theories as Todorov's and Eric S. Rabkin's,[4] and partially because of the suspicion that any theory would limit the range of questions we might ask. Perhaps my most useful guides have been Northrop Frye's *Anatomy of Criticism,* Mircea Eliade's *Myth and Reality,* and George Steiner's *After Babel,* especially chapter 3, "Word against Object."[5] In my essays, I usually ask questions in the following three areas. First, what is the literary creation of the fantasy: how is the fantasy established through literary elements? Second, what feelings are engendered by the text? What is the manipulation of desires? What is the psychological appeal? Third, what are the explorations of thought: what ideas, what concepts, what mythologies are suggested by the work? In each of these three areas the questions are a way of illuminating the work and a way of seeing how literary elements, feelings, and ideas are part of the medium into which the fantasy is cast.

For psychological appeal, I look at emotions, both positive and negative; I suggest that there are parallel fantasies, "fantasy of affirmation" and "fantasy of denial," which hold our interest. The uses of thought are both an exploration of concepts and an exploitation of them, a source for themes, concerns of the characters, and dialectics of thesis and antithesis. Thus fantasy in books such as Calvino's is not pure, it seems to me, but mediated by the very medium of the fiction, the language, the characters, and the themes. These aspects of the medium help to make the fantasy vital, full, alluring to readers. I like to think of pure fantasy, or the musing of a speculative mind, as the pointed end of a cornucopia, an origin without any real substance or power, until it is incarnated, down the cone of the cornucopia, into fiction. At the mouth of the cornucopia I see inscribed around the rim the three resources: literary elements, feelings, ideas. The fruits emerge, taking substance and form, in a much more interesting ontology than the original musings. For a fuller discussion of such theoretical matters, I refer the reader to chapter 2 of my 1971 dissertation.

For this discussion, I am more interested in the critical discussion of Calvino's works, with an emphasis on ways he develops fantasy in different forms; thus my subtitle, "metamorphoses of fantasy," suggests that Calvino's art has been an ambitious succession of embodiments, all ad hoc to the individuality and integrity of the works. For all of the striking images and bizarre characters and plots, Calvino's work is always thoroughly thought out and consciously ordered: at least three books have elaborate counting games in their structure. Calvino was a slow, methodical worker who rewrote much, and who, especially in the later works, plotted, calculated, and schemed, we might almost say. When I asked him in 1971 what he was working on, he would say very little, beyond that it was "much thought out" ("molto pensato"—the book turned out to be *Invisible Cities,* in which the numbering scheme alone is an intricate bit of structure). My emphasis is on the artistry that creates the fantasy and the skill that explores many versions of fantastic effects. I am particularly interested in the ways fantasy appears to subsume other realms, even, paradoxically, "nonfantastic" realms, such as realism. For example, the history in *The Baron in the Trees* is a realistic mode of thinking that becomes one of the ways of creating the fantasy of the arboreal hero. The notion of history itself then becomes suspect as an oversimplification, especially in a fantastic context.

How we are led, then, from the known to the unknown, from the probable to the fantastic, from the conventional to the unusual, lies at the heart of this study.[6] The implied question—*why* we are led (what keeps us reading, what delights us, what captivates us)—is less directly faced, but worth keeping in mind, especially with the growth of reader response criticism.

2

Who Was Italo Calvino?

Of modern authors writing in Italian, Italo Calvino (1923–85) was probably the most esteemed. Indeed, he was one of the most respected writers in Europe. He did not have the popularity or the notoriety of Alberto Moravia or Günter Grass; his writing will probably never be made into movies. Calvino was, rather, something of a writer's writer, a close student of literary possibilities and an assiduous experimenter. (At the same time, he was a collector of Italian folktales, which, when published as a volume, drew a large audience.) Calvino was a productive and persistent point in the literary avant-garde of the mid–twentieth century, as he explored linguistic, narrative, and combinatory experiments in his fiction. Some of his later works may remind us of the work of the Argentinian Jorge Luis Borges; both men specialized in polished, intricate, literarily ambitious fiction. As an editor, reviewer, and translator for the Turin publisher Einaudi from the late 1940s, Calvino was in touch with many intellectual, creative, and aesthetic currents, many of which he used in his fiction. His canon, stretching from the 1940s to the mid-1980s, reflects many interests and aesthetics; in the words of a description of a novelist in *If on a winter's night a traveller* (*Se una notte d'inverno un viaggiatore*): the one thing that is the same in different works is that he is different. And yet, amidst the aggressive evolution of his art, there are continuities we may follow; because, specifically, much of the literary interest of his work derives from his uses of fantasy, this study concentrates on fantasy in Calvino's art.

Italo Calvino was born near Havana, Cuba, of Italian parents, scientists doing field research there.[1] The birthdate of this, their firstborn, was October 15, 1923, just before their return to Italy. Calvino grew up in San Remo, a Ligurian town on the Mediterranean, a scant ten miles from the French border. In his twenty uninterrupted years there he completed his academic education through the *liceo* (high school); because his parents were freethinkers, he did not have a religious education. He enrolled in the Faculty of Agriculture at the University of Turin, where his father was professor of tropical agriculture, but completed only the first few exams there. During the twenty months of the Ger-

man occupation, Calvino joined the partisans of his region in seeking to rees-
tablish Italian control. His experience of guerilla warfare in the Ligurian mountains provided material for his first fiction, short stories such as "Last Comes
the Crow" ("Ultimo viene il corvo," written in 1946, published in a collection
in 1949) and his first novel, *The Path to the Nest of Spiders* (*Il sentiero dei nidi
di ragno,* 1947). Following the war, Calvino continued his university education
at the University of Turin, this time in the field of literature, graduating with
a thesis on Conrad in 1947. Active in the literary-journalism spheres of Turin
and Milan, Calvino came to know Cesare Pavese, Elio Vittorini, and the editor
Giulio Einaudi, who published the first book, *The Path to the Nest of Spiders.*
Calvino began to work for Einaudi in various capacities, beginning a long and
fruitful relationship: Einaudi published almost all of Calvino's fiction, and Calvino became one of the directors of the firm. It was an arrangement that many
writers would love to have: Calvino could write his manuscripts by hand, send
them to Turin to be typed and returned for correction; he would edit the typescript and return it for publication. Such a system could be abused by an author
seeking maximal exposure, but Calvino was a strict taskmaster of his composition, writing and rewriting laboriously. His "Note" to *The Castle of Crossed
Destinies* gives a sense of the years of involvement that went into one of his
books.[2]

In the late 1940s, Calvino's political interests were to the left, and he
sided with the Communist party. Questions of social justice appear directly or
indirectly in his earlier work especially, and specifically in his short fiction.
Calvino traveled to Russia in the 1950s and wrote a series of articles for the
magazine *ABC;* he left the Communist party in 1957, after the Russian invasion
of Hungary. Deciding over the years that neither politics nor journalism would
be his career, Calvino turned more and more to writing. He started a novel *I
giovani del Po,* still in the line of social realism, but became dissatisfied with
it; as a break he wrote rather quickly *The Cloven Viscount* (*Il visconte dimezzato,* 1951). *The Cloven Viscount,* with its happy blend of history and fantasy,
was well received: a new dimension to his art opened up, one that would take
him a long way.

In the 1950s, Calvino spent more time in Rome, the cultural center of the
country, and continued his political writing (notably "The Marrow of the
Lion," a paper delivered in Florence in 1955 and published in *Paragone,* "Il
midollo del leone," 66, 1955); he also continued to work for Einaudi. While
editing *Italian Fables,* now available as *Italian Folktales* (*Fiabe italiane,*
1956), Calvino found he had new interests in different forms of story, folk literature, and even nineteenth-century philology. Enamored of the eighteenth
century as well, Calvino wrote *The Baron in the Trees* (*Il barone rampante,*
1957) as a romance parody with elements of political allegory. In the same year
Building Speculation (*La speculazione edilizia*) came out, in a more realistic,
although satirical vein.

Calvino would remark on his need to be writing two contrasting things at the same time. Some critics have taken the two sides as schizophrenic opposites, both in his work and as literary principles, such as realism and fantasy, or classicism and romanticism. Other critics, myself included, take the two sides as poles of a dialectic, stressing the constructive interaction of the two poles, not the disparity.

I racconti ("The Tales"), a 572-page collection of Calvino's stories, appeared in 1958, including most of the stories collected as *The Difficult Loves* (*Gli amori difficili*, 1970), followed by *The Watcher* (*La giornata d'uno scrutatore*) in 1963. The "watcher" is a poll watcher, a narrator who reflects on the social and political lives of the persons voting at the bizarre place he has been assigned to observe. Both books are largely of a realistic texture; *The Watcher* was the last clearly realistic volume from Calvino's pen, with the possible exception of *Mr. Palomar*. In 1963, also, *Marcovaldo* was published, a collection of children's stories about a sad-sack character who seeks the beauty of nature even in the midst of the industrial city.

From 1959 to 1966, Calvino collaborated with Elio Vittorini in editing *Il Menabò*, a journal publishing commentary on literature, politics, and ideology.[3] Calvino contributed several essays ("Il mare dell'oggettività," 2, 1960; "La sfida al labirinto," 5, 1962, and "L'antitesi operaia," 7, 1964), but seemed to find increasing complexity in the issues and a growing resistance to making what he regarded as simplifications. In later years, Calvino wrote less and less on such subjects and even withdrew his own introduction (1960) to the trilogy *I nostri antenati* ("Our Forefathers"; includes *The Cloven Viscount, The Baron in the Trees,* and *The Nonexistent Knight*), which offered an interpretation of the novels. The interpretation itself was surely an adequate rendering, but Calvino wrote to me that he found it too limiting, preferring to leave the reader entirely free to interpret in any direction. His later books, *Cosmicomics* (*Le cosmicomiche,* 1965), *t zero* (*Ti con zero,* 1967), *The Castle of Crossed Destinies* (*Il castello dei destini incrociati,* 1969), and *Invisible Cities* (*Le città invisibili,* 1972), have almost no political message and considerable openness to literary interpretation.

Calvino told me in a 1969 interview that in the 1950s he liked knowing a wide circle of people in Rome, but in the 1960s he kept more to himself, moving to Paris in 1964 (and returning to Rome in 1980). Similarly, his fiction moved from overt external action in the early work to states of mind, cerebral games, and abstract progressions of thought. The late novel, *If on a winter's night a traveller* (*Se una notte d'inverno un viaggiatore,* 1979), uses political questions, but generally in satiric ways. The last novel published in Calvino's lifetime was *Mr. Palomar* (*Palomar,* 1983), which follows the musings of a single character who has no political interests. The last four novels (*The Castle, Cities, If on a winter's night,* and *Mr. Palomar*) are intricately wrought, so that the ways of presenting and organizing the fiction become more important than the narratives.

In 1964 Calvino married an Argentine woman, Chichita Singer, a translator, and settled in Paris; in 1965 the couple had a daughter. Calvino lived for some sixteen years in a town house on an out-of-the-way street in the Montparnasse section of Paris. When I visited his home in 1969, the house was decorated by his wife's collection of African art—prints, cartoons, and reproductions—as well as art by his young daughter. (I believe his interest in modern art is a source of inspiration for his writing; it is a good guess that Calvino controlled the art decorating his books, by M. C. Escher, Henri Matisse, Paul Klee, Victor Vasarely, Albrecht Dürer, and Pablo Picasso. *The Castle of Crossed Destinies* is, of course, a book virtually about seeing art, since it is built on the interpretation of enameled tarot cards.)

Calvino's studio was on an upper floor, overlooking the roofs of Paris, something of a concretization of the conceit basic to *The Baron in the Trees.* It was a large room, with one side full of windows, the opposite wall full of books. At one end was his desk, at the other were a coffee table and comfortable chairs, where our interview took place. For the most part, we found it efficient for each to speak in his native tongue, Calvino in Italian, I in English. Besides being well read in English letters, Calvino visited the United States several times, giving seminars at Columbia University and Harvard University. He gave the Morris Gray Reading at Harvard in the spring on 1983 and was scheduled to give the Norton lectures there in the fall of 1985.

Calvino's *Eremita a Parigi*[4] ("Hermit in Paris," 1974) gives a rare glimpse into some of his ideas about his writing, his sources, his changes in attitudes over the years. (This little-known book is not, to my knowledge, translated into English; indeed there may be only half a dozen copies in the United States, according to the library from which I borrowed it. It is a rare bibliography of Calvino's work that even lists the title.) *Eremita a Parigi* is a 3,500-word evocation of the meaning of Paris for Calvino; it is a personal essay of a lyricism not usually seen in later Calvino, something of an intimate and slightly mannered description of his relationship with Paris. (That the book was produced in collaboration with Radiotelevisione della Svizzera Italiana suggests that the text was originally a radio broadcast; certainly it has the air of a personal monologue.) The title gives the theme: Calvino treasured the anonymity of the big city, not just Paris, but all cities as they merge as interior landscapes:

> My writing desk is something like an island: it can be the same here as in another country. And, moreover, cities transform into a single city, an uninterrupted city in which all the differences that once characterized each are lost. This idea, which runs through my book *The Invisible Cities,* has come to me from a way of living which is by now common with many of us: a continuous passage from one airport to another, making life nearly the same in whichever city that we find ourselves. (P. 9)

As the real world has less importance as a place to write, so too the real world becomes less important as the subject of writing. Calvino wrote that he relied more and more on books as his sources. The world of the bookcases not only took precedence over the outside world, but it became the model for reality: Paris itself was some kind of "encyclopedia," "a museum," "a collective memory," "a library of dreams." Drawing the text to a close, Calvino paid tribute to the surrealists and the small movie theatres of Paris, both of which had freed images to operate on some purer level of desire. The piece is lyric and evocative, gently presenting the abstract figure of the writer as an observer-participant in life, and more observer than participant. The book reminds us of Calvino's range of interests, his intelligence, and his increasing proclivity for abstraction.

It should be clear that Calvino's art drew from many sources: from his war experience, from his intellectual interests, from his aesthetic interests. One of his continous sources of inspiration was the sixteenth-century poet Ariosto, whose great epic *Orlando furioso* Calvino edited for Einaudi in 1970. Calvino said:

> Of all the poets of our tradition, the one I feel nearest to me and at the same time most abstrusely fascinating, is Ludovico Ariosto, and I never tire of rereading him. This poet, so absolutely limpid and cheerful and problemless, and yet, at bottom, so mysterious, so skillful in concealing himself; this unbeliever of the sixteenth century who drew from Renaissance culture a sense of reality without illusions and . . . persists in creating a fable.[5]

Other authors Calvino admired include Voltaire, Edgar Allan Poe, Stendhal, Ernest Hemingway, Massimo Bontempelli, and Jorge Luis Borges.[6] He was interested in the range of art forms, from graphic art to cinema. He suggested something of the breadth of influences upon his *Cosmicomics:* "The *Cosmicomics* have behind them above all Leopardi, the comics of Popeye, Samuel Beckett, Giordano Bruno, Lewis Carroll, and the painting of Matta and, in some cases, Landolfi, Immanuel Kant, Borges, engravings of Grandville."[7]

It is no surprise that Calvino once offered a definition of a novel that emphasizes the notion of combining different sorts of meaning: "a narrative work, enjoyable and significant on many intersecting planes."[8] The notions of enjoyment and significance remind us of the traditional *aut prodesse aut delectare* of Horace: to instruct and to please are the duties of literature. While enjoyment extends throughout Calvino's work, the notion of significance shifted, as discussed above, from direct allegorical or political meanings to indirect explorations of the meaning of significance itself. We might find applicable to Calvino's later works the famous phrase of Marshall McLuhan that "the medium is the message." *The Castle of Crossed Destinies,* for example, is very much about the nature and interpretations of signs; further, Calvino aggressively explores the freedom with which signs may be combined and recombined.

A late 1960s' article "La letteratura come proiezione del desiderio"[9] ("Literature as a projection of desire") discusses the Italian translation of Northrop Frye's *Anatomy of Criticism;* Calvino is interested in Frye's complex, encyclopedic patterns and would extend them even further to include a nonfiction work such as Stanley Edgar Hyman's *The Tangled Bank*. Thus, paradoxically, while Calvino's works seemed to narrow in focus and subject to artificial, self-enclosing worlds, they nonetheless opened onto wider vistas of meaning—the workings of the mind and the possibilities of literary art. Not only was Calvino eclectic in his literary interests, but the title of the essay on Frye contains a phrase that seems helpful in considering the nature of fantasy: "projection of desire." The term "projection" to discuss the interplay of writer, character, and reader in fiction does not require us to be strict Jungians; the cinema's sense of projection is also suggestive.

By the late 1960s, Calvino's reputation was gaining worldwide stature, and critical commentary began to grow quickly.[10] He had, for example, won several literary prizes in Italy, although these, per se, were not of much interest to him; he refused the Viareggio in 1968. Gore Vidal's "Fabulous Calvino," which appeared in the *New York Review of Books* in May 1974, shows something of Calvino's acceptance in America.[11] In this long (some 9,000 words) piece, Vidal covers seven of Calvino's books, introducing them to American readers. An exacting critic, Vidal has excoriated many authors, but this essay is a rare rave:

> I fear I must trot out that so often misused word "masterpiece." Or, put another way, if "The Argentine Ant" is not a masterpiece of twentieth-century prose writing, I cannot think of anything better. (P. 14)

> On his own and at his best, Calvino does what very few writers can do: he describes imaginary worlds with the most extraordinary precision and beauty (a word which he has single-handedly removed from that sphere of suspicion which the old New Novelists used to maintain surrounds all words and any narrative). (P. 19)

> During the last quarter century Italo Calvino has advanced far beyond his American and English contemporaries. As they continue to look for the place where the spiders make their nests, Calvino not only found that special place but learned how himself to make fantastic webs of prose to which all things adhere. In fact, reading Calvino, I had the unnerving sense that I was also writing what he had written; thus does his art prove his case as writer and reader become one, or One. (P. 21)

Vidal, writing in 1974, could not touch *The Castle of Crossed Destinies* or *If on a winter's night a traveller,* of course, but on the basis of the canon through *Invisible Cities,* which he calls "a marvelous invention," he feels that "The artist seems to have made a peace with the tension between man's idea of the many and the one" (p. 20).

Cosmicomics was widely reviewed and gained fame in the United States when William Weaver's translation won the National Book Award for translation. Next, *t zero,* continuing the tales and adding others, probably had a smaller audience. *The Castle of Crossed Destinies* is quite a curiosity, a series of stories told by using tarot cards. There are two editions (both in Italian and in English): a sumptuous coffee-table edition with color reproductions of the playing cards, and one in an ordinary format with line drawings only. The former edition is more interesting but prohibitive in price for any mass audience (in the range of $50). *Invisible Cities* (*Le città invisibili,* 1972) is an elaborately structured series of prose poems, *If on a winter's night a traveller* (*Se una notte d'inverno un viaggiatore,* 1979), a funny mixture of narrative and novel fragments. In reviewing *If on a winter's night,* John Updike praised Calvino's work, suggesting that Günter Grass and Calvino would have but to wait for the Nobel prize to fall into their laps.[12]

Calvino avoided the limelight for the most part, disliking literary competitions and granting interviews only occasionally. Francine du Plessix Gray interviewed him in Rome for the *New York Times Book Review* (June 21, 1981) and captured something of the wit, sophistication, and bonhomie that prevailed in the Calvino household. She described Calvino as "meditative," "self-effacing," "courteous," and "impish."[13] A note he wrote for the Italian edition of *The Castle of Crossed Destinies,* gives a further idea of his personality:

> I was born in 1923, under a sky in which the shining sun and the gloomy Saturn were guests of the harmonious Scales. I spent the first twenty-five years of my life in the then verdant San Remo, which brought cosmopolitan and eccentric aspects into a difficult union with rustic concreteness; from each of these points I remain marked for life. Then I stayed in the industrious and rational Turin, where the risk of going crazy (as did Nietzsche) was not less than elsewhere. . . . Now and then I have known other famous metropolises, both Atlantic and Pacific, falling in love with all at first sight, some giving me the illusion of having understood and possessed them, others leaving me out of touch and a stranger. . . . Finally I chose to marry and live in Paris, a city surrounded by forests of beech and hornbeam and birch in which I walk with my daughter Abigail, and surrounding in its turn the Bibliothèque Nationale, where I go to consult rare texts, using my Carte de Lecteur n. 2516. Thus, prepared for the Worst, always harder to please regarding the Best, I now savor the incomparable joys of growing older.[14]

It seems to me that Calvino often promoted an asymmetrical relationship between himself and his readers: he played something between a trickster, an artist in ambush, a puppeteer, and a secret admirer who wishes to keep us on our toes. In the 1981 interview he said,

> In each of my separate books, in each different part of each book, I want to constantly add to the image that my reader has of me. That is like being a good lover, that is definitely an erotic relationship. And of course there is always something sadistic in the relationship between writer and reader. In this new novel (*If on a winter's night a traveller*) I may be a more sadistic lover than ever. I constantly play cat and mouse with the reader, letting the reader briefly enjoy the illusion that he's free for a little while, that he's in control. And then I quickly take the rug out from under him; he realizes with a shock that he's *not* in control, that it is always I, Calvino, who is in total control of the situation. (P. 23)

The control, of course, is through the words of the novel and not through any force of personal egoism.

Calvino always gave primacy to the literary experience. When I originally wrote to him in 1969 to ask about an interview, he cordially responded that, yes, I could call on him, but he warned me that meeting an author was usually "a big disappointment" ("una grande delusione") since, presumably, the literary achievement was the most interesting projection of an author, not the author's personality or chitchat or responses to questions. My discussion thus focuses on Calvino's literary canon and not on his intellectual life, his psychology, or his evolution of a theory of literature—any of which would be extremely interesting to know and extremely difficult to chart in any detail. (As I was finishing this manuscript, I wrote to Calvino. He responded that he was glad about my writing but that I should not bother with biographical details. "Biographical information never corresponds to truth, above all if such is taken from newspapers," he wrote; "even when the author himself provides the information, it is a question, always, of *fiction,* of invented news." "Only when an author is dead can you undertake a work of *history,* searching through documents, gathering testimony, etc. And then one discovers that all which was written before was false.")[15]

This brief introduction to Calvino's life and work oversimplifies many issues and ignores others completely, but perhaps it suggests that Calvino was a writer who liked, even encouraged, complexity and who enjoyed the notion of infinite freedom in the possibilities of writing, reading, and theorizing. He was suspicious of attempts to reduce his work to formulas and, I should imagine, of attempts to abstract his intellectual and aesthetic life from his work. My approach, therefore, is not biographical. What interests me, and what comes through in translation, are the ways in which Calvino directs the reader's parallel creation of the fantasy through literary conventions, manipulation of desires, and explorations of thought.

3

The Path to the Nest of Spiders and "Last Comes the Crow": Fantasy as Serious Business

This chapter explores the emergence of fantasy in two of Calvino's early works which are generally realistic in texture. After a brief discussion of *The Path to the Nest of Spiders* (*Il sentiero dei nidi di ragno*, 1947), we shall turn to a close reading of "Last Comes the Crow" ("Ultimo viene il corvo," 1949).[1] *The Path* uses fantasy in direct, rudimentary ways; these uses are expanded in "The Crow" to actual bases of the narration. Both stories are set in World War II Italy, reflecting Calvino's experience as a young man fighting with the partisans against the German occupation. *The Path*, Calvino's first novel, helped establish his reputation as a writer of neorealism in postwar Italy, but we can see in it the seeds of the fantasy that made "The Crow" one of his most famous short stories. The fantasy in both stories is not the cheery fantasy of the children's literature in which "they lived happily ever after"; rather we find fantasy that deals with the serious business of being human: maturation to adulthood, confrontation with evil, sex, war, and death. Fantasy can be a way of dealing with the deepest of human concerns.

Critics have often approached Italo Calvino's early writing as a mixture of fantasy and realism that would soon split apart into two distinct modes of narrative. "The Crow" has been seen as a historical representation of the partisan struggle, with, however, lyric and poetic overlays.[2] Carlo Annoni, in his "Italo Calvino: La resistenza tra realtà e favola," suggests that the partisan stories represent two directions in Calvino's work, the neorealistic and the fabulous; "The Crow" represents the latter.[3] Teresa de Lauretis, however, argues against dividing Calvino's corpus into neorealism and fantasy as if there were "divided impulses or irreconcilable interests in the author."[4] Using concepts from, among other sources, structural linguistics, she argues that, on the contrary, realistic and fantastic elements in Calvino's works are in "a dialectic process reflecting his awareness of the very nature of culture as the highest and unique form of human 'doing.'"[5] I would agree with Professor de Lauretis.

The Path is the story of young Pin; he is perhaps twelve to fourteen years old, between the worlds of childhood and manhood. Pin lives in the slums of a Ligurian town with his sister Rina, a prostitute; his parents are dead or long departed. Pin tries to shift for himself, working for a shoemaker, stealing fruit from the market, and trying to join the men of the local tavern by entertaining them with song and repartee. Thus he is potentially in a modest way a clown or an artist, a kind of counterpointing role that the unnamed hero of "The Crow" definitely assumes. Pin has a nascent fantasy of belonging with the men by means of his singing and chatter, but the fantasy is not fully fleshed out by artistry, craft, or practice. In the course of his involvement with the partisans, Pin steals a pistol from a German. As we might expect, the pistol symbolizes for Pin power, war, and, in general, the adult world of authority, strength, and responsibility. But since he buries the pistol for safekeeping, these concepts are not realized by him. (By contrast, the hero of "The Crow" gets weapons with ease, shoots them as much as he likes, and reflects on the conundrums of seeing and destroying, connecting from afar, hitting apparently impossible targets.) The place where Pin buries the pistol is, of course, "the path of the nests of spiders" (the exact translation of "Il sentiero dei nidi di ragno": as opposed to Colquhoun's rendering, "The Path *to* the *Nest* of Spiders"). It is a place that only Pin knows about, where spiders make nests in the earth: "It's the only one in the whole valley, perhaps in the whole area. No other boy except Pin has ever heard of spiders that make nests" (p. 19; "un posto, c'è, dove fanno il nido i ragni, e solo Pin lo sa ed è l'unico in tutta la vallata, forse in tutta la regione: mai nessun ragazzo ha saputo di ragni che facciano il nido, tranne Pin," p. 51). For him, the place is magic: "the magic place which only Pin knows. There he can weave strange spells, become a king, a god" (p. 138; "È un posto magico, noto solo a Pin. Laggiú Pin potrà fare strani incantesimi, diventare un re, un dio," p. 187). Or so he says. Actually, he is still a confused, immature young man: his fantasy of magic never gains power, in contrast to the kinetic action in "The Crow."

There are two brief discussions of fantasy. At the opening of chapter 7 we read that the hungry partisans dream only of food.

> Only when the men's stomachs are full, when the fire is lit, and there has not been too much marching the day before, can they dream of women and wake up in the morning with spirits free and soaring, gay as if anchors have been drawn." (P. 74)

The Italian has not just "women," but "a nude woman":

> Solo quando lo stomaco è pieno, il fuoco è acceso, e non s'è camminato troppo durante il giorno, ci si può permettere di sognare una donna nuda e ci si sveglia al mattino sgombri e spumanti, con una letizia come d'ancore salpate. (P. 114)

The second discussion of fantasy, in chapter 9, is more complicated; Kim and Ferriera are discussing why men go to war. Kim sketches a range of urges, motivations, even fantasies that send men to fight. After parting from his fellow, Kim continues to muse on war and his own reasons for fighting. He thinks, "I love you Adriana" ("Ti amo, Adriana," p. 151), just as other soldiers, be they Italian or German, think of their beloved; he worries that he is not thinking analytically about the battle:

> Now, instead of escaping into fantasy as I did when I was a child, I should be making a mental study of the details of the attack, the dispositions of weapons and squads. But I like thinking about those men, studying them, making discoveries about them. What will they do "afterwards" for instance? Will they recognize in postwar Italy something made by them? (P. 107)

"Fantasticare" is the pivotal word in the Italian:

> Certo io potrei adesso invece di fantasticare come facevo da bambino, studiare mentalmente i particolari dell'attacco, la disposizione delle armi e delle squadre. Ma mi piace troppo continuare a pensare a quegli uomini, a studiarli, a fare delle scoperte su di loro. Cosa faranno "dopo," per esempio? (P. 151)

Calvino has great sympathy for the character Kim; indeed the dedication (missing in the English version) is "To Kim, and to all the others" ("A Kim, e a tutti gli altri"). When Calvino gives him this uneasy mixture of strategic and fantastic thought, it is, I believe, to show Kim's intelligence (in the usual, rational sense) as well as his sensitivity and emotional wisdom about himself and others. I do not wish to comment on this passage or the previous one about dreams further, since these issues are handled with more depth in later works; mainly I want to signal their presence in this first novel as a point of departure: elements of the fantastic are embedded in Calvino's work from the beginning.

In 1964, Calvino wrote a preface to the novel; it is not an interpretation (like the suppressed introduction to *I nostri antenati*) but a discussion of the literary forces that shaped his creation of the story. It is a rather extraordinary preface: Calvino feels that in writing *The Path* he prematurely fixed one version of his war experience so as to preclude other versions, other books: "One book written will never console me for those that I have destroyed in writing it: that experience, which keeps through the years of a life, will perhaps help me to write the last book, and it wasn't enough for me to write the first one" ("Un libro scritto non mi consolerà mai di ciò che ho distrutto scrivendolo: quell'esperienza che custodita per gli anni della vita mi sarebbe forse servita a scrivere l'ultimo libro, e non mi à bastata che a scrivere il primo," p. 24; this and the following are my translations, since the Beacon Press edition of 1957 does not, obviously, have the 1964 preface). Thus, "The literary projection where all is solid and fixed once and for all, has henceforth taken over the field, has made it lose color, has squashed the vegetation of memory," and "The writer finds himself the most impoverished of men" ("La proiezione letteraria dove tutto è solido e fissato una volta per tutte, ha ormai occupato il campo, he fatto sbiadire, ha schiacciato la vegetazione dei ricordi"; "Lo scrittore si ritrova ad essere il piú povero degli uomini," p. 23).

This analysis, written after the trilogy *I nostri antenati* and just before the publication of *Cosmicomics,* shows Calvino's growing interest in the many literary combinations, inventions, recastings, and variations that dominated his later books, even, as he suggests, "his last." As he put it in the preface: "in youth, every new book that is read is like a new eye that is opened and modifies the view of the other eyes or book—eyes that one had had before, and it was in such a new notion of literature that I craved to revive all the other literary universes that had enchanted me from infancy forward" ("in gioventú ogni libro nuovo che si legge è come un nuovo occhio che si apre e modifica la vista degli altri occhi o libri—occhi che si avevano prima, e nella nuova idea di letteratura che smaniavo di fare rivivevano tutti gli universi letterari che m'avevano incantato dal tempo dell'infanzia in poi," p. 17). The favorite books of Calvino's youth included Hemingway's work and Stevenson's *Treasure Island*.

Can various literary worlds be revived? Calvino's famous short story "Last Comes the Crow" ("Ultimo viene il corvo") may signal such a renewal, a revision of his war experience, since "The Crow" presents similar material in a different literary universe than we found in *The Path*. There are some very specific motifs that recur, but with much more symbolic and fantastic power. Besides the obvious expansion of the power of shooting in "The Crow," which I shall discuss in detail, there are some interesting resonances between the two stories that I shall only list here. In *The Path,* the cook strangles a hawk that has served as a mascot for the band of partisans; in "The Crow," birds are shot, first with no symbolic overtones, then with many, as the boy shoots the eagle on the soldier's uniform. In *The Path,* Dritto and Giglia pursue their games of love in counterpoint to the demands of warfare; in "The Crow," the boy's sense of marksmanship is a game that does not fit the partisans' sense of duty and purpose. In *The Path,* nature is a somewhat neutral background, with aspects of mystery and magic and the ability to hide; these notions are expanded in "The Crow." And, for all the expansion of literary evocation in "The Crow," it is but 5 pages long, in contrast to some 150 pages of *The Path*.

I would like to offer a close reading of "The Crow," emphasizing how the realistic and fantastic elements *interrelate,* mutually supporting each other in the development of the narrative. Calvino's exploitation of literary elements takes us smoothly from a realistic texture to a mixture of realism and fantasy. The fantasy of this tale derives from a young boy's riflery, a realistic enough wartime pursuit; while this skill seems at first nothing unusual, Calvino extends it to superhuman proportions. The protagonist is, in E. M. Forster's term, a flat character, an apple-cheeked boy. He is differentiated no further, not by age or even name. We know him only through action. He joins a group of Italian partisans in the woods who discuss dynamiting a trout stream to catch fish. He borrows a rifle, fires it into the stream, and stuns a fish. He has improved on the crude method they were going to use, and they are impressed. He repeats the action and, like a chorus, the men praise his marksmanship. Their continued praise gives the boy further stature, while the narrator, always neutral, does nothing to diminish it.

The sixth paragraph adds a more theoretical interpretation, giving a new kind of support to the boy's actions. We read that the strange separation of the self from objects is easily overcome by "the direct and invisible line, from the mouth of the rifle to the thing." This line is a locus of potential, a hypothesis for a direction of power. As if to make this theory more concrete, the sentence runs on into an example, a falcon, which is immediately shot down, despite "the wings which seemed steady." The falcon falls "like a stone," a disarmingly common simile that makes the bird's demise seem all the more natural. Calvino continues with abstract questions, the kind the boy might ask. (The use of impersonal constructions and imperfect tenses in the Italian helps to generalize the train of thought.) The questions about whether the pine cones would make good targets help to build tension and doubt about whether the boy can hit them. When he does so, his inordinate skill in shooting becomes even clearer, to the point of fantasy. The marksmanship is fantastic, both because of its supreme precision and because of its ability to fulfill a mental conception: the boy hypothesizes or fantasizes the hitting of an object, and then he enacts that idea with his shot. That he is so young and innocent-looking further intensifies the fantastic character of his skill: it is not the product of years of practice.

Calvino plays with the sense of emptiness of space and the direct line of fire to one, two, three, four more objects, at an accelerating rate of fire. This repetition further confirms the boy's skill, establishing it as an invariable norm. Again the men affirm the boy's skill. "This one doesn't miss a one" is said with a sense of awe; "no one had the courage to laugh" ("Questo non ne sbaglia una" and "nessuno aveva il coraggio di ridere," p. 61). In fact, the partisans value his skill so highly that they want him to join them, to serve their military aims; thus the attitude of awe continues to grow around the powerful, apple-cheeked boy.

By the time we reach the sentence that reflects on the joys of going away ("Andare via . . ."), the verb "to see" has been redefined. We might well expect the truism that travel is broadening because one sees new things, but we also know that for this boy seeing new things and shooting them can be equivalent. Distance between him and objects, as the sentence makes clear, is but "faked" since he can overcome it with a squeeze of the trigger. This equivalence is a fiat, what Philip Wheelwright calls the "King's Nod," only here in a destructive form: "Let there be nothing," and there is nothing.[6] The boy does not have to speak, merely to think and point. This superrefined, supernatural marksmanship reaches full fantastic proportions as the boy becomes a little god with an ironic, smiling face and the unerring power to "strike from afar," as the Homeric epithet goes, with his eye and gun. Calvino reaches this level slowly and surely, building up meanings from examples, comments, hypotheses, so that the boy's power can gain fantastic dimensions without disturbing the realistic conventions of the story.

After this early climax in the development of the boy's marksmanship, the realistic demands return briefly to mediate the development of the fantasy. The men make clear that their interest in the boy's shooting is not in the aesthetics of the spatial game, but in its usefulness to their purpose: war. There is a conflict here, since the boy, following his fancy, wants merely to shoot at difficult targets, particularly birds on the wing, presumably because they are more challenging. The men take the rifle away from him when he does not adopt their norms. This paragraph, by paragraph count, is the exact middle of the story; the boy's powers and his variance with the realistic norms of the adult world are both clear.

The next half of the story finds the boy freed of the men, shooting birds, mice, rats, mushrooms. For him it is a game, a game with the boundless potential of such romances as *Orlando furioso,* since he wanders arbitrarily, without obstacle, from target to target: "It was a great game to go that way from one target to another: perhaps you could go around the world" ("Era un bel gioco andare cosí da un bersaglio all'altro: forse si poteva fare il giro del mondo," p. 62). The boy wanders into "unknown meadows," but he does not escape the war.

German soldiers come with rifles leveled at the boy, but upon seeing him apple-cheeked and smiling, they seek to greet him. Instead he shoots one of them. The irony of the dangerous child here combines both the notion of the wanton, playful gods from the *Iliad* to Thomas Hardy with the notion of the powerful child king, as in Virgil's "Fourth Eclogue" or the New Testament. The boy's youth intensifies the fantastic aspect of his deadly game. He rejects both the aims of the partisans and the greetings of the Germans to follow his own whims, and such whims fully accord with the notion of the fantastic as nonutilitarian and arbitrary.

It is a different kind of irony, however, that at this point the boy's game and the efforts of the partisans coincide; indeed the partisans' warfare seems another sort of game by contrast. Fantasy has a way of making everything else look like fantasy also, as in Grass's *The Tin Drum,* in which Oskar, the dwarf with fantastic powers, appears to be related causally to the historical events of World War II. The realistic intrusion of the partisans' arrival—they have heard shots—makes possible the escape of one German. The boy pursues him, playing with him, as a cat plays with its prey.

The last quarter of the story is presented from the point of view of the German soldier as he confronts death. This shift in point of view is fundamental to the effect of the story and to its fantastic elements. First we looked at the boy from the men's point of view. Then we looked down the barrel of the rifle with the boy, enjoying with him his powers. Now we must look through the German's eyes at the muzzle of the gun. The story thus leads us from the growth of a fantasy to an exaltation of it and, finally, to tragic realization of the implications of this fantasy. Once established, the fantastic force is a fixed point within the story that governs all later events.

At paragraph eighteen ("There, for the instant"; "Là per ora," p. 63) begins a technique Calvino was fond of, the presentation of a character who faces an extreme situation and makes hypotheses about it. This technique is especially useful for the creation of fantasy, since the character apprehends and takes seriously a threat of fantastic proportions, affirming its existence and creating his own personal fantasies to deal with it. And since these two mental operations are akin to a reader's reaction (apprehension and interpretation), an author can use the endangered character to direct a reader's responses.

At first the German feels quite secure: he is well hidden behind a large, impenetrable rock, and he has his own weapons, hand grenades. Unsure of what the realities are, the soldier thinks hypothetically, trying to understand his position. His first idea is that since the boy cannot approach him, he is safe. His premise is valid, but he does not know yet how well the boy shoots. His next idea is to escape, but he immediately questions it, wondering about the boy's skill and patience. The soldier makes a test only to find his helmet shot through, but, lacking the reader's knowledge, he does not lose heart. Rather he hypothesizes that a moving target would be harder to hit. When the boy shoots two birds out of the air, the soldier reacts with physical symptoms of fear, much as the partisans in the beginning had reacted with a chorus of praise. There is another acceleration of pace as more birds fall, intensifying the drama. Accordingly, the soldier forms another hypothesis, that the boy would be too busy shooting birds to bother with him. This time the reader himself may not be sure, for he knows about the boy's marvelous accuracy, but not about his speed. The soldier, a careful perceiver and thinker (and thus a better Horatio figure), makes another test. When this test not only affirms but carries further the range of the boy's fantastic skill, the soldier tastes lead in his mouth. This common image of fear has further meanings of irony and terror because bullets are made of lead and because this reaction balances the earlier, reverential comment that there was "a good smell of powder."

Having formed and rejected hypotheses of escape, the soldier returns to his earlier line of reasoning, that he is safe where he is, with his hand grenades. He follows this strategy, throwing one as best he can, and in fact succeeding in a good throw, but the boy shoots this missile down as well. When the German ducks to avoid the shrapnel from his own weapon, he is beginning to act out a concept that becomes clearer as the story ends, that he is his own enemy.

With the arrival of the crow, the point of view is doubled, as if to separate further the German from a comprehensive view of the action. The narrator says, "When he raised his head, the crow had come" ("Quando rialzò il capo era venuto il corvo," p. 64). Then the soldier sees it from his point of view: "There was in the sky over him a bird that was flying in slow turns, a crow, perhaps" ("C'era nel cielo sopra di lui un uccello che volava a giri lenti, un corvo forse," p. 64). It is clear that the narrator, but not the soldier, knows that the bird is a crow—not only *a* crow, but *the* crow; it appears to come as if expected (the title of the story, of course, helps to reinforce this idea). When the boy does not fire, the soldier (and the reader), who has been trained to accept the boy's behavior as normal, begins to wonder, creating a new series of hypotheses to explain why for the first time in the story the boy does not fire immediately.

Although the crow itself is not described as a particular crow, it is differentiated from the other birds as bigger, black, and ominous, a traditional sign of death, since crows are scavengers. That it flies in slow circles around the soldier is portentous, when we recall the linear flight of the other birds. The crow's motion brings a deceleration of action, a prolongation of the tense, unresolved moment. As it circles it descends, circling about the soldier, who becomes a focus for this mysterious development. These circles are not the free wanderings the boy made earlier, but a restrictive encompassing, more typical of an ironic, even Gothic framework.

By this time the soldier's thoughts become more desperate, and the hypotheses become more fantastic, to match the fantastic situation in which he finds himself. Increasingly frantic, he first doubts the boy: perhaps he does not see the crow. He quickly discards this idea and instead doubts himself: perhaps he is hallucinating. Instead, he is destroying himself through his own doubt. Indeed he next frames a hypothesis to explain his imminent (in his own mind) death, naming the crow as the last sign—such is his own fantasy of death, a last resort of his mind to make sense of data that cannot otherwise (certainly not realistically!) be interpreted. His mind controlled by this fantasy, he decides he must act consistently with it, to direct the boy's attention to his own person. Possessed by his own fantasy, the German breaks the realistic frame of his safety behind the rock, jumps up, points at the bird, and shouts. His very act of rising is an ironic aspiring upwards; his pointing at the bird with his finger is feeble compared to the way the boy points at birds.

The next-to-last sentence has several interesting elements, thanks to the values previously established in the story: "The projectile caught him in the middle of an eagle with spread wings, which was embroidered on his jacket" ("Il proiettile lo prese giusto in mezzo a un'aquila ad ali spiegate che aveva ricamata sulla giubba," p. 64). First, the words "il proiettile" use the same device of the definite article we saw earlier ("il," not "un"). The very mention of the bullet is unusual, since previously it had been the locus in space, the line of fire, not the actual bullet that was important; the game was more theoretical than fatal. Now this abstraction becomes concrete, and we follow the realistic implications of the fantasy: destruction, suffering, death. The notions of power that the reader had reveled in are now, quite literally, brought home to the German, over whose shoulders we are forced to look. Next, the adverbial components that specify the accuracy of the shot come as no surprise, since they affirm this power, but they do serve to delay the ironic climax of the sentence. Last, the embroidered eagle that the bullet strikes provides a focus for many meanings. The usual connotations of an eagle are its lordliness and its mastery of heights. Another tradition, as in the Psalms, is its final glorious flight before its death. Here instead, the bird is fixed, sewn to the jacket with its wings spread-eagled in an ambiguous way that could be seen as impotent. Indeed, the bird has been fixed in the sense that it cowered behind the rock with the soldier. If the soldier's leap up to point out the crow is at all parallel to the final flight of the eagle, it would be in the most ironic and pathetic sense. If the eagle is the Nazi Kriegsadler, it is one doomed to defeat—but I do not suggest that the story is an allegory for World War II as a whole.

That the crow, in the last sentence, continues to circle is problematic. Is it the last reflection of the soldier before he dies, or the last comment of the narrator, or both? Will the boy shoot it, or does he no longer figure in the story? If it is not shot, we can assume the crow will conclude its focusing movement by settling on the German's corpse. We do not know. In any event, the crow completes the frame of nature with which the story opened, providing a background of rather neutral value, easily taken for aloofness or detached sovereignty, depending on the reader. The fantasy begins and ends with this simple frame.

What is the fascination of such a story? Why do we keep reading? The answers to such questions lie, at least in part, in noticing how desires are being manipulated. If we thought that fantasy dealt only with good fairies and helpful beasts, we are reminded that fantasy can also treat the dangerous, the threatening. The first part of the story comes closest to the innocent or friendly sort of fantasy, what I call fantasy of affirmation: the boy is friendly and helpful to the partisans, and he has vital, applelike cheeks. We side with him, find his shooting acceptable as a game without ordinary restrictions. It is an easy sort of wish fulfillment to look over his shoulder, to enjoy his fantastic power as if it were our own. Moreover, his shooting is not subject to the moral control of the adults who want him to be a soldier; the boy is free, and we are free with him as we wander from target to target, even into "unknown areas." On the other hand, he has the praise of all the adult characters in the first part of the story; he is accepted, even sought after for his gift. That he should rebel against his admirers further increases his stature and independence. His gift is purer for not being compromised by a practical use. It is a game, a sport that we affirm, assuming it exempt from serious consequences. As a fantastic hypothesis, the boy answers our desires for power, freedom, safety, control, innocence, and an uncanny purity of action. He also personifies our repugnance for narrow-minded adult opportunism. He is a praiseworthy figure who is above the partisans' praise.

But when the boy begins to chase the German we find that an abstract game that seemed attractive can also be most dangerous. The fantasy of affirmation gradually shifts to a fantasy of denial. We find the values to which we readily assented becoming redefined. We may have expected this reversal, of course, since we are used to the tragic concept of nemesis that corrects man's hubris, as in *Oedipus Rex, King Lear,* or *Faust.* But the twist in this story is that the boy is not punished. The victim is a relatively innocent man, randomly selected and unnamed, a *pharmakos,* or scapegoat. The reader is put in the difficult position of having to identify with the ill-fated German. In a sense the reader is punished for affirming so readily an unnatural power, more dangerous than it first appeared. As the German's thoughts work toward his own death, so the reader is hypothetically killing himself as he watches the bullet come toward him, the sort of bullet he earlier took pleasure in firing. The mood of the story changes from an easy, optimistic sense of affirmation to a progressively more awesome fear of a power that seems increasingly sublime, and we move from security toward terror.

When the crow continues to circle at the end, it is perhaps for the reader's death. The contract of the story has been suspended (broken or fulfilled?), and the reader is left stranded in a countryside, approximately where he started, but much more alone. Why should this second, bleaker half appeal to us? Why should a reader consent to annihilate himself on the symbolic level we have been considering? Perhaps the basic appeal is the desire to confront and experience death through the safety of the literary form. The notion of our death somewhere in the future is a fascinating one, which we ignore out of fear and laziness; the literary presentation of death breaks this habit (taboo?) with our permission, encouragement even, since we welcome the chance to reflect on the death of this stand-in, this scapegoat, this mask. Our naive desire to stay alive is fulfilled by having someone else die while we watch, but our deeper desire to know about death is also fulfilled, if only in part, by the ritual presentation of a death. By enacting this rite through reading a fantastic account, we make death more familiar to us in symbolic terms that manipulate and satisfy our emotional sense as no mortician's handbook could.

The thematic power of "The Crow" is largely in its presentation, in story form, of death as the ultimate coincidence of a person and an inexorable, lethal force. The story form allows us to watch a controlled revelation of the nature of this force and to ponder, to reflect, to think about death, nemesis, oblivion. Since we participate in the creation of this force by watching its genesis (at least in this particular situation) we gain some control over it in a mythic sense, in Eliade's terms.[7] This complicity between story and reading is somewhat alarming: we partially own something that we cannot fully understand. As we have seen, this creation uses exaggeration of a realistic skill, extending it to a fantastic degree. Our sense of awe grows with this extension, especially as we follow the attitudes of the other characters reacting to the boy, and the mood shifts as we explore the serious implications of the force. The reduced space between the muzzle and the target is oppressive, not generative, and we may well feel a paranoia that such a skill would destroy, a fear that there is such a mysterious and inexorable sort of destruction possible in the universe. Whether such a force exists per se is not important; what is important, clearly, is that our ability and apparent need to imagine and affirm the possibility of its existence are enough to suggest our interest and concern.

We affirm a kind of truth in our recognition of the fascination of such an ultimate, perfect force, a metaphoric extension of powers we do understand. Moreover, the fantasy is especially forceful because of the suggested partnership of nature throughout the story, from the first sentence to the last. Nature appears to cooperate with the force, sending over birds, providing unknown meadows and valleys, and sending the scavenger crow as a messenger of death. The boy may be the agent of the shooting, but his skill seems mysteriously a part of some larger order. That this order is only suggested, not spelled out, is vital to the story, as a kind of subliminal mood of oppression, as opposed to a simplistic sort of naturalism. The thematic power of the fantasy of "The Crow" could be summarized as the affirmation of our ignorance about and our fear of death, which seems predetermined, an inexorable part of a mysterious and efficient natural system that can be fantastically accurate in its power and brutal in its toying with its victims, allowing them to aid in their own destruction. As we might expect, this discursive formulation is oversimple, too allegorical; the range of truth exists elaborately in the story as a variety of insights we find and affirm for a variety of needs which, however personal, are always human.

4

The Cloven Viscount: Fantasy and the Grotesque

With his *The Cloven Viscount* (*Il visconte dimezzato,* 1952), Calvino continued his narrative experiments on a larger scale.[1] He had been writing primarily realistic short stories and a realistic short novel, *I giovani del Po,* which appeared serially in *Officina,* but the latter left him unsatisfied, as he remarked in his introduction to it. He had taken more than a year and a half to write it, but in the next two months he wrote *The Cloven Viscount,* "to make up for the punishment inflicted on fantasy" ("per rifarmi del castigo imposto alla fantasia").[2] He added parenthetically that he had sought in *The Viscount* "to describe a mutilated and alienated man and his aspirations toward wholeness" ("dare dell'uomo mutilato e alienato e della sua aspirazione all'interezza," p. 331), in a more approximate and arbitrary manner than in *I giovani.* Calvino wrote further on *The Viscount* in his 1960 preface to *I nostri antenati* ("Our Forefathers"), the trilogy of *Il visconte dimezzato, Il barone rampante,* and *Il cavaliere inesistente.* Some of the commentators, especially J. R. Woodhouse, have used this preface at great length, but Calvino himself tired of it and omitted it from later editions.[3] The preface is certainly sensible enough, perhaps too sensible, since it limits the theoretical scope of the *novella.* Calvino was a good critic of his own and others' work, but he preferred to see his works as "bouteilles jettées à la mer," free for anyone to read and comment upon, without the limitations of authorial intent.[4] Thus the critical statements of the preface (and of the critics who follow it) are not so much wrong as limited.

The fantasy of *The Viscount* begins abruptly, in contrast to the slowly built-up fantasy of "The Crow." A cannonball cuts a man exactly in half, not only physically but, it seems, morally. One half is decidedly good, the other evil. The peasants in the story are divided as well; I shall call them the "good half" and the "evil half," the names given by the peasants, commenting later on the extent to which the names are inexact. This division is fantastic not only in medical and biological terms, but also in psychological and moral terms, and there are many physical and mental details that are left unclear. (Some are ignored; others, like sexual problems, are pleasantly ambiguous.) Such an immediate presentation of extreme fantasy gives the reader an early choice of whether or not to continue; the interest of the book will be less in the extension of the unknown to the unknown as in "The Crow" and more in the implications of the fantasy within the relatively realistic world of the novel.

The fantasy of "The Crow" is relatively easy to discuss because it is slowly shaped and has a clear central abstraction to which everything else relates. There is, furthermore, a unified direction of mood, and an ultimate tragic conclusion. In *The Viscount,* however, the fantasy is harder to discuss in an orderly fashion because it is so disorderly itself and because, strangely enough, it has allegorical pretensions that are parodied within the story. *The Viscount* seems to have a clear direction, but an allegorical reading will fail to account for a good deal of this story, the manipulations of expectations, the changes of mood, the mixed nature of the conclusion. The central question is the nature of the grotesque. Not only is the grotesque a difficult enough notion itself, but this novella does some surprising things in testing and redefining the term.

We may start with some of Wolfgang Kayser's ideas on the grotesque to describe evil in this story, but the novella pushes us beyond this point of view. Kayser's study, *The Grotesque in Art and Literature,* emphasizes the more horrible aspects of the grotesque; if there is humor, it is a humor to be transcended by the deep forces of the horrible.[5] But in *The Viscount* the opposite happens: we start with a brutal setting of war, full of grotesque effects lightly tinged with macabre humor, and we follow the evil Medardo for about two-thirds of the book. Then, with the arrival of the good half of Medardo, the book turns into a lively dialogue, not only of the two halves, but of grotesque and humorous effects. Finally, the many reconciliations, reintegrations, and restitutions at the end give us a mythos of comedy, as Northrop Frye describes it. Kayser's theory of the grotesque is unable to account for this movement, but a discussion in terms of fantasy can treat both the dark and light sides and, most important, the mixture of the two.

In discussing the graphic arts, Kayser suggests a distinction between the "fantastic grotesque" and the "satiric grotesque" (p. 173). Although his vast historic and generic scope does not allow him to explore this distinction at length theoretically, it is clear that for him the "fantastic grotesque" is the horrible, demonic dream world of repulsive objects created through capricious and malevolent combinations. The "satiric grotesque," on the other hand, is a mode of comic distortion based on cynical and caricatural principles (p. 178). In terms of fantasy, the latter would be a fantasy highly mediated by realism. If it were comical and pleasant, it would be fantasy of affirmation; if it were bitter and tragic, it would be fantasy of denial. If it were serious (to deny Kayser's distinctions), it could describe "The Crow." The other grotesque he describes would be, in our terms, fantasy of denial mediated as little as possible by realism, tending toward dreams of evil or nightmare. If such a dream shifted from evil to good (as Kayser would be reluctant to allow), it would be changing the direction of desire as treated by fantasy, leaving the grotesque within the larger realm of fantasy. Such is the movement of *The Viscount.*

For Kayser, the grotesque has many guises, but there is a constant theoretical thrust toward the ominous and estranged world. Aiming at completeness, he ends his historical survey with a reminder that "grotesque" in the day of Francisco Goya or of Jacques Callot had the meanings of caprice, capriccio, whim (p. 78), but his emphasis of the estranged, frightening world of the grotesque limits his discussion of the lighter side, and his final conclusion can only be that the grotesque is a world of fear and horror. "It may begin in a gay and carefree manner," he grants, "but it may also carry the player away," he emphasizes (p. 187). Kayser finds a positive side at last, calling the grotesque an attempt to "subdue the demonic aspects of the world" (p. 188), but he does not, to my satisfaction, recognize how often and how triumphantly this attempt succeeds.

To discuss *The Viscount* strictly in Kayser's terms would be to misuse it. Rather, the novella forces us to see a closer link between the grotesque and the comic than Kayser specifies. If we discuss the grotesque as a kind of fantasy, the transition toward comedy should be easier. I will follow the usual approach, starting with the creation of the fantastic, using Kayser's final definition of the grotesque, "an attempt to invoke and subdue the demonic aspects of the world" as my entry point. And by "demonic aspects," I mean not just evil in general, but malicious and fiendish forms of evil in particular.

Despite the mixture of grotesque, humorous, and philosophical effects, the creation of the fantastic in *The Viscount* depends upon several ordinary elements and conventions. The style is clear and expository. The narrator (introduced in chapter 3) quickly earns our trust; he is modest, neither ironic nor self-aggrandizing. The first chapter opens in a matter-of-fact sort of way, with a question-and-answer dialogue to bring out the oddities of the war with the Turks. Our first point of view, Medardo, is, like us, a newcomer to the scene; a good Horatio figure, he asks a series of questions of his experienced squire Kurt (Curzio in the Italian). The dialogue brings out by gentle steps that the many storks, flamingos, and cranes now eat human flesh on the battlefield because the crows and vultures have been killed off by the same plague that killed the men they ate; both dead men and dead crows and vultures remain in grotesque heaps. Next Kurt explains that all the cadavers of horses are a result of disembowelment by scimitars; further on the way it becomes the men's turn, he explains.

Up to this point there are two reactions built into the story, that of Medardo and that of the horses. The first, somewhat indirect, is expressed through Medardo's aggressive questioning, which the narrator explains as part of Medardo's youthful confusion between good and evil, his indiscriminate love of life—even the parts of it that are macabre and inhuman. Not only is this confusion between good and evil important thematically, but in taking such aggressive interest in anything new, Medardo becomes an excellent character to explore fantasy with, a daring investigator who will take the risks for us. The second reaction is that of Medardo's and Kurt's horses; Kurt explains that the horses do not like to smell the bowels of the dead horses. The emotional impact here is mixed. There is a primal animal fear of death that helps make more immediate the horrors of war, but there is also the ironic comparison of the horses with the men—who have not smelled anything. The horses have a more biologically realistic fear of war than the men do; the men take death as a sort of occupational hazard. Calvino does not make much of this; fantasy often works best when the readers complete the sketch for themselves.

The rest of the opening chapter continues the introduction to the world of the war without any noticeable technical innovations, except the last paragraph. The squire continues to answer questions, even when Medardo does not ask them specifically, so that we learn about the soldiers' cutting fingers off corpses to get rings, the harem of the camp, the sieving of the earth to recover gunpowder. The range of these details runs from the gruesome to the carnal to the absurd; the soldiers are barbaric, animalistic, ridiculous. Calvino is slowly building up a strange combination of values around the war that Medardo has come to join and around Medardo himself, who takes a vital interest in all he sees. By the last paragraph of the chapter, we may already be feeling a tension between this brutal world of potential violence and Medardo's willingness to participate in anything, come what may.

Chapter 2 opens: "Battle began punctually at ten in the morning" (p. 152, "La battaglia cominciò puntualmente alle dieci del mattino," p. 15). Such a designation is comical, since the battle sounds more like a business meeting or a radio program than the horrendous event we have been prepared to expect. Despite the evident danger, Medardo, predictably, is swept away by his enthusiasm and curiosity; he rushes toward the Turks. Shortly thereafter his horse is disemboweled by a scimitar; this scene is grotesque because of the description of the horse's entrails upon the ground and pathetic because of the horse's show of heroism. The next step, we remember from chapter 1, will be the death of the rider.

Undaunted, however, Medardo plunges ahead toward a cannon, not knowing enough to attack it from the side. At this crucial and dangerous moment Calvino introduces a comical description: the artillerymen are "like astronomers" as they turn their gun. This unlikely comparison robs the cannon of much of the power of its usual connotations of concrete force and material destruction; the artillerymen are players both in the battlefield of vicious soldiers and in the quiet, abstract world of an observatory. The cannon is not the source of flames and destructions, but the receiver of cold, distant light delicately focused for the human eye. This abstraction reminds one of the locus of power between rifle and target in "The Crow." When Medardo jumps toward the cannon to frighten the two "astronomers," he shares with the reader an uncertain estimate of danger. The astronomy simile might or might not have come from his mind in the first place; Calvino avoided saying "it seemed *to him*." Yet when Medardo intends to frighten the two "astronomers," it is his thoughts we read. If, however, we join him in this simile, we also stand aloof in the irony of our, not his, realization of the danger at hand, while he "entusiasta e inesperto," plunges ahead. To have him shot through immediately is something of a relief from the tension built up in these two chapters through the descriptions of war, Medardo's lack of experience and acceptance of everything, the foreshadowing, the comparisons, the strange mixture of danger and humor and of pathos and aloofness.

The break in the text (p. 155; p. 17) provides a shift in point of view from that of the soldiers fighting that afternoon to that of the men cleaning up after the battle that evening, although we still have the continuity of our unidentified narrator. The result is suspense, since we left Medardo flying through the air. We come upon his mutilated remains with only our normal expectations that he is dead. The title of the book, however, and our faith that such a carefully established protagonist would not be wasted encourage us to expect something unusual to happen. What we learn first, however, are the processes the doctors go through to save a wounded soldier, drastic measures that would seem more appropriate to mechanical things. There is a Bergsonian sort of humor in plugging leaks in bodies or turning veins inside out like gloves (p. 155; p. 18). This kind of description is important for establishing the norms according to which Medardo will be treated in the camp. When he finally arrives, the narrator slowly catalogues what is missing, concluding that exactly half is gone and half is saved. The doctors, fascinated with such a "fine case" ("bel caso"), let minor wounds kill other patients while they turn their attention to Medardo alone. (The theme of technical excellence that lacks human compassion recurs throughout Calvino's corpus.) The miracle of saving Medardo is, however, much less documented than, for example, the creation of Frankenstein's monster in Mary Shelley's novel. Calvino gives only a token explanation: "They sewed, kneaded, stuck; who knows what they were up to" (p. 156; "Cucirono, applicarono, impastarono: chi lo sa cosa fecero," p. 19). That Medardo should survive is a leap into the fantastic, a surprise that will call for more surprises. We have been prepared to accept as norms humor, exaggeration, extremes of mood, action, and language.

If "The Crow" moved from the known to the unknown and back again, always emphasizing realistic implications, *The Cloven Viscount* starts out much more directly in the fantastic, then brings the fantastic to a (relatively) normal society, creating a living dialectic. Chapter 3 describes the introduction of the evil Medardo to his native Terralba; this is the last chapter I want to discuss in detail before treating the inhabitants of Terralba. The Terralbans know even less than the reader; they are a whole chorus of Horatios who must encounter, question, accept, and evaluate Medardo in this new condition. First Calvino establishes a specific point of view, that of the narrator, in Terralba, making clear the narrator's youth. Next we have a brief sentence full of atmospheric details, standard melodramatic stage directions: a dark October evening, with covered sky. The narrator and his friends are harvesting grapes; this activity not only gives local color, placing the people close to the land, but it also marks the end of the life-giving summer and the beginning of autumn, in preparation for the winter of Medardo's bizarre reign.

The Terralbans have been awaiting Medardo, thinking every sail might be his, building the tension and expectation. They know he has been horribly wounded, but not the exact extent; we know the physical extent, but not the implications. We could guess from our own experience the implications of such impairments as blindness, loss of legs, or paralysis, but a fantastic injury is something else. Our own fantasy may jump ahead to picture what will happen next, but more likely we are content to wait, trusting the author's ingenuity and control. Everyone comes out to meet Medardo. Such a crowd, a small society, immediately creates the norms: Medardo is to be welcomed by a curious, suspenseful group. Only the old viscount, Aiolfo, does not come to greet him; he is a recluse, an eccentric lover of birds.

In the dramatic scene that follows, we can see the importance of visual details in creating the fantasy that will control the book. Through the villagers we see first an eye, then a hand. Finally Medardo leaps to his "feet" (one of which is a crutch). He has resurrected himself in stages: a dot of life, a limb, a body. The face is halved, but the crowd cannot yet see the body, because of the drapery. Then this too is revealed; Medardo's empty half is like a ghost, a simile that will have further meaning later. Calvino accents the discovery with a branch groaning in the rising wind, a wind that blows back the cloak. And then, in what may be a parody of nature's reaction to the picking of the fruit in *Paradise Lost,* the animals react to the horrible sight. Calvino builds the climax: the goats shuffle uneasily; the pigs, "more sensitive," shriek and run; and the crowd can no longer hide its fear, Sebastiana crying out, "My son!" and then "Wretched boy." The mood of this melodrama is mixed; exaggerated terror is carefully manipulated and parodied. Calvino had used horses in chapter 1 to give their reaction to war, but without the continuity between man and beast we find here. That the pigs are "more sensitive" is not, as far as I know, a biological fact, but rather another instance of Calvino's deft use of hypothetical premise.

Medardo seems physically able, mentally alert, but will he be able to return to his castle as a social and political leader? Kayser's idea of the grotesque as estranged must be mediated here by the narrative aim to play off the fantastic Medardo against a community that is, at least so far, normal. When Medardo insists on paying the stretcher-bearers only half the expected sum, we know that his halved brain retains a definite acuteness. He is still an active person, physically and mentally, and throughout the book he will act suddenly, with a speed and surprise that give him an aura of constant energy. As Kayser notes: "Suddenness and surprise are essential elements of the grotesque" (p. 184).

Although the chief fantastic device of this novella is the dual lives of Medardo, we learn about them almost entirely from other characters, not through Medardo's thoughts. Some of these characters are a bit fantastic themselves, and they vary in their ability to come to an understanding of Medardo. In general they are flat characters, having one or two motivating urges, useful chiefly for the development of the fantasy. The old nurse, Sebastiana, for example, is something of a carefully managed cliché. She is a Mother Earth figure, both lover and nurse. Having closed the eyes of many, she is knowledgeable about life and death. It is she who first recognizes that the half of Medardo that has returned is the bad half, and she is the only person who will stand up to him and bawl him out. Thus she provides the strength of moral judgment that Aiolfo might have given, until Medardo turns against her as well. A strong and resourceful figure, Sebastiana sets many of the moral norms of the book: patience, kindness, strength in declaring what is right, and ingenuity in difficult situations. Her banishment to the leper colony lets Medardo run unchecked, but her return allows her to attend his resurrection. It is she, in fact, who sees the first signs of life in him again. As a character of experience and moral strength, Sebastiana is important in defining the fantastic Medardo and in limiting his power.

Sebastiana is removed from action at the end of the first half (by chapter count) of the story; the first paragraph of the second half of the story presents us with Pamela, another, but much younger, primal female. A shepherdess, she combines the standards of pastoral virginity with the shrewdness and emotional responses of Samuel Richardson's Pamela. She interprets immediately the signs left by her unusual lover, knowing that half a bat and half a jellyfish mean an evening rendezvous with Medardo at the seashore. Like Sebastiana, Pamela has no delusions about Medardo's nature. When her parents try to smooth things over, suggesting that the viscount has improved, Pamela knows better (p. 199; p. 58). Like Saint Francis with his animals, like Esmeralda with her goat, and like Aiolfo with his birds, Pamela retreats from the world of people who cannot understand her and lives out her own fantasy in the forest, courted by the evil Medardo and, later, by the good Medardo. By her native common sense and openness, she is the first to make clear (although Dr. Trelawney has realized it) that there are two Medardos, and she is the first to declare that the good one is too good, too tender, too meddlesome. She has little else to say for the rest of the book, as she waits patiently, hoping for the best, coping with the well-intended but untoward suggestions of her parents and both her strange lovers.

Like Célimène in *Le Misanthrope,* Pamela is the bond that links the protagonist to the society he is trying to oppose. Medardo may say that he chose to love her, but he had also felt "a vague stirring of the blood" (p. 193; "un indistinto movimento del sangue," p. 53), evidence of a biological force that continues despite his cloven condition. As a girl who is beloved and who speaks her mind, Pamela helps define the nature and limits of Medardo's fantastic state. In a book that says little about the sexual implications of being cut in two, it is she who says at the end, in candid understatement: "At last I'll have a husband with all the attributes" (p. 245; "finalmente avrò uno sposo con tutti gli attributi," p. 100). Although her wedding to the good half at first denies our hopes of something more interesting, her final union with the whole Medardo is the classic comic marriage pattern that Northrop Frye discusses, a pattern that resolves conflicts and reunites the society.

That Dr. Trelawney should abandon his practice in favor of chasing will-o'-the-wisps and return to medicine later gives us some grounds for an allegorical interpretation, but this is not the only nor even perhaps the pervasive meaning. Certainly Pietrochiodo sets the problem rather explicitly, asking why he should use his mechanical genius to make instruments of torture. But another side of the problem becomes clear when the good half of Medardo presents his idealistic plans for an organ-mill-furnace that Joris-Karl Huysmans' des Esseintes and Karl Marx could not have dreamed up together. If one implication would be that technology needs moral guidance, another might be that machines of destruction are easier to create than those of construction. But we oversimplify. Pietrochiodo's crutches and Trelawney's skills are neither good nor bad in themselves, and the reunion of Medardo results in not a perfect but a complicated being, a mixture of good and evil. The narrator says that Pietrochiodo would make mills and not gibbets, while Trelawney would work with humans, not will-o'-the-wisps. But we also know that Trelawney will play cards and drink his wine. Furthermore, when he says this, the narrator is both idealistic and melancholic; his mind is in a complicated state. Finally, the solution of Medardo's problems, however fantastic, does not guarantee a happy ending for anyone; we do not find "and they lived happily ever after." Rather, the narrator says life changed not for the best but for the better: "Some might expect that with the Viscount entire again, a period of marvellous happiness would open, but obviously a whole Viscount is not enough to make all the world whole" (p. 245; "Forse ci s'aspettava che, tornato intero il visconte, s'aprisse un'epoca di felicità meravigliosa; ma è chiaro che non basta un visconte completo perché diventi completo tutto il mondo," p. 100).

But if it is "better," the new society is also more boring. The narrator can no longer visit Pietrochiodo to find him making machines of torture, and Trelawney will chase no more will-o'-the-wisps with him—such were the voluntary attempts to trip the light fantastic. And, of course, the interruptions of Medardo as involuntary diversions into the "heavy" fantastic are finished. With these sources of fantasy gone, the boy must make up his own, telling himself stories. But at certain points he becomes ashamed of these *fantasticherie*, these daydreams or foolish fancies, and he escapes from this escape. It is while he is telling himself stories that Trelawney sails away, leaving the narrator "in this world of ours full of responsibilities and will-o'-the-wisps" (p. 246; "in questo nostro mondo pieno di responsabilità e di fuochi fatui," p. 101). This final phrase of the book is unsatisfying, and intriguingly so: it is the narrator's last attempt to bring order to the complicated world he has experienced, and he can do no better than give another formulation of the mixture of realism and fantasy. On the other hand, he is perfectly right in the abstract: the world is so made. But the problem is defining specific situations, distinguishing the two, finding elements in common. The confusion between the two is profound and unavoidable. Terralba has not become a utopia: the lepers and the Huguenots, although tokenly represented at the final duel, have not been reincorporated into the new society. The good half of Medardo may have put an end to the orgies of the lepers, but what their new pursuits are is not stated, and the Huguenots are left with their patriarch ranting and raving as before.

Thus the fantastic is created largely by fiat: Medardo is split, and the rest of the book follows the implications of this fantastic event, largely through the fast-paced and dramatic interaction of a wide range of characters. The two halves of Medardo and the society of Terralba enter into a dialectic that is further complicated by social problems of rank and subgroups (the lepers, the Huguenots) and by Medardo's love for Pamela. The chief and most dramatic problem is, of course, Medardo's obsession with division, especially of the most precise sort. This monomania (hemimania?) provides a physical expression of his psychological division. There is token authority granted to medical and mechanical arts as means to accomplish the fantastic events of the book, but the fantasy of Medardo's exact division and his ability to divide objects into precise halves goes far beyond the conventions of realism. From start to finish, before and after the division of Medardo, there is a broad spectrum of the emotions (including animals') proper to the conventions that we may recognize in romance, "black humor," satire, allegory, the grotesque. But there are variations: we expect the wedding to be delayed, à la Gothic romance, but then Pamela uneventfully marries the good half; we expect her to be married, but there is not an allegorical ending; we expect a neat solution to everything, but the ending is bittersweet. The fantasy has even played havoc with our expectations of the grotesque, not only subduing it, but making it a corrective to the good Medardo, who turns out to be not so good.

As a variation upon the Doppelgänger, in the tradition of *The Strange Case of Dr. Jekyll and Mr. Hyde* and *The Picture of Dorian Gray,* Medardo is a most efficient device for exploring the extremes of good and evil simultaneously, to show a community reacting to him, and to show his extension of himself in the physical division of pears, flowers, octopi, with metaphoric exactitude. As a study of the hypothetical, the fantasy is doubly satisfying. On the one hand it is an escape from realistic rules (such as those of medicine that would say Medardo could not live), a rejection of the limitations upon our lives. On the other hand, beyond this rejection of the negative, fantasy also affirms a positive belief in conceptual freedom, in the power to imagine changes and to create and control new worlds, especially, in this case, a demonic world.

Our feelings toward evil are at least twofold: we have a desire for it in the sense that we want to know it, to understand it, even to the point of breaking taboos in order to experience it. But we also have a repugnance for evil in the obvious sense that we wish to be free of it, to conquer it, to control and exorcise it. The grotesque is a safety valve through which we may consider the worlds of crime, nightmare, and willful evil. Medardo, with his original willingness to encounter all aspects of life, is an ideal figure to follow on his energetic and unpredictable way, scheming and punishing arbitrarily. At the same time, his evil is buffered by the literary framework, the shields of humor, the narrative form, and the clear understanding that the work is fantastic.

At the other extreme is the good Medardo. As a parody through exaggeration, he demolishes the ideal of the perfectly good man. Indeed, in case one might think of Jesus, there is a subtle current of religious parody between the good Medardo and the Huguenots, including what seems a burlesque on the entry into Jerusalem in chapter 8 (cf. Luke 19). Not only does this irreverence toward perfection allow the grotesque more sway, it also relieves us of the responsibility of trying to follow the example of the good Medardo, by the rationale that life is too complicated to allow us ever to be perfect. This formulation is obviously appealing since it relieves us of responsibility, but it is balanced thematically in the book by the many characters who do learn something (if not everything) about responsibility. The fantasy in this story affirms both poetic miracles and the complexity of life in which some good is possible.

Powerful characters closely linked to moral concepts usually suggest allegory, and the cloven Medardo is no exception. We have spent some time discussing him as he is dramatically created and limited by the other characters; now let us see how he creates and limits himself in his two speeches about his divided self. The first speech comes from the evil half as he strokes a writhing portion of an octopus he has just cut in half:

> If only I could halve every whole thing like this, . . . so that everyone could escape from his obtuse and ignorant wholeness. I was whole and all things were natural and confused to me, stupid as the air; I thought I was seeing all and it was only the outside rind. (P. 191)

> Cosí si potesse dimezzare ogni cosa intera, . . . cosí ognuno potesse uscire dalla sua ottusa e ignorante interezza. Ero intero e tutte le cose erano per me naturali e confuse, stupide come l'aria; credevo di veder tutto e non era che la scorza. (Pp. 51–52)

If the boy is ever cut in half, Medardo continues, he will see everything more clearly: "And you too would find yourself wanting everything to be halved like yourself, because beauty and knowledge and justice only exist in what has been cut to shreds" (p. 192; "E tu pure vorrai che tutto sia dimezzato e straziato a tua immagine, perché bellezza e sapienza e giustizia ci sono solo in ciò che è fatto a brani," p. 52). Medardo's description of his clarity of vision shows two main points: (1) ordinary existence is most complex, to the point that we do not really understand it, and (2) his new vision gives him a zeal to "liberate" other objects by slicing them in half. The other speech is made by the good half. Looking, as always, on the bright side, he says the good of being halved is that he understands the *incompletezza* that everyone suffers from. Like him, everyone is "a split and uprooted being" (my translation; "un essere spaccato e divelto," p. 74), and Medardo in his cloven condition feels a brotherhood with others that he never knew before. Parallel to the appeal of the evil half to the boy, the good half offers Pamela an understanding of the ills of others and a relief from her own ills by the curing of others. This offer comes not through violence but through education. Taken as a matched pair, the speeches can easily be taken allegorically. Woodhouse, for example, generally sees the fantasy as mediated strongly by such moral and thematic concerns. An allegorical reading is possible, but I would prefer to see a broader range of meanings in what Wheelwright calls poetic assent, which can be allegorical, mythical, or fantastic. To take the Medardos as symbols of clairvoyant division and integration is to miss much of their literary complexity.

Fantasy can also be mediated by *préciosité*, the use of literary traditions refined to the point of affectation or cliché. There is indeed a precious side to *Il visconte,* in the high degree of organization and control. After the carefully introduced division of Medardo, there are three crowd scenes, one for his return and two for the final climaxes of the wedding and the duel, which create two nodes for the opening and the closing of the action at Terralba. There are two groups of outcasts, the lepers and the Huguenots. Pamela's two parents side with different halves of Medardo. The weapons, the signals that the two Medardos use, the medical feats, the use of literary characters—all give the book a witty surface of symbols that the reader can readily remember, match, and balance. This mediation both helps create the fantasy and limits it from the wilder, freer range of an author like William S. Burroughs.

With the schism of Medardo, this novella contracted very early to work on a fantastic plane. If we accepted the contract it was because of our willingness to give credence to another sort of narrative than realism; this is an act of faith that what is mysterious can also be rewarding. We take this risk for a number of reasons, all of which are forms of desire: desire for wish fulfillment, desire to explore evil through the relative safety of the literary frame, desire to subdue the demonic of the grotesque, desire for a conceptual expansion of our minds.

The grotesque is called into being, exercised, and, finally, resolved. It is tempting to claim a moral for the novel, along the lines of Woodhouse's reading; indeed, an allegorical reading is surely within the range of responses readers may have. But such an approach limits the novel by interpreting it solely as an allegory of schizophrenia; furthermore, the thematic suggestions of the story are, throughout, tempered by satire, the levity of exaggeration, and the general mood of playfulness. The aesthetic is reminiscent not of Aesop's *Fables* but of cinematic cartoons in which the energy of an exaggerated separation animates spectacle, entertainment, exploration of the possible. Our urge for the unusual is satisfied, and so is our urge for closure. The grotesque has been created, attended to, and brought back within the bounds of the norm. The story is satisfying in offering a model that succeeds in controlling the grotesque; it does not promise that this will always be the case, but it shows, with wit and glee, that it is at least possible in a well-managed narrative such as *The Cloven Viscount*.

5

The Baron in the Trees: Fantasy as History

It is easy to call a book such as *The Baron in the Trees* fantastic when the hero, as a 12-year-old boy, climbs into the trees to live there for some 50 years. But what if the hero is also involved with the persons and events of European affairs from, say, 1770 to 1810, including Voltaire, Denis Diderot, Napoleon Bonaparte, the French Revolution, the conflict between the Jesuits and the Freemasons, and the Napoleonic wars? Calvino has taken great pains to develop a rich historical background not only of persons and events, but also of books, customs, foods, languages, even garden trees and flowers. These details, which give occasion for abundant footnotes in the school edition, often pass unobtrusively, so naturally does Calvino work them in.[1] On the other hand, such details can give us pause to consider how they relate to the fantasy that unfolds in the midst of a history we thought we knew. "The Crow" and *The Cloven Viscount* used nominal forms of history—World War II, the Crusades—to help place the narrative action in time and space, to answer the most obvious questions. But *The Baron* explores historical details aggressively, confronting them with Cosimo Piovasco di Rondò, the man who lived in the trees, and we are continuously comparing our senses of history and fantasy.

Fantasy seeks to explore the hypothetical nature of all times, past, present, future, and perhaps never to be. When it explores times past it enters into competition with our conventional form of exploration, history. If we return to Mircea Eliade's book, *Myth and Reality,* we can consider the similarities between fantasy and history.[2] Since Eliade sees myth as a serious attempt to discover the nature of the past, he is able to discuss history as a survivor of mythical thought (p. 133 and chapters 6 and 7, especially pp. 108–13, 119–25, 134–38). After reviewing some of the famous names of historians from Augustine to Marx to contemporary writers, Eliade writes, "these systems set out to discover the *meaning* and *direction* of universal History," history being an ultimate order. Leaving aside the nature of this ultimate order, he is interested in man's efforts to present it in "historiography itself—in other words, the *endeavor to preserve the memory* of contemporary events and the desire to know the past of humanity as accurately as possible" (p. 135). Eliade concludes that there is a "common element" between history and myth: "both types of *anamnesis* [memory] project man out of his 'historical moment' and true historiographic *anamnesis* opens, too, on a primordial Time, the Time in which men established their cultural behavior patterns, even though believing that they were revealed to them by Supernatural Beings" (p. 138). Eliade does not neglect the differences between history and myth, nor the validity of history in its truest form. He summarizes:

> If we succeed in understanding a contemporary Australian, or his homologue, a paleolithic hunter, we have succeeded in "awakening" in the depths of our being the existential situation and the resultant behavior of a prehistoric humanity. It is not a matter of a mere "external" knowledge, as when we learn the name of the capital of a country or the date of the fall of Constantinople. A true historiographic *anamnesis* finds expression in the discovery of our solidarity with these vanished or peripheral peoples. (P. 135)

The Baron, more than the other works of the trilogy, presents "our ancestors" in historical as well as fantastic terms. They may be drawn bolder than life, something like the eighteenth-century "originals," but they are nonetheless imaginable, credible, and worthy of our familiarity. (Indeed they do not seem any odder than some of our oddest relatives.) The ease with which the book moves through history and fantasy simultaneously invites us to reconsider the easy distinctions we make between the two. Again, the fantasy is interactive, using, incorporating, even creating history as we read. In discussing the creation of the fantastic, I shall spend most of my time on the first two chapters to show the extensive bases Calvino establishes for later action. Then I shall take up some of the adventures from the middle of the book (especially the political and the amorous events) and the resolutions of the final pages. Throughout I will emphasize the roles of history and the narrator as sources of mediation between the fantastic Cosimo and us.

The rhetorical function of the first chapter is to enlist our sympathy with the rebellious Cosimo, who breaks with his family and life below tree level. Primarily two devices help build this sympathy: the mediating narrator just mentioned and the development of the rebellion through a series of small, carefully prepared conflicts. The two devices are related, but we may examine them separately for ease of discussion.

The narrator, Biagio, is throughout the book a most useful interlocutor, as Woodhouse and others have pointed out.[3] On the one hand, Biagio stands close to the reader as an observer, a questioner, an amateur historian in his own right, who makes Thucydidean comments on the reliability of information and the problems of reconstructing events not directly witnessed. Biagio is passive, conservative, loyal to social norms. On the other hand, he is sympathetic to many of Cosimo's aims and, in varying degrees, amused and excited by

Cosimo's adventures, which constitute alternatives to orthodox living. Especially in the first pages, Biagio often tells us how he looked up (literally and
metaphorically) to his older brother, admired him, and wished to follow him
even when he was unable. Four years younger and much less daring, Biagio
is often sorry he did not have his brother's courage and daring. Biagio is more
personally involved than a traditional Horatio figure, and his opinions about his
brother change over the course of the book, from the admiration of youth, the
puzzlement and temporary rejection of conservative middle age (chapter 20), to
a final respect and nostalgia at the end. Throughout, however, he strives to be
a good historian.

In the first chapter Biagio sets about reporting and explaining Cosimo's
flight to the trees. The action is simple enough, even plausible: confronted with
an oppressive, stiff-necked family who indulges his sister when she serves a
loathsome snail dish, Cosimo remonstrates, is reprimanded, becomes angered
beyond words or reason, leaves the house, and climbs a tree, refusing to come
down. Such events would probably not be taken as fantastic (not, at any rate,
more fantastic than many actions of unruly children). Nor, from a historical
point of view, do any of the details, from clothing to genealogy, seem to ring
false, except for some mild satire (as in the name Von Kurtewitz). And
Biagio's account seems clear and authoritative. The first sentence reads as a
model topic sentence, answering the journalistic questions of who, when, and,
indirectly, where, leaving the what defined negatively: "It was on the fifteenth
of June, 1767, that Cosimo Piovasco di Rondò, my brother, sat among us for
the last time," (p. 3; "Fu il 15 di giugno del 1767 che Cosimo Piovasco di
Rondò, mio fratello, sedette per l'ultima volta in mezzo a noi," p. 9). Beginning immediately with a precise date, the story makes its claim to historical authenticity, a claim it will constantly maintain through many details but which
it will also deny through the fantasy.

This double movement of history and fantasy begins immediately in the
first chapter, working away from the balanced first paragraph, a domestic scene
with historical authority. The progression from a precise date to Cosimo's action of rejecting the snails provides the structure for six climaxes of the chapter,
each expanding the scope of Cosimo's rebelliousness, showing by turns the
characters against whom he rebels. This technique of repetition and expansion
is most useful in building suspense, moving from the known to the unknown,
making material familiar through repetition; furthermore, it has the authority of
ritual repetition. As Eliade puts it, "The apodictic value of myth is periodically
reconfirmed by the rituals" (p. 139).

Having shown the vagaries and banality of the Abbé, the old-fashioned
stiffness of his father, and the humorous eccentricities of his scolding mother,
Biagio saves the worst offender of Cosimo's peace until last, the sister. She is
also a humor character, boldly overdrawn, with a short, unusual history to

suggest how she got that way: a rumored attempt on her virtue ended in a promise of marriage, provided she stay inside, dressed as a nun. The parents spoil her further by allowing her the freedom of the kitchen, a freedom she abuses, especially from the point of view of her brothers. As much as anything in the book, her cooking is fantastic; indeed we find the word *fantasia* twice in the Italian to describe it (pp. 15, 16). Not only does she disregard the usual rules of nutrition and custom, but she combines unusual elements and arranges them with an inappropriate amount of care for appearance, with all the arbitrary decadence of Trimalchio's cooks in the *Satyricon*. Having presented such dishes as mouse liver and whole porcupine, she has now embarked upon a series of snail dishes, which particularly annoy her brothers. Indeed they rebelled once, out of hatred of the cooked snails and out of pity for them imprisoned, releasing them from a barrel in the basement, but the snails were recovered and the boys punished by being whipped and imprisoned for three days with minimal food. Calvino builds the climax: and what is served at the first meal upon their release? Snail soup and a main course of snails.

And now, finally, after all the preparation of historical setting, domestic conflict, and a series of unusual characters, we have the full action in dramatic presentation. Cosimo refuses to eat the snails, is ordered away, but found to be leaving already; he takes his tricorn hat and his small sword, leaves the house, and climbs the holm oak mentioned in the first paragraph. At this point Biagio gives us some realistic reasons for Cosimo's behavior. Biagio remembers how Cosimo and he had shared the joys of tree climbing, concluding: "So I found it quite natural that Cosimo's first thought, at that unjust attack on him, was to climb the holm oak, to us a familiar tree" (p. 13; "Trovai quindi naturale che il primo pensiero di Cosimo, a quell'ingiusto accanirsi contro di lui, fosse stato d'arrampicarsi sull'elce, albero a noi familiare," p. 19). The subordinate phrases that follow are exemplary in their mixture of seemingly natural description and the storyteller's ability to make what seems to be fortuitous useful: the tree is in just the right place, the boughs at just the right height for Cosimo to display through the windows of the dining room "his disdainful and offended countenance to all the family" (p. 13; "il suo contegno sdegnoso e offeso alla vista di tutta la famiglia," p. 19). The adjectives direct and heighten the action toward comic melodrama, but when the story turns immediately to the reactions of the family, there is a change of tone. The mother, the more comic and less cruel parent, wants Cosimo to be careful; her concern here gives a hint of her later acceptance of Cosimo's new lifestyle. The father, however, says he will punish Cosimo when he comes down. Cosimo retorts, "I'll never come down again" (p. 13; "E io non scenderò piú!" p. 19). And when Biagio immediately closes the chapter by adding that Cosimo kept his word, we are left in suspense, left to hypothesize about the implications and to await the solutions the story will bring. It is important that the father and Cosimo had spoken of "changing ideas" about whether to come down; in the idiomatic sense of "changing one's mind" it is ordinary enough, but the word *idea,* with its full sense of mental activity in Italian, is most important to this book, in terms of Cosimo's many aims and plans and his rational pursuit of the knowledge of the Enlightenment. His original ascent into the trees is a hasty, impulsive act, but as the book progresses he gives much thought to the implications.

Is the story fantastic yet? It depends on readers' definitions, of course, but the physical events in simple terms (an angry boy climbing into a tree) are probably not fantastic. More important, however, are the clues that this is not going to be an ordinary historical novel, such as the presence of humor characters, from whom we expect unusual actions. These originals are also perceptive, and they are ready to recognize the fantasy they help create. As "one of us," the narrator stands closer to the reader, but he is nonetheless sympathetic to the others, especially Cosimo. Furthermore, the text shows us that a careful and adventurous author is in charge, one who dares to mix moods, to create bold characters, to combine various kinds of authority, from narration, satire, and history. Thus we should be prepared to see the following chapters move further into both historical and fantastic realms.

Two major conflicts structure much of the action in the rest of the book: Cosimo's rejection of the old society, and the confusion within Cosimo of reason and emotion. The first conflict, in Frye's terms, gives the book much of its tragic and comic impetus, as Cosimo is separated from a society he would in some ways like to join, but, on the other hand, he is in many ways master of his own utopia. The second conflict joins the story with a long tradition of "heart-versus-head" literature from Greek dramas such as *Antigone* to sentimental English novels of the nineteenth century. The two conflicts in themselves do not, of course, guarantee either a good or a fantastic tale, but they provide a lot of material with which we are already familiar in Western literature, and we can readily see the variations in this tale, the games Calvino plays with literary traditions in his historic-fantastic format.

We have seen, in chapter 1, Biagio's historical sense of Cosimo's reasons for his rebellion. In chapter 2 we have an ample introduction of the heart-versus-head conflict as Cosimo meets Viola. Throughout their encounter, she pressures him into assuming a wider and wider role for himself in the trees. Like his family, she is a strong influence on his career in the trees, but whereas Cosimo rejected them out of desperation and dislike, he stays in the trees now, to a large measure, to fulfill standards of conduct Viola has helped him establish. We understand these ideals imperfectly, of course, since we see the external formation of them through dialogue, not through Cosimo's more complex psychology. Viola pulls him two ways: to maintain his stance above to impress her, and to come down from the trees to "fall" into her power. Following the rules of the game and his own need for self-direction, Cosimo stays aloft, fleeing temptation. But a cup of chocolate is a petty temptation compared to the greater temptation to which Cosimo has fallen, that of self-love and self-direction to the exclusion of normal social interaction. Cosimo banishes himself from the edenic gardens of aristocratic Ombrosa with its easy life of rules and conventions; he chooses the curse of work in trying to construct a small, personally conceived and executed world that moves toward, but does not reach, the status of a utopia. After these two chapters, we have the foundation for the rest of the book. The first conflict (the old, aristocratic society versus Cosimo's new, arboreal society) provides the basis for much of the confrontation of history and fantasy, while the second (the internal conflict of Cosimo's reason and emotion) gives the book a more personal and intimate dimension, not to mention a rough suggestion of Cosimo's motivations for his fantastic acts. Much, if not all, of the rest of the book can be seen in terms of these conventional conflicts, which give the story continuity—at the risk, however, of too little variation, which can become boring.

The history in *The Baron* serves first to reinforce our sense of history as a true and absolute version of what happened in the past. We take the historical ambient as a given, true frame for the fantasy to build upon and within. The details of time, place, and cultural milieu give us means of continual comparison; Cosimo may live in the trees, but they are specific kinds of trees in a specific time and in a space that is at least approximate. The given society around him, however, is a mixture; we recognize the historicity of Napoleon, Voltaire, and types of people (nobles, peasants, soldiers), but Cosimo's immediate family is clearly made up of fictional characters. The family serves as a transition perhaps more than we realize, since we see them in contrast with Cosimo through our "historical" narrator.

In general, the conflict between Cosimo's new society and the old moves between confrontation and compromise, as Calvino works the device of Cosimo's life in the trees both ways: we get the fantasy of escape but also a reintegration of fantasy and history through their interaction. After Cosimo's initial boasts to Viola of being a fruit thief, he attempts to make true this hypothesis. But his efforts to join this subgroup of society fail (as did his boasts), and he must create his own society, just as he had to make up his subsequent boast about living in the trees. He rejects the society "below" and seeks to stretch his own powers of action, as we read in the opening of chapter 8: "In those days Cosimo often challenged men on the ground to compete in aiming or skill, partly to try out his own capacities and discover just what he could manage to do up there on the treetops" (p. 58; "In quei giorni Cosimo faceva spesso sfide con la gente che stava a terra, sfide di mira, di destrezza, anche per saggiare le possibilità sue, di tutto quel che riusciva a fare di là in cima," p. 70). He even challenges the fruit thieves he once tried to join.

Later he meets Gian dei Brughi, the brigand leader Cosimo had boasted to be; by this time, however, he has established his own style of life, his own intellectual habits, and it is Gian who tries to join Cosimo's society. The result is disastrous to Gian, who is captured because of the insatiable appetite for novels which Cosimo has instilled in him; the high comedy (Gian's cronies threaten him by tearing pages out of his *Clarissa,* pp. 95–96; pp. 110–11) turns to high melodrama as Cosimo tells Gian at the gibbet the outcome of *Jonathan Wilde,* and Gian executes himself, fulfilling the literary parallel. Abbé Fauchelefleur[4] does not even have to read Cosimo's books to get into trouble: an unopened copy of Bayle in his cell is enough to have him taken off to prison for life. In both cases, Cosimo's educational utopianism fails completely, in a bittersweet parody of Schillerian literary idealism. It may be safe for Cosimo to read what he pleases away from everyone else, but Gian and the Abbé were still involved in a society that made certain demands.

If we look more closely at Cosimo's private life, we can consider to what extent he succeeds in creating a new society. The attention Calvino gives (in chapter 10, especially) to the practical side of Cosimo's life is both careful and delightful. Such attention answers many realistic questions we have about food, shelter, and the like. There is a light touch to some of the mechanics, for example the "torrente oscuro" used for his sanitary needs, aptly named the "Merdanzo" (p. 72; p. 86).[5] Such mild levity helps point up the difference between Cosimo and the literary character who is perhaps the most famous of all men in nature, separated from society, Robinson Crusoe, who is briefly mentioned later (p. 155; p. 179). The major difference, of course, is that for Crusoe solving such problems was a matter of survival; for Cosimo it is almost pure game, since he can always come down from the trees and since even while he is aloft his friends and relatives can bring him hot food, medicine, and the like. The likeness, however, is the happy combination of luck and skill, found especially in such robinsonades as *The Swiss Family Robinson,* that allows tree houses, libraries, and Cosimo's walkways, improved by pruning and grafting. (There may be historical reference here to the Florentine walkway of Cosimo de' Medici from the Palazzo Vecchio across the Ponte Vecchio to the Palazzo Pitti.)

To be sure, there are some serious challenges to Cosimo's mastery of the trees, such as fire and the invasion of the wolves, but he meets these heroically and brilliantly, conquering them with a combination of luck and skill that we may surely call fantastic and that makes his status as a hero ambiguous. He is indeed intelligent, physically adept, and a good leader, but many of his triumphs depend on luck (from the early fight with the wildcat in chapter 6 to the fight against the wolves in chapter 14), and once his salvation is entirely gratuitous: falling with no wish to save himself, Cosimo is caught by his coat on a branch, leaving his face inches from the ground (p. 42; p. 52). This sort of situational irony relieves Cosimo of the burdens of high heroism, makes him closer to us, and raises the power of the guiding hand of the author.

It takes more than one person, however, to create a new society, and the more complex questions of Cosimo's existence turn upon his relations with others. First there is his family. As we have seen, Biagio acts as an intermediary, participating in both realms. The father is at first hostile, later patiently acceptant, if not enthusiastic. Such reactions, typical of many characters, are standard enough; they create a double movement of acceptance and rejection to make a lively play of values, creating norms for and against fantasy. Apart from these reactions, however, there are two women (Cosimo's mother and Viola) who strongly participate in Cosimo's world, creating, to some extent, a small society. We might expect the baronessa to have a mother's interest in him, but she goes far beyond such realistic expectations, joining Cosimo's world as fully as she can with binoculars and signal flags. More than anyone else in the book she accepts his new life and continues her contact with him on a new basis. Biagio, who cannot quite understand it all, is at least able to observe: "But our mother, the most removed from Cosimo in a way, seemed the only one who managed to accept him as he was, perhaps because she did not try to give herself any explanation" (p. 40; "Ma nostra madre, la piú lontana da lui, forse, pareva la sola che riuscisse ad accettarlo com'era, forse perché non tentava di darsene una spiegazione," p. 50). She could never enter the trees physically (like Biagio, or even the Abbé!), but she was able to create a parallel fantasy to join his, abandoning rational explanation. They remain close, Cosimo entertaining her even in her last hours. Biagio is surprised to see the serious nature of the games, but it is he who has missed the point.

With the death of the baronessa and the return of Viola from Paris, we have, as in *The Cloven Viscount,* the removal of an older, understanding woman and the immediate prominence of a younger, attractive woman. Viola is not the pure, pastoral lass Pamela was, but she is like Pamela in serving as a link between a fantastic hero and ordinary human behavior. Upon her return, she and Cosimo continue the earlier rules and fulfill the edenic aspects of their first meeting, making love in a walnut tree (chapter 21). However normal this consummation may be as part of a love affair, the text soon emphasizes the fantastic elements of their liaison, as Viola takes to tethering her horse up in the trees. A gossip sees and reports the strange trio, but he is taken for a *fantastico,* and the lovers remain safe (p. 166; p. 189). Still humorous, but more serious psychologically, is Cosimo's war of jealousy against his rivals; a yet more serious variation is his rage at Viola's departure à la *Orlando furioso* (p. 179; p. 203). She joins him for a while, but Cosimo's new society will not include her; they can share physical needs and spatial games, but their concepts of love are too different.

In sum, we have a widely fluctuating relationship between Cosimo's fantastic world and the sociohistorical world around him, two worlds that overlap in many ways. At one extreme, Cosimo is a madman in feathers who prefers birds to men (chapter 14); at the other, he is a member of the provisional government and a protector of the people during war (chapter 28). Within a single chapter, there are often two or three events that differ widely in mood; the book moves rapidly between different levels, following different sorts of hypotheses pushed to extremes and then dropped in favor of others. Calvino's ingenuity keeps the book varied and intriguing, although perhaps the Spanish episode pushes the frame too far. We are told Cosimo stayed almost a year, but the fast pace of the episode does not let us get to know the characters sufficiently, leaving them as caricatures. Stick figures certainly have their uses, but in fantasy it seems more important to have characters who can give human values to a world that is already difficult to assess. Don Sulpicio recurs, but Cosimo's fortuitous victory over such a cardboard villain is hardly heroic.

Of all of Calvino's writings, *The Baron* is the most episodic, the most indulgent, the closest to romance in its most naive (i.e., for Frye, nonclimactic) form. Some critics have found the book too long and episodic, too lacking in ultimate meanings, and I agree that the Spanish episode tests the continuity of the book. Ultimately, however, I think that the fantastic nature of the story justifies such a rich variety of experiments and that, among other conventions, the single, major protagonist and the historical narrator give the book the unity we customarily expect. And if the tale lacks a basic quest in Frye's sense, Cosimo's arboreal life itself becomes a realized ideal, the one thing he believes he did well (p. 213; p. 241). After all, he has in many ways been able to realize his fantasy. The end of the book provides an unusual exaltation of the hero—something akin to Elijah's fiery chariot?—when we might have thought Calvino had exhausted his ingenuity. The ending is neutral, however, in the sense that it is not fully fantastic or historical, but a blend of the two; Cosimo dies in space and time, but he does not have to return to terra firma!

The Baron explores a hypothetical world of escape into the trees, with all the delightful details of daily life, high adventure, travel, and enjoyable, even useful social roles. Cosimo takes us on a curious trip through time and space, dominating nature and overcoming enemies. He is not like a divinity, supreme in power, but nature is generally friendly, saving him fortuitously a time or two and arranging his happy disappearance at the end. The fantasy is affirmative, the wish fulfillment of childish rebellion that leads to the creation of another world. The ritual is the praise of freedom and exploration of nature, society, and history. Cosimo is free to meet on an equal plane some of the greats of his day, from Napoleon to, we take it, Andrej Bolkonskoy of Tolstoy's *War and Peace*. But Cosimo also has a dark side, his animal sexuality. This Achilles' heel (not quite a true *hamartia*) denies him complete utopian rationality. Furthermore his sexual frustrations motivate some of his most fantastic moments, both humorous and awesome (the tactics against his rivals; his "destructive furies"), until he matures to quiet middle age, passing beyond the rash lusts of youth. In the story there is only one true villain, the rascal Enea Silvio Carrega, who meets with a violent end through poetic justice. The other treatments of evil are light and satirical, as in the opening presentation of the oppressive family and Cosimo's rejection of them. But he is later reconciled to them, just as his sexuality cools off, and we may conclude that fantastic treatment of evil in this story is much less pervasive than in *The Cloven Viscount,* but useful in motivating some of the action. Even in Carrega's punishment, the book generally transcends evil to affirm positive values.

Such a story prompts our recognition that history and fantasy lie much closer together than we habitually believe. We can abstract a mechanism to represent how history and fantasy inform each other, taking the metaphoric principle of moving from the known to the unknown. We have already seen this movement from history to fantasy, but we may also consider the other way around, recognizing the literary conventions (such as the robinsonade or a *Bildungsroman*) that provide order for the historical details, or our reactions to such human problems as pride, idealism, or sexuality. Such literary and psychological assents with the exaggerations of fantasy allow us to humanize the history as we bring human values to an artificial frame of reference. Since ordinary historical novels, such as Thackeray's *Henry Esmond,* also use this sort of humanization of history, we should specify to what extent a fantastic tale differs.

The ritual or conventional side of the story is primarily the search for meaning in the past, as it is hypothetically recreated by a combination of history and fantasy. Keeping in mind the citations from Eliade that opened the chapter, we can see how the story suggests our "solidarity" with these ancestors. First, we find a great abundance of historical details which remind us of our habitual way of exploring the past, history. Second, we recognize literary conventions as ritual forms of hypothetical experience that can also shape the past; "the past" becomes, from this point of view, anything written in the past tense (and possibly anything written in any tense, since the act of writing is not only a creation at a point in time but of creation of time itself). Third, we recognize the specifically fantastic directions of the story and make comparisons with the historical frame; if the contrast seems too extreme, we reject the invitation and stop reading. Fourth, if we continue, we must create for ourselves a union of the two. This union is at times uneasy, since Calvino stretches the device to test its limits, but usually it seems so natural that we may wonder if history itself is not a form of fantasy, a form of hypothesis specialized by literary and philosophical conventions. Or, in broader terms, we can see history and fantasy as two forms of myth. The ritual of the story, then, is the testing of our forms of thought about the past, a purposeful blurring of our conventional distinctions of fact and fiction. Fantasy has many advantages over realism (especially realism of averages, as William Dean Howells understood it) in exploring extreme forms of desire, since it can combine new and old elements, heighten them, or create new ones. There must be sufficient coherence for the reader to follow it, and in this story of highly mediated fantasy, Calvino has used history as a major source of recognizable order.

The mythic truth of *The Baron in the Trees* can be described in several ways. As a kind of history, the story reminds us of historical phenomena we take as true and absolute; as an expansion of history, it shows us that history is readily open to reinterpretation, even in fantastic ways. As fantasy, the story reminds us of our need for change, for freedom, for escape into hypothetical realms, for reconsidering the forms of thought we generally take for granted. As fantasy set in a historical milieu, the story reasserts human values in a chapter of history we may have assumed was closed.

6

The Nonexistent Knight: **Fantasy and Self-Creation**

With the publication of *The Nonexistent Knight* in 1959, Calvino was using plot and event less and exploring the mental processes of his characters more. This shift in literary emphasis increased in the following works (even the fairly realistic *The Watcher,* 1963), and especially in *t zero* (1967). In *The Nonexistent Knight,* we find as before the device of a major fantastic character, but this time with a more extensive exploration of that characters' values and ideas. In "The Crow," to be sure, we followed the ideas of the soldier, but his recognition was of limitation, of death; for the characters in *The Nonexistent Knight* it is a recognition of freedom, as they learn about themselves, even to the point of self-creation.[1]

There are two basic processes. First, characters lose the old, unworkable values through their interaction with Agilulf, who represents these values in their extreme forms, demonstrating them to be arbitrary and trivial. Second, characters discover their freedom to decide, to operate according to new, hypothetical values. Agilulf himself changes his ideas and acts accordingly because of his interactions with other characters, especially at the end of the story. The values of all the characters become so involved in hypothesis and fantasy that one of the best ways to approach this book is through a discussion of how characters understand, maintain, and redirect themselves—in short, how they create or recreate themselves according to their own notions of fantasy.

The literary creation of the fantasy is threefold. First the central character, Agilulf, is established as fantastic; second, the personal values of the characters are fantastic per se or come to seem so in a new context; and, third, new personal fantasies allow characters to face the future. The creation of the main character, Agilulf, does not require much comment. There are two ways in which he is fantastic: he is nonexistent in the sense that he has no physical body, and his mentality is a precise codification of the chivalric and military values around him. The physical nonexistence is given to us by fiat immediately, without even the explanations of origin we found in *The Viscount.* Again, after such a jump into the fantastic, there is the usual exploration of implications, but this specific fantastic device does not develop or extend itself as Medardo, Cosimo, or the boy in "The Crow" all did—not, that is, until the very end. Agilulf's fantastic nature is provided largely for the others to react against. More than any of Calvino's earlier fantastic heroes, Agilulf is a stable, predictable character, whose fantastic nature, made clear from the start, provides a sort of conceptual mirror for the other characters of the story.

We learn about both kinds of fantasy immediately, without a transition. Indeed there is a short, dramatic build-up to emphasize Agilulf's disclosure of himself to Charlemagne in the midst of the review of the troops. The precision of Agilulf's mind takes a little more time to present, but by the end of the first chapter, we know clearly about the two fantastic sides, both body and mind, of the nonexistent knight. There are the customary uses of physical detail, comments by minor characters, and a recognizable literary convention (chivalric romance) as a source of continuity, all of which we examined in detail in Calvino's earlier stories. Instead of detailing these features here, we may pass to the new emphasis in Calvino's art of the fantastic, the manipulation of characters' personal fantasies.

Calvino had long been an admirer of Ariosto, as we noted in chapter 2. Ariosto's great chivalric epic, *Orlando furioso,* provides Calvino with the general background of *The Nonexistent Knight* and some of the characters. Roland, Astolfo, and Oliver appear in cameo performances. Charlemagne has a slightly larger role, but still is quite a flat character. Bradamante/Sister Theodora is the only character taken from *Orlando furioso* whom Calvino develops elaborately, changing her, of course, quite a lot from the original figure. Torrismund, Raimbaut, Gurduloo, and Agilulf are all Calvino's invention, quietly inserted into the larger canvas. Calvino seems to draw on the same aesthetic he sees in Ariosto: "Ariosto seems a clear poet, merry and without problems, and yet he remains mysterious: in his obstinate mastery in constructing ottava after ottava he seems occupied, above all, in hiding himself."[2] The two sets of characters, the borrowed and the new, break down in another fashion, however. The originals represent a world that no longer works, while the new ones are active, seeking, questing. I will discuss Agilulf first, then Torrismund, Gurduloo, Raimbaut, and, finally, Bradamante/Theodora.

Agilulf is first in chronology, prominence, and purity. He provides an abstract paradigm of self-creation and also serves as both a model and a foil for other characters. We never know how he gained control of his armor, which serves as his mask, but we learn how his career began with the rescue of a young girl. Whether his protection was by the book (i.e., whether she was a virgin) becomes the question that serves as a nominal focus for action. In having to prove the authenticity of his knightly status, Agilulf finds he must prove to himself his right to exist socially, a right that he had taken for granted. It is Charlemagne, himself, who first asks the obvious question: how does Agilulf get along, if he does not exist? Agilulf answers: "By will power . . . and faith in our holy cause!" (p. 7; "Con la forza di volontà . . . e la fede nella nostra santa causa!" p. 12). Thus he maintains himself mentally, not physically, but we are not told much more. We do see him later battling the indeterminacy of the world through mental exercises, especially mathematical problems, to maintain "a sure consciousness of himself" (p. 30; "una sicura coscienza di sé," p. 25). His form of self-creation is his maintenance of himself according to abstract perfection; his guiding fantasy is one of exaggerated purity. Not only does he insist on mathematical models (which might not be so unusual), but his concerns for bureaucracy, history, and traditional knowledge are so extreme and uncompromising that he becomes a parody of an intelligent man: a pedant, an idiot savant. He is successful in many ways, maintaining, even advancing, himself in military life; he does wonderfully well satisfying the eager Priscilla, but in general he is an annoyance to his colleagues, and he finally meets a knight who does not believe in his carefully maintained reputation.

Thus when Torrismund challenges Agilulf's right to exist according to the narrow rules Agilulf so carefully follows, his whole right to exist (insofar as he does so) is brought into question. As a result, Agilulf's quest is at once humorous and pathetic: it is an archetypal sort of search for origins, as in the birth-mystery plots in Euripides, Menander, Fielding's *Tom Jones,* and Dickens. But here the reason is so legalistic as to be trivial: can he prove that the girl he rescued was a virgin—after a lapse of fifteen years! Agilulf may have been living by an inauthentic fantasy—a hypothesis that is inimical to his sober way of thinking. He must know the truth, even if it should destroy him. Ultimately, of course, it is not the truth (which he never learns), but his own conception of it that kills him. Of all the characters, Agilulf is the one who is least capable of changing, learning to live according to a new set of values. He clings to his old fantasy to the end; in this case fantasy, as a fixed mental construct, becomes a prison.

The character who challenges Agilulf lives by his own fantasy, which is equally preposterous. Torrismund believes everyone a fake except the knights of the Holy Grail. Rejecting the "matter of France," he swears by the "matter of Britain," to use the terminology of romance. His challenge, that Sophronia was not a virgin, is no less a hypothesis than Agilulf's succession of titles, which had been based on the opposite premise. This time, however, Agilulf cannot carry the day by argument; for the first time he himself is not sure of the truth. Furthermore, Torrismund's presentation of his own fantasy about his origins is most effective, a fine coup de theatre borrowed from the most melodramatic of Wagnerian productions (p. 83; p. 83). Like Agilulf, however, Torrismund must also seek the truth of his origin if he is to maintain his sociomilitary position according to the conventions of birth.

While seeking to substantiate this hypothesis, however, Torrismund discovers another that seems more attractive: to become a knight of the Holy Grail himself, forgetting about who his father might have been. More flexible than

Agilulf, Torrismund tries to adjust himself according to this new hypothesis, even though it turns out to be more fantastic than he foresaw. When the knights are exposed as frauds, they are no longer attractive to him, either as presumptive fathers or as future comrades. Their fantasy may sustain *them,* but it will not do for him. He resorts to a relatively instinctive sense of justice in fighting them, but since he cannot (yet) adopt the norms of the nearby villagers, he flees. After meeting Sophronia, Torrismund's conceptual flexibility allows him a series of realizations: that he has committed incest, that he has not (we may think of *Tom Jones*), and so forth. Once his ancestry and love are straightened out, he marries and returns to Koowalden (Curvaldia in the Italian) as a count. The Koowaldens, however, do not wish a count; in the spirit of the conclusion of *Candide,* they have decided to cultivate the land by themselves; they have found that they can live without knights and nobles. They explain the new values to Torrismund, who first recalls the norms of Charlemagne but then reconsiders. Although he does not explicitly decide to stay, it appears likely that he will do so, since Sophronia wants to stay, and even Gurduloo will learn to be an equal in the new democracy.

Gurduloo, of course, will attempt to become anything; after all, he has already attempted to become a pear tree, a duck, and a pot of soup. In his mind, apparently, he actually creates a union with the thing he is captivated by, but physically it rarely works (with the delightful exception of the visit to Priscilla's maids). As a complement to Agilulf, after the pattern of Sancho Panza, Gurduloo is perhaps overplayed, but his performances are brief and good, particularly in the burial scene (pp. 56–59; pp. 58–61), which would be worth extended discussion. In sum, Gurduloo is continually trying to change himself according to his fantasies. If he is not successful in becoming other objects, he is successful in a variety of social relationships, not only with the maids but with the many folk who know him by several names: Gudi-Ussuf, Ben-Va-Ussuf, Ben-Stanbul, Pestanzoo, Bertinzoo, Martinbon, Omobon, Omobestia, the Wild Man of the Valley, Gian, Paciasso, Pier Paciugo. He is a passe-partout figure, much like the translator in *If on a winter's night a traveller,* Hermes Marana, and Qfwfq—he is a figure that seems to go everywhere, do everything. Gurduloo is the earthy complement to the cerebral Agilulf, the plenitudinous complement to the single-minded man. A question emerges: does Gurduloo even have fantasies apart from action, or are his fantasies all immediately carried into action, much in the fashion of a child?

Raimbaut's course is somewhere between Agilulf's and Torrismund's, but closer to Torrismund's. Like Torrismund, he arrives at the battlefield with a pre-established set of values. Raimbaut's chief hypothesis is that he should carry out his revenge according to chivalric custom. The vengeance itself, despite its conventional origin, becomes fantastic as the story exploits it through exaggeration, with battleground interpreters, officers who arrange duels, and so forth. Indeed it becomes so complicated that even when carried out "successfully," it lacks the importance he was sure it would have. And, like Torris-mund, while in search of one goal, Raimbaut becomes sidetracked by another: Bradamante. Once he has fallen in love with her, his values become quite sim-ple: follow her. He then becomes a simple and predictable character in the tra-dition of faithful lovers like Major Dobbin in Thackeray's *Vanity Fair* or Casper Goodwood in Henry James's *Portrait of a Lady*. Knowing she loves Agilulf (and this is how Agilulf chiefly influences him—indirectly), Raimbaut waits until she has changed her mind to win her.

But his quest succeeds by more than his faithfulness. He has help from the narrator, who is in some ways the most fantastic person in the book. More than all the other characters, she can surprise us, especially with her revelation that she is Bradamante.[3] Her relationship to the fantasy of this story is the most complicated of all: as Sister Theodora, she is creating the entire literary world; as Bradamante, a lone attractive woman surrounded by admiring warriors, she loves the perfect warrior who is, however, a most imperfect man. As one sol-dier puts it, since she can have any man she wants, the only wish left is for a man who does not exist (p. 66; p. 68). Like Raimbaut, Bradamante becomes a simple character in her desperate love for Agilulf, following him in order to realize her fantasy. When the old comic device of mistaken identity (Boccaccio and Shakespeare come to mind) allows the consummation of Raimbaut's love for Bradamante, she believes she has been successful for Agilulf: "Yes, I was sure of it! . . . I was always sure that it would be possible" (p. 135; "Oh, sí, ne ero certa! . . . Ero sempre stata certa che sarebbe stato possibile," p. 130). She believes her fantasy has been fulfilled at last, only to find that she has been tricked by Raimbaut, who was fulfilling his own fantasy. Disappointed, she flees.

Until we get to the end of the book, we take Sister Theodora to be yet another character. From the very moment of her introduction to us in chapter 4 she is a curious figure. Take for example her sarcasm as she declares her in-nocence:

> Apart from religious ceremonies, triduums, novenas, gardening, harvesting, vintaging, whip-pings, slavery, incest, fires, hangings, invasion, sacking, rape, and pestilence, we have had no experience. What can a poor nun know of the world? (P. 34)
>
> fuor che funzioni religiose, tridui, novene, lavori dei campi, trebbiature, vendemmie, fus-tigazioni di servi, incesti, incendi, impiccagioni, invasioni d'eserciti, saccheggi, stupri, pes-tilenze, noi non si è visto niente. Cosa può sapere del mondo una povera suora? (P. 38)

How can she write battles, she goes on, when there have been only four or five under their castle windows? Her fantasy appears to be that she can convince us that she is an ignorant nun! True, we do not yet know what else she is or has been, but we do know, even on first reading, that she protests her innocence too much. Thus I think Woodhouse is wrong in calling Bradamante "as naive a personality as anyone in the trilogy."[4]

Sister Theodora takes to addressing comments to us at the beginnings of chapters (chapters 4–8, 12), somewhat in the style of *Tom Jones* and *Vanity Fair*. These offerings are not so much critical, moral, formal commentary as personal reflections on her motives for writing the story, reminiscent, on a small scale, of *Tristram Shandy*. From the point of view of fantasy, this is quite important. Why is she writing? Why is there a fantastic personage in her story? Why does the narrative turn out to be about herself? After her introductory statement about her innocence, she expands the reason for her writing, from the religious point of view. Her task, like the tasks of the other nuns, is supposed to guarantee the health of the soul.

If not (yet) sure herself about her goal, she does seem sure of her method: *immaginare*. She is especially adept at using the noise of the convent as raw material, says she (chapter 5). She takes up the problem of imagination again in the next chapter (chapter 6), saying she can only imagine amorous passion, from which, she says, "my vow, the cloister, and my natural shyness have saved me until now" (p. 61; "il voto, il chiostro e il naturale pudore m'hanno fin qui scampata," p. 63). She moderates this statement with another joke about how the nuns would listen carefully to pregnant girls' confessions, but we know, upon second reading, that this good sister is not telling the truth about herself! She is maintaining the fiction that she is and has been for some time a virtuous nun.

Closer to the truth would be to say that her current fantasy is to recreate herself as a virtuous, cloistered, but still playful soul who wishes to digest her adventures. Apparently her life goes in cycles of heavy action in war and love, then a retreat to this same convent for rest, relaxation, and narration. She makes these decisions to wage war or to go on retreat as a way of creating her life, her self, and makes few claims on advancing wisdom: "The art of writing tales consists in an ability to draw the rest of life from the nothing one has understood of it, but life begins again at the end of the page when one realizes that one knew nothing whatsoever" (p. 61; "l'arte di scrivere storie sta nel saper tirar fuori da quel nulla che si è capito della vita tutto il resto; ma finita la pagina si riprende la vita e ci s'accorge che quel che si sapeva è proprio un nulla," p. 63). But there is knowledge and there is knowledge. Bradamante is a vitalist, an instinct-driven character, a person of primal desire. "Did Bradamante know more?" (p. 61; "Bradamante ne sapeva di piú?" p. 63), she ingenuously asks. Hell yes, we might answer upon second reading, and it is her depth of understanding of war, passion, action and retreat, writing, and the irrational nature of knowledge that makes her one of the deepest figures of the book, certainly the "roundest" in Forster's sense because she can surprise us. She is, finally, the character who most aggressively plunges into the future. Gurduloo is more plastic in immediate action, but Bradamante is the self-creator par excellence who projects forward and backward into time.

If writing the story is supposed to be her means to salvation, Sister Theodora finds the opposite happening: the more she compares her present life with the life outside, the more she escapes from both into her book, "another world" (p. 72; "un altro mondo," p. 72). The book will be worth no more than she values it, she muses, but she doubts she will save her soul (p. 72; p. 73). From the point of view of fantasy, this is an important reflection. Her task of writing forces her to compare her life with the life possible outside and in her story; she denies herself the outside life, plunging into the book. We learn later that these are in some ways the same, since she has already lived what she is recounting, and the action of the story finally joins her private realm. In abandoning herself to the book she is, as she says, already lost. In evaluating the book as something all-important, she rejects her religion and follows her fantasy.

But is it fantasy? By her comments, she feels she can tell us she is racing after the *truth:* "'Tis towards the truth we hurry, my pen and I" (p. 87; "È verso la verità che corriamo, la penna e io," p. 87). At the end, we see in what sense she is right. We can accept the cathartic value she specifies, that she will reach the truth after burying "all the disgust and dissatisfaction, the rancor" (p. 87; "tutte le accidie, le insoddisfazioni, l'astio," p. 87). But there is a new urgency about her task, as she and her pen run along. Her next thoughts (chapter 9) reaffirm the hurry; she must avoid all extras, all the usual intricate adventures of chivalric romance. Even if she thinks of these sidelines, the actual tools of her trade, the paper and ink, are unwilling to record them—her writing is becoming more and more a power in its own right.[5]

She is finally able to compromise, using the paper not as a locus for the written word, but as a map representing western Europe and northern Africa, with lines, dots, dashes for her characters' trips. This symbolic shorthand allows rapid manipulation of the characters (including herself). Her power becomes ever more obviously fantastic as she manipulates time and space symbolically, drawing an ocean, drawing a whale (which Agilulf's boat runs into), drawing a larger boat for the return trip to avoid another such accident. But her power is not absolute. Her symbols have proliferated to such a degree that they are beyond her control; there are so many lines that the boat is wrecked. The verb Calvino uses to describe how the lines "intersect" ("si intersecano," p. 111; Colquhoun renders it "crisscrossing," p. 113) is the same verb he used to describe the varied riches of a novel.[6] The novel, like Sister Theodora's map, maintains many terms simultaneously; it is the observer who chooses to consider any particular sequence as a hypothetical sequence in time.

In her crescendo of action, Sister Theodora refrains from commenting at the beginning of chapters 10 and 11 in order to bring the action of all characters to the focal point of the cave. With the resolution of these lines of action, she can take up her own story, both in the ordinary present she has used when speaking directly to us and in the past, which has now caught up to the present.

The fusion of the two times is partly due to her speed in writing, which has assumed epic proportions. She bares her identity, explains her haste, and says that she is now open to the future, to new adventures. More than any other character, she is fantastic in her ability to consider and follow new hypotheses, to accept whatever the future may bring. (Gurduloo may be better moment by moment in trying to change himself, but the wider conceptual outlook is Bradamante's. She can use a rational mind and literary gifts as part of her fantasy, but he cannot.) Obsessed with order and perfection, she loved the fantastic Agilulf and lovingly recreated him in her narrative, although she managed, in reflective fairness, to show his faults as well. With his disappearance, which gave her time to reflect, to reexamine and recreate her past, she now can see that Raimbaut should be her love. She has reshaped her fantasy and herself.

The psychological appeal of such a book is wide, since there are so many characters with variable fantasies. Indeed, feelings, fantasies, and values are constantly changing, the romance frame is parodied, and the story passes from one character to another, each with his changing goals. Most important therefore is the fantasy of affirmation, with its search for freedom through the manipulation of hypotheses. The characters do not change themselves to suit an authority, a family, or any such external order; they do it for themselves, to gain what they want.

Bradamante, as Theodora, gives the clearest example of self-creation through fantasy. She knows her writing is supposed to have a most moral end, following the nuns' point of view (fantasy?), but she loses her heart to the enterprise per se, which is no surprise, since she is recreating herself, analyzing herself, exploring the past in order to understand the present. She does this so well that she can join past and present and stand ready for any possible future. She gains her freedom in time and space, jumping over continents with her pen, following a variety of characters through a wide range of actions.

A more difficult case is Agilulf, who is much less free; his goals of perfection, although following social models, are ultimately asocial. In the banquet scene, for example, Agilulf is clearly a bother to the waiters who must serve him constantly, but from his point of view, he is following his own urge toward perfection, purity, geometric rectitude. He is pushing customs of eating to their extremes, playing the game to the limits. For us this is both a parody of social conventions and a hypothetical exploration of the limits of excellence narrowly conceived.

The clearest realm of fantasy of affirmation, however, is the general world of the novel. This world allows the characters to live their adventures without some repressive form of fate, since it is the narrator who is in charge, allowing herself much (although no absolute) control. Thus there can be the accident of the boat striking the whale, but Theodora is able to lubricate Agilulf properly (to keep him from rusting) and supply Gurduloo with a tortoise. She can speed Raimbaut toward her by recounting the story faster, even if she cannot, it seems, alter the general plan. Although we cannot be positive, the ending of the story for all the characters (except Agilulf) seems happy; it is at least full of promise, and Bradamante gladly looks forward to new adventures. The narrative is witty, bright, and fast, with surprises that inspire hope, not fear. The close is not, however, the conventional "they lived happily ever after" of fantasy of affirmation in its purest form. Here instead we have the characters with a good chance to be at least partially happy.

Fantasy of denial is here too, but less pervasively and in subtler forms (leaving aside the obvious suspension of natural laws). First there is a side of Agilulf that is perverse in its uncompromising purity, comparable to the evil Medardo. When Agilulf interrupts the knights as they recount their deeds (chapter 7) he is a pedantic spoilsport. But we also enjoy the brilliance of his arguments and his deflation of the bragging heroes. (At least Agilulf is not a hypocrite in the same way the knights of the Holy Grail are. The problem becomes complex, because from their point of view the Holy Grail knights are not hypocrites either; they are consistent to their way of thinking. What does make them hypocrites is the obvious disparity between their ideals and their oppression of the Koowaldens, their lack of self-analysis and self-criticism. Once Agilulf's reputation is challenged, on the other hand, he honestly seeks the truth for himself.)

The fantasy of denial in Agilulf lies in the extremes of his thought and action; it is evil in its uncompromising inhumanity. He separates himself from other humans. He does not play by the same rules, ultimately, risking himself in social discourse. Rather he plays by very specific and narrow rules, by which he always wins, whether at play or war: he rescues people when they do not want to be rescued and forces his own inflexible values on others, often haughtily. With Priscilla he does better, but that encounter is an exception, rounding him off a bit as a character. Another exception would be his offering sympathy to Raimbaut (end of chapter 2). Thus the fantasy of denial is the exaggeration of a few forms of human tyranny through inflexible values: Agilulf breaks the social laws of forgiveness, fair play, camaraderie; the knights of the Holy Grail break the laws of honesty, humility, sharing, and the precepts of Christianity in general. These evils are exorcised in the book by Torrismund's rejection of and fight against the knights, and by Agilulf's noble suicide.

Thought, as a structure for the creation of fantasy, seems less important in *The Nonexistent Knight* than in the rest of Calvino's fantasy. With the arbitrariness of the story and the lack of a clear, rational pole for dialectic, the tale appears to exist more for its own fun than for any new sorts of understanding. Like Ariosto's *Orlando furioso*, this novella is a complicated, vibrant mixture of tone and narrative line, more admirable for its ingenuity, design, and parody than for its means to insight. There are, however, some sources of order to reflect upon. First, we may consider the chivalric world as a world of conventional norms, values, forms of behavior. The book as a whole uses chivalric romance as a basis for parody, a source of conventions the reader can recognize, seeing how they are reworked to show their arbitrary nature, as in the duels on the battlefields with translators and eyeglasses bearers. Within the story, we find the military code per se inadequate in various ways, through Agilulf's "perfection" of it, Raimbaut's conception of revenge, and Torrismund's awe of the knights of the Holy Grail. Even near the end, Torrismund clings to the chivalric tradition, offering his rank and abilities to the Koowaldens, who reject him in favor of self-rule. This episode comes close to allegory, but we may follow Torrismund in thinking it over before we decide whether the Koowaldens are right. This ability to be flexible about authority, norms, values—whatever form order may take—is most important to the complexity of the book.

Clearly the chivalric world of *The Nonexistent Knight* is over the hill. The knights are old and tired; Agilulf is a mannered parody of the chivalric code. As the various characters take their leave for the merry chase of the last five chapters, Charlemagne thinks of the "days when the departures were of Astolfo, Rinaldo, Guidon Selvaggio, Roland, to do deeds that later entered the epics of poets, while now the same veterans would never move a step unless forced by duty" (p. 86; "tempi in cui a partire erano Astolfo, Rinaldo, Guidon Selvaggio, Orlando, per imprese che finivano poi nei cantari dei poeti, mentre adesso non c'era verso di muoverli di qui a lí, quei veterani, tranne che per gli stretti obblighi del servizio," p. 86). He concludes: "'Let them go, they're young, let them get on with it,' said Charlemagne, with the habit, usual to men of action, of considering movement always good, but already with the bitterness of the old who suffer at losing things of the past more than they enjoy greeting those of the future" (p. 86; "'Che vadano, son giovani, che facciano', diceva Carlomagno, con l'abitudine, propria degli uomini d'azione, a pensare che il movimento sia sempre un bene, ma già con l'amarezza dei vecchi che soffrono il perdersi delle cose d'una volta piú di quanto non godano il sopravvenire delle nuove," p. 86). (This theme will return in the conversations of Kublai Khan and Marco Polo in *The Invisible Cities*.) What we see now is a mannered, almost decadent world, in which the perfect knight, Agilulf, is no knight at all. Calvino has commented on this dilemma in Ariosto's original poem:

> The word "game" has returned again to our discourse. But we must not forget that games, whether those of children or those of adults, always have a serious base, are always techniques for training faculties and attitudes that will be necessary in life. That of Ariosto is the game of a society that feels itself both the elaborator and the depository of a vision of the world, but also feels a chasm growing under its feet, between the tremors of earthquakes.[7]

The question becomes: what should be the sources of order, and for what ends? Agilulf, who has most strongly internalized and exaggerated the chivalric norms, is the least capable of change, except to remove himself from the game of chivalry when he feels he has violated the rules beyond restitution. Gurduloo, at the opposite extreme, has so little conception of social structure (or any other) that he is a protean clown of material anarchy. Agilulf seduces Priscilla spiritually, not carnally, while Gurduloo waylays the servants seriatim. Agilulf finds himself to be an unworkable hypothesis; Gurduloo never seems to find himself—but he survives. Evidently Gurduloo's vitalism is more practical than Agilulf's idealism.

After chivalry, the second and third controls on the world of the story might be the narrator's writing and our reading. The act of writing is worthy of assent as an effort to understand and evaluate. By changing the rules of her existence and entering a convent, Bradamante has given herself time to reflect, to recreate herself through understanding her past. She learns that writing is not the salvation her colleagues think it will be; indeed she is lost to it. Ultimately, though, it *is* her salvation, in a different way. By remembering, reconsidering, recounting her past, Bradamante reaffirms who she is much in the manner Eliade shows that myths of origins give knowledge and control. To the end, her writing creates this control. But we should notice too that her dream, her desires, become more and more pervasive, as the past joins the present: her art at last frees her. This extension of desire prevents the book from becoming too controlled, too precious. With the revelation of who Sister Theodora is, we may feel it is all too neat, too controlled, but the immediate jump toward the unknown future opens the frame up again.

By our reading, we allow our desires to be manipulated. We start with several conventions (narrative, chivalry, doctrinaire excellence), and we see them explored, extended, forced by the fantastic device of Agilulf, inviting us to look more closely at society and ourselves, especially our desires. Thus we are invited to reflect upon our wishes (1) to be taken on a trip to another world, to be controlled by this unusual narrator, (2) to be shown the nature of duty and faithfulness as human responsibilities, not merely legalistic ones, (3) to see what happens to an extreme personification of social norms, and (4) to understand the ultimate freedom available to any who realize the arbitrariness of social norms (which may still be useful, within limits). Our assent to the end of the story is not to a formulaic ending tying everything up neatly; we leave characters on the brink of the future, ready to make their decisions. They have gained power over themselves, in Eliade's terms, by studying their origins. Bradamante knows she is ready to love the faithful Raimbaut, having exorcised her love for military order as personified in Agilulf. Agilulf realizes he is a contradiction, an impossibility, and destroys himself; I think his ending is a ritual murder in which we willingly participate to rid ourselves of the ideal of perverse "excellence," a source of both humor and pain. Like the characters, we may leave the end of the book ready for something new, our faith renewed in our ability to see values as conventional, not absolute, to accept and explore freedom, to take a more active hand in self-creation. Unless characters can maintain the capacity to create themselves, they wither. The old knights from *Orlando furioso* can be directed only by Charlemagne's commands. Agilulf's suicide represents their failure to look ahead, to have desires, to take action. The knights of the Holy Grail are particularly corrupt in their hypocrisy and exploitation of the Koowaldens. Torrismund's rejection of their knightly code parallels Agilulf's destruction of himself. Torrismund, Raimbaut, and Bradamante, on the other hand, all have energy, hope, vision, and the personal resolve to "get on with it," in Charlemagne's phrase. Without pushing the book too hard as a psychological allegory, we may observe that much current psychology, both popular and scholarly, speaks of our personal abilities to imagine, to "script," to visualize possible futures for ourselves. The power of personal fantasy for self-creation is important not only thematically, but narratively, since it can enliven and direct such narratives as *The Nonexistent Knight*.

7

"The Argentine Ant," "Smog," and "The Watcher": Fantasy and the Mundane

These three long stories were written over the period of a decade, but, because of similarities in subject and technique, they go well together as collected in the English volume *The Watcher and Other Stories*.[1] All three deal with the basic question: how do our fantasies, our thoughts, our dreams interact with the oppressions in daily life? The order of the collection is: first, "The Watcher" ("La giornata d'uno scrutatore," 1963), second, "Smog" ("La nuvola di smog," 1958), and, last, "The Argentine Ant" ("La formica argentina," 1952), but I will discuss them in the opposite order, the chronological order, which is more instructive about Calvino's variations of fantasy and the mundane. "The Argentine Ant" and the "Smog" are first-person narratives; "The Watcher" is third-person, but in a Flaubertian-Jamesian kind of way that keeps the main character's thoughts very close to us. In short, we have tales that are primarily in the minds of three male characters, all modern Italians, who ruminate on how to deal with the daily pressures of jobs, civic duties, women, art, neighbors, and so forth. Each story increases the burden of reality upon the protagonist, making his thought more unclear, more desperate; yet each story ends with an unexpected moment of clarity and affirmation, something like a Joycean epiphany. These positive visions are interpretations by the narrators of their current environments; the extent that the visions are fantastic says something about the inner desires of each character. Externally the tales are, on the face of it, primarily realistic. Only "The Argentine Ant" has an apparently fantastic premise: an exceedingly large number of ants in a given neighborhood. But in all three stories, our protagonists' responses take on fantastic dimensions as these characters respond to the mundane elements of their lives, to the ants, to the smog, to the asylum where an election is taking place (in "The Watcher").

These stories are less obviously fantastic than most of the rest of Calvino's works discussed in this book, certainly in the external settings, but the fantasy, which we can still follow, and which is central to the art and meaning of these stories, is the inner lives of the characters. These stories help us understand that fantasy is not just the "self-indulgent" narrative of an author who wants to have a character shot in half, aloft in trees, or lacking a physical body. Fantasy is also part of the imagination, the vision, the daily hypothesizing and searching that we all share, that we all must do if we are to survive. In each case the narrator has given, largely, a rational philosophy that turns out inadequate for the complexity of reality. Thus, curiously enough, rationalism is revealed as a kind of personal fantasy, and reality, for all of its mundanity, has its own fantastic quality that may, on occasion, "shine forth" (to recall the original Greek sense of *phantasia*). Our discussion, therefore, will focus on the minds of the narrators as they deal with reality, both mundane and mysterious.

"The Argentine Ant" is easily the funniest of the three stories, a macabre tale of a man, woman, and child taking up a dwelling in the rural setting, upon the recommendation of their Uncle Augusto, then finding it to be ant-infested. Indeed the entire neighborhood is full of ants, and the inhabitants react to the ants in various ways that seem to give life meaning. We may well begin to wonder if we are not reading an insectoid parody of Camus's *La Peste* (1947)! The Reginaudo couple, for example, laugh at the ants, perhaps in the fashion of Camus's beloved Sisyphus, whom we must imagine as happy. Captain Brauni, the inventor, creates fantastic inventions to kill the ants; he himself, with his steel-framed glasses, false teeth of steel, and bicycle clips that clamp his trousers, seems to have become a kind of machine (p. 156; p. 101). At one point it appears that he has used his wife as bait for the ants (p. 163; p. 107)! The landlady, Signora Mauro, has adopted the stoic attitude of bearing all pain with dignity. Others drink to excess. Our unnamed narrator ponders all these responses and seems most drawn by temperament to stoicism, but, then, he has a wife to deal with, one who wants *action* against the ants.

The heart of the dilemma for our narrator is a conflict within him between freedom through fantasy and the limitations of duty and bourgeois oppression, as symbolized by his wife and child. (None of the characters of this family has a name: this is a generalized, universal kind of family that is easy for readers to identify with.) In his reveries, for example, our narrator can readily cast himself into the mind of the distant Uncle Augusto, whom he fantasizes as the natural man, who ate and slept where and when he wished. After all, "this had been Uncle Augusto's ideal countryside" (p. 163; "questo restava il paese ideale dello zio Augusto," p. 108). Our narrator fills a paragraph trying to imagine himself as Uncle Augusto, but must conclude "he was a different type, a man who never had my worries: a home to set up, a permanent job to find, an ailing baby, a long-faced wife, and a bed and kitchen full of ants" (p. 164; "lui era un tipo diverso, e non avrebbe mai sopportato i miei pensieri: una casa da metter su, un lavoro continuato da trovare, un bambino mezzo malato, e una moglie che non ride, e il letto e la cucina pieni di formiche," p. 109).

The narrator envies both Augusto and the ability of the locals to incorporate the ants into their local world view that all adventure and freedom are somehow possible. For himself, he sourly reflects, "What prevented me from entering their state of mind . . . was my wife, who had always been opposed to any fantasy. And I thought what an influence she had on my life, and how nowadays I could never get drunk on words and ideas anymore" (pp. 165–66; "L'ostacolo per me a entrare in quella mentalità . . . era mia moglie, sempre nemica delle cose fantastiche. E pensavo pure a quanto essa avesse inciso nella mia vita, cosí che ormai io non riuscivo piú a ubriacarmi di parole e pensieri, perché mi veniva subito in mente il suo viso, il suo sguardo, la sua presenza, che pure m'era cara e necessaria," p. 110). Unfortunately, the last phrase in Italian, starting at "perché mi veniva," has been dropped in English: "because suddenly there came to mind her face, her look, her presence, which were all still dear and necessary to me," a phrase that helps her not be a villain.

It is hard to judge from the story whether his blame of his wife is justified, but he clearly feels that she has killed his fantasy, his intoxications, his insight. Interestingly enough, it is his wife, the least prone to fantasy, who takes the most direct action of any character against the apparent source of the ants, the ant man himself: Signor Baudino, the exterminator, seems to be *feeding* the ants, making their infestation possible. Baudino's very name is similar to the word "budino" ("pudding"), like the sweet molasses he sets out for the ants, supposedly to poison them; furthermore, he looks and acts like an ant, at least according to the narrator. When, at the end of the story the narrator's wife berates and manhandles Baudino, the neighbors, curiously enough, do not join in. They have a chance to follow a real leader, even to extirpate the source of the ants, but, no, they do not want to change the reality whence they have derived their fantasies, their reasons for existence. The bystanders call out in complaint, but ambiguously, so that they seem both beleaguered by the ants and proud of that predicament. The ants provide structure, give meaning to their lives (pp. 179–80; p. 124). The inhabitants close their windows and doors to return "to their wretched lives with the ants" (p. 179; "la loro misera vita assieme alle formiche," p. 125). Their lives are their own, and they resist the wife's attempts to change them.

The narrator finds no solutions from any of the characters and, gratuitously enough, takes his family on a walk to the sea. In these last four paragraphs of the story, he finds everything away from his ant-dominated neighborhood to be picturesque, beautiful, perfect. If he had feared earlier that he could not "get drunk on words and ideas anymore," he now manages it here with ease:

> The sea rose and fell against the rocks of the mole, making the fishing boats sway, and the dark-skinned men were filling them with red nets and lobster pots for the evening's fishing. The water was calm, with just a slight continual change of color, blue and black, darker farthest away. I thought of the expanses of water like this, of the infinite grains of soft sand down there at the bottom of the sea where the current leaves the white shells washed clean by the wave. (Pp. 180–81)

> Il mare andava su e giú contro gli scogli del molo, muovendo quelle barche dette 'gozzi',
> e uomini dalla pelle oscura le riempivano di rosse reti e nasse per la pesca serale. L'acqua
> era calma, con appena uno scambiarsi continuo di colori, azzurro e nero, sempre piú fitto
> quanto piú lontano. Io pensavo alle distanze d'acqua cosí, agli infiniti granelli di sabbia sot-
> tile giú nel fondo, dove la corrente posa gusci bianchi di conchiglie puliti dalle onde. (Pp.
> 126–27)

The grains of sand seem the ameliorated analogue of the ants, the shells
perhaps a poetic analogue to houses or even persons. Our narrator, despite all
the hell of the ants and his disappointment in the kinds of fantasy generated by
the inhabitants, is still able to project his own interpretive fantasy on the details
of his surroundings. These details—women with baskets, palm trees and stone
benches, the fishermen—are mostly mundane, but the narrator, like his
"child . . . turning around in amazement at everything" (p. 180; "Nostro figlio
si voltava stupito a vedere ogni cosa," p. 126) evaluates them favorably. The
narrator joins his capacity for fantasy with the visual stimuli as he describes the
way he and his wife "had to pretend to take part in his [the child's] marveling;
it was a way of bringing us together, of reminding us of the mild flavor that
life has at moments, and of reconciling us to the passing days" (p. 180; "toc-
cava prendere parte alla sua meraviglia, ed era un modo per riaccostarci al
blando sapore che ha a momenti la vita e riindurirci al passare dei giorni," p.
126). The most apparently logical solution for the ants, the rejection of the ant
man, does not come about to resolve the main external conflict of the story, but
we rejoice at the internal resolution of the narrator's paralysis of fantasy and
his reborn ability—however temporary—to sustain fantasy. The ants may full
well continue as mundane nuisances, but he has, we take it, regained something of his personal freedom.

If "The Argentine Ant" is a pastoral gone wrong, "Smog" is a tale of urban
horrors, using not ants, but dirt as the central evil. But while the ants were
rather clearly fantastic, the dirt may not be fantastic at all, because big industrial cities *are* dirty, and because the perceiving, evaluating mind of our narrator is possible unreliable. Again unnamed, this narrator sees dirt, noise, and
squalor everywhere. He admits to us that he is nervous, young, and uncertain,
and that he actually chooses to experience the dirtiest, least glamorous places
of the city "because that wear, that exterior clashing kept me from attaching too
much importance to the wear, the clash that I carried within myself" (p. 79;
"tutto perché quei logorii e stridori esterni m'impedivano di dar troppa impor-
tanza ai logorii e stridori che mi portavo dentro io," p. 11). Furthermore, when
his girlfriend Claudia comes to visit, she finds plenty to admire, while he sees
only the worst: "The sky was leaden; Claudia praised the light, the streets'
color" (p. 108; "La giornata era di piombo; Claudia lodava la luce, i colori
delle vie," p. 46). Our poor narrator is aware that her world is different: as they
drive out among the green hills and see the gold of autumn, he relates: "I em-

braced Claudia, in that taxi; if I let myself give way to the love she felt for me, perhaps that green and gold life would also yield to me, the life that . . . ran by at either side of the road" (p. 109; "Abbracciai Claudia, in quel taxi; se m'abbandonavo all'amore che lei mi portava, forse mi s'apriva quella vita verde e oro che correva . . . ai lati della strada," pp. 47–48).

High above his city they look out on the Alps, but he is fascinated by the pool of smog down the valley, hovering over his city, "the cloud that surrounded me every hour, . . . the cloud I inhabited and that inhabited me, and I knew that, in all the variegated world around me, this was the only thing that mattered to me" (p. 111; "la nuvola che abitavo e che m'abitava, e sapevo che di tutto il mondo variegato che m'era intorno solo quella m'importava," p. 49). The actual, external smog that one would find in Turin or Milan, particularly in the 1950s, is not as important as the image of smog in the mind of our bizarre narrator, an image that takes on fantastic dimensions in a humor that is both witty and macabre.

When Claudia virtually forces him to take her to his dingy little apartment, their sexual interaction is mediated in his mind by dirt:

> I was looking at her breasts, still those of a young girl, the pink, pointed tips, and I was seized with torment at the thought that some dust . . . might have fallen on them, and I extended my hand to touch them lightly in a gesture resembling a caress but intended, really, to remove from them a bit of dust I thought had settled there. (P. 113)

> Io guardavo il suo seno ancora da giovinetta, i rosei culmini appuntiti, e mi prese lo struggimento che vi fosse calata della polvere . . . e avanzai le mani a sfiorarli in un gesto che somigliava a una carezza ma era invece un voler toglierle quel po' di polvere che mi pareva ci fosse caduta. (P. 52)

He then leaps on her to protect her from further dust! His behavior assumes fantastic dimensions because of his obsession with dirt.

All the other major characters can be characterized by their attitude toward dirt, much as the characters in "The Argentine Ant" could be charted according to their understanding of ants. In "Smog," however, we have the continuing problem of the unreliable narrator, who sees, for example, the character Avendero almost exclusively in terms of his neatness. Our narrator has come to this city to write for a magazine, *Purification,* which purports to advance ecological concerns. In fact, it is a bit of hypocrisy by big business, notably Commendatore Cordà, who was chairman of the board of several industries and thus could only devote his odd moments to the institute (p. 91; p. 26). Our narrator realizes that his own ideas and Cordà's—their philosophies, assumptions, and fantasies are divergent: "Everything that was, for me, the substance of general wretchedness, for men like him was surely the sign of wealth, supremacy, power, and also of danger, destruction, and tragedy, a way of feeling filled—suspended there—with a heroic grandeur" (p. 95; "Tutto quel che per me era sostanza d'una miseria generale, per gli uomini come lui dovera essere segno di ricchezza supremazia e potenza, e insieme di pericolo distruzione e tragedia, un modo per sentirsi investiti, a stare lí sospesi, d'una grandezza eroica," p. 30). Curiously enough, he also feels that he can play the chameleon as a writer, mouthing Cordà's platitudes and truisms. Eventually, he finds the game, even in his perversions of it, empty. His own game is empty, since it is Cordà who runs the whole show: the journal, the office, even the smog itself which his companies blow over the city (p. 117; p. 57). It is the journal that promotes the successful fantasies of the possibility of a better life and, simultaneously, a celebration of the present one, certainly the kind of manipulation often used by defenders of a society's status quo.

Two other characters illustrate other responses to the smog through forms of fantasy. One is Omar Basaluzzi, the union worker, who sees smog as an indication of social injustice that will be resolved, "come the revolution." As Basaluzzi puts it, "it's man's conscience that will change . . . we'll be new inside ourselves, even before we are new outside" (p. 127; "è la coscienza che cambierà, da noi come da loro, saremo nuovi dentro, prima che fuori," p. 71). Thus a new collective fantasy, a mythology perhaps, will give society its new order. The other character is the landlady; although she acts in isolation, in contrast to Basaluzzi, her own understanding of smog, of dirt is one shared by many householders in many countries. The kitchen, where she actually lives, is filthy; she leaves the rest of the house a kind of museum, perfectly kept by her in her role as cleaning woman, not mistress of the house (p. 90; p. 24). In other words, her life, like Basaluzzi's, like Cordà's, like the narrator's, takes most of its meaning from the fantasy she has developed around the central topic of the story, dirt.

Like "The Argentine Ant" this story is not highly structured by plot, climactic action, or dénouement. Rather, both tales are like sketches that have a surprising shift in the last few pages, an epiphanic vision of perfection. In "Smog" there is a bit more of a transition. The narrator becomes aware that the laundry carts he has been seeing were an antidote for his usual vision of dirt; they had "a soothing effect" on him, reminding him "that the world is never all one thing" (p. 134; "un effetto rasserenante"; "il mondo non è mai tutto in una maniera," p. 78). Following a cart to the countryside (a *functional* pastoral, in opposition to the ant-damaged land of "The Argentine Ant"), he comes upon a redemptive scene. Again, as in "The Argentine Ant," the concluding four paragraphs are a favorable vision of persons and nature in picturesque and productive harmony, with cleanliness a central part of the mood:

> I wandered through the fields white with hanging laundry, and I suddenly wheeled about at a burst of laughter. On the shore of a canal, above one of the locks, there was the ledge of a pool, and over it, high above me, their sleeves rolled up, in dresses of every color, were the red faces of the washerwomen, who laughed and chattered; the young ones' breasts bobbing up and down inside their blouses, and the old, fat women with kerchiefs on their heads; and they moved their round arms back and forth in the suds and they wrung out the twisted

sheets with an angular movement of the elbows. In their midst the men in straw hats were unloading baskets in separate piles, or were also working with the square coarse soap, or else beating the wet cloth with wooden paddles. (P. 136)

Io giravo tra i campi biancheggianti di roba stesa e mi voltai di scatto a uno scoppio di risa. Sulla riva di un canale, sopra una chiusa, c'era la sponda d'un lavatoio e di là con le braccia rimboccate, le vesti di tutti i colori, s'affacciarono alte sopra di me le facce rosse delle lavandaie e ridevano e ciarlavano, le giovani coi petti sotto le bluse che andavano su e giú, le vecchie grasse coi fazzoletti in capo, e muovevano avanti e indietro le braccia rotonde nella saponata e strizzavano con moto angoloso dei gomiti i panni attorcigliati. In mezzo a loro gli uomini coi cappelli di paglia scaricavano le ceste in mucchi separati, o ci davano dentro anche loro col quadrato sapone di Marsiglia, o battevano con le palette di legno. (P. 81)

The narrator of "Smog" is, however, more skeptical than the narrator of "Ant": he still watches where he steps to avoid dust on his shoes! And his last sentence is rather self-conscious: "It wasn't much, but for me, seeking images to retain in my eyes, perhaps it was enough" (p. 137; "Non era molto, ma a me che non cercavo altro che immagini da tenere negli occhi, forse bastava," p. 81).

Thus the narrator of "Smog" realizes that his dialectic of fantasy with smog, with cleanliness, is part of his own search for wholeness, for maturation. The opening of the story ("That was a time when I didn't give a damn about anything," p. 77; "Era un periodo che non m'importava niente," p. 9) suggests that there would indeed come happier times later on. Perhaps the conscious work on his fantasy of dirt helped him to a higher plane of consciousness. Perhaps this epiphanic and somewhat hilarious vision of laundering helped purify his soul as his writing for *Purification* never could. We do not really know. Will he and Claudia marry? Again, we do not know. Will there ever be less smog in that city? Not likely. Like the ants, the smog is not an obstacle to resolve in the story, but each narrator makes a mental breakthrough in his feelings and thoughts, in his ability to change how his fantasies relate to such mundane obstacles.

"Ant" is some 40 pages; "Smog," some 60. With "The Watcher" we approach novella length, 70 pages. This longer format is not, however, due to an expansion of action. The original Italian title is more specific: "La giornata d'uno scrutatore" ("the day of the watcher"), something like Solzhenitsyn's *One Day in the Life of Ivan Denisovich* (1963). Ivan Denisovich's day, however, was a slice of life, a day as ordinary as all the other days of his imprisonment, while our watcher's day is clearly extraordinary, as he observes an election in an asylum and has, as did the other narrators, something of an epiphany at the end of the day. Thus the expansion comes not from further action but from further explorations of the mind of our protagonist. This time he is a named man, Amerigo Ormea, who has specific and extended reveries about the meaning of society, governance, aristocracy, health, history, and so on, as he spends a day at an asylum where both the caretakers, nuns primarily, and the inmates are allowed to vote. In contrast to the vagueness of setting in the first two stories, "The Watcher" is specifically set in Turin, in 1953. Furthermore, an author's note informs us that "The substance of *The Watcher* is based on fact, but the characters are all entirely imaginary" ("La sostanza di ciò che ho raccontato è vera; ma i personaggi sono tutti completamente immaginari.") The mundane, worldly basis of fact is set most certainly in place, time, and event (an election). The fantasy, to the extent that it exists, will be in the thoughts of our guide Amerigo.

"Amerigo" reminds us directly of Amerigo Vespucci, the Renaissance Italian explorer of the new world, whose name became transformed to America. He is the explorer of the new worlds, even if according to the ideals of a previous time. He favors (as did Calvino, frequently) the Renaissance and the eighteenth century for his guides; his fantasies of order and perfection draw on humanism and the Enlightenment. America, of course, was to be the new land where the Enlightenment ideals of John Locke and Jean-Jacques Rousseau, among others, were to rule everything: Amerigo thinks he knows what he wants. His function as a watcher gives him a clear point of departure: elections *should, ought, must* be run a certain way. He will give up a day of his time to be sure that they are. His last name "Ormea" reminds me of "ormai," Italian for "by now," "at last," or "henceforth," suggesting once again time, in some climactic or pivotal sense. Indeed, his initials A. O. look a lot like alpha and omega, the beginning and the end; we shall find secular and mythic time contrasted later on.

The place where Amerigo ends up "watching," however, is the very antithesis of the orderly, informed electorate that would "make a democracy work." It is not just any ship of fools, to recall one tradition; it is an asylum (Cottolengo) for the insane, the infirm, and the deformed—a true *grotesquerie.* The setting is something like that of Peter Weiss's play *Marat/Sade,* in which the inmates of the Charenton attempt to stage a play. Amerigo, the consummate man of thought, finds that his political ideals are compromised, indeed exploded one after another. Early in the story he broods that the church has entered the political arena, checkmating the Enlightenment dreams of human rationalism with the intrusion of God's grace: "Election watcher Amerigo Ormea felt he was a hostage, captured by the enemy army" (p. 19; "Lo scrutatore Amerigo Ormea si sentiva un ostaggio catturato dall'esercito nemico," p. 27). Much as the mental life of characters in the earlier stories revolved around the mundane problems of ants or dirt, Amerigo's thoughts, feelings, fantasies are controlled by his environment. In this story, however, neither ants nor smog are parlayed into fantastic dimensions; Cottolengo is entirely real and based on fact; but the fact is so unusual that it seems a kind of fantasy, a kind of alternity (Steiner's word) to Amerigo's rationalist humanism. His current philosophy, however, is insufficient to comprehend this new reality.

The second important conflict for Ormea is in his relationship with his girlfriend Lia. When she phones to tell him she is pregnant, he rationally responds with the thought that "procreation represented, first of all, a defeat for his ideas" (p. 53; "la procreazione, per prima cosa, era una sconfitta delle sue idee," p. 69), much as the election at Cottolengo diverges from his ideas. But, more important, news of the pregnancy also releases a turmoil of feelings within him, telling him that his head does not rule his heart. The continuance of the species—in some ways the most mundane of all biological facts—conjures for him the image of India, the land where procreation leads to social and biological disaster. So Lia's pregnancy sets off in him emotions of guilt, fear, irresponsibility, and anger. Amerigo cannot solve these problems; the question whether she should abort the fetus is never resolved in the story, much as the plague of the ants and the urban smog are not resolved. But in a way he transcends the conflict, at least for a while, when he has an insight about the nature of love.

Amerigo has been watching the work of a nun, who has given her life to caring for the inmates, and an old peasant, who has come to visit his idiot son. In watching—ever his function—the old man and the young son looking at each other, Amerigo has three thoughts:

> "There," Amerigo thought, "those two, as they are, are necessary to each other."
> And he thought: "There, this way of being is love."
> And then: "Humanity reaches as far as love reaches; it has no frontiers except those we give it." (P. 64)

> Ecco, pensò Amerigo, quei due, cosí come sono, sono reciprocamente necessari.
> E pensò: ecco, questo modo d'essere è l'amore.
> E poi: l'umano arriva dove arriva l'amore; non ha confini se non quelli che gli diamo. (P. 83)

These touching lines help set up the reflections in the next pages that the love between Amerigo and Lia is not so very different from the love shown to the hospital inmates:

> In fact, for the space of a second (that is to say, forever) he thought he had understood how the meaning of the word "love" could comprehend a thing like his affair with Lia and the peasant's silent Sunday visit to his son at Cottolengo. (Pp. 66–67)

> Anzi, per lo spazio d'un secondo (cioè per sempre) gli sembrò d'aver capito come nello stesso significato della parola amore potessero stare insieme una cosa del genere di quella sua con Lia e la muta visita domenicale a "Cottolengo" del contadino al figlio. (P. 87)

Indeed, Amerigo perceives, all persons are bound by love, in "strings of the knot or tangle in which—often (or always) painfully—people are tied together" (p. 66; "lacci dello stesso nodo o garbuglio in cui sono legate tra loro— dolorosamente, spesso (o sempre)—le persone," p. 87). The power of his insight, however, is not sufficient to sustain him in his next phone conversation with Lia: they end up squabbling.

The insight is momentary *and* permanent, however. Calvino says so with the phrase, "the space of a second (that is to say, forever)," which suggests the transitory nature of privileged insights, something like Marcel's in Proust's oeuvre, and at the same time the eternal nature of their depth and importance. We do not know how the pregnancy will end up, but we may hope that Lia and Amerigo will continue to love each other in their own fashion, regardless of the outcome. The concept here, "forever," is much like the sense of mythic time in Eliade's phrase *in illo tempore* ("in that time") which is apart from mundane, historical time. The rare occasions that we touch into this "forever" time may be enough to sustain our ideas, our hopes, our fantasies through the rest of mundane time.

So it is with the ending of "The Watcher," as with our other stories: the narrator has a vision of perfection. This time, however, it is not a different neighborhood, the laundering suburb as opposed to the soiling city, but the same Cottolengo that has been assaulting Amerigo's senses and sensibilities for some 70 pages. Amerigo hears the testimony of a man with no hands, who says that the nuns have taught him and the others everything. "The nuns taught me. Here at Cottolengo we do everything for ourselves. Workshops and everything. We're like a city" (p. 72; "Sono le suore che mi hanno insegnato. Qui al 'Cottolengo' facciamo tutti i lavori da noi. Le officine e tutto. Siamo come una città," p. 94). This word "city" occurs eight times in the last seven, short paragraphs.[2] The first mention is in the speech just cited; the other seven mentions are in Amerigo's reflections as he wonders about Cottolengo as an image of the perfect society. For most of the story we have felt the tension of Amerigo's idealism of rationalist utopias and his disdain for the asylum, a kind of dystopia. Now he sees the asylum as an image of perfection. Always a watcher, he looks down from a window onto a courtyard to see in the sunset "perspectives of a city that had never been seen" (p. 72; "le prospettive di una città mai vista," p. 95).

> Women, dwarfs, passed by in the yard, pushing a wheelbarrow of twigs. It was a heavy load. Another woman, huge, a giantess, came and pushed it, almost running, and she laughed. They all laughed. Another woman, also huge, walked in sweeping, with a twig broom. A very fat woman was pushing a kind of cauldron between two poles, on bicycle wheels, perhaps the evening soup. Even the ultimate city of imperfection has its perfect hour, the watcher thought, the hour, the moment, when every city is the City. (Pp. 72–73)

> Donne nane passavano in cortile spingendo una carriola di fascine. Il carico pesava. Venne un'altra, grande come una gigantessa, e lo spinse, quasi di corse, e rise, e tutte risero. Un'altra, pure grande, venne spazzando, con una scopa di saggina. Una grassa grassa spingeva per le stanghe alte un recipiente-carretto, su ruote di bicicletta, forse per trasportare la minestra. Anche l'ultima città dell'imperfezione ha la sua ora perfetta, pensò lo scrutatore, l'ora, l'attimo, in cui in ogni città c'è la Città. (Pp. 95–96)

The City with the capital "C" is raised to some powerful level of abstraction, but there are no clues as to what that level is: a platonic archetype of the Republic, an image of Marxist perfection after the revolution, a New Jerusalem— it is not specified. But we may observe that it is not future but present, not dependent upon some profound change but a current, mundane scene, washed over by "a certain slant of light" and the particular perceiving consciousness of the watcher, who, for a moment, entertains a fantasy of perfection. As in his reflection about love, in which a second was like forever, the hour, the moment here is a different order of time, when the mundane time enters some kind of fantastic, or mythic time (something like T. S. Eliot's intersection of time and eternity in *The Four Quartets*). Perhaps it is here that the alpha-omega resonance of Amerigo's initials reinforces the collapse of ordinary time (and perhaps even the concept of the New Jerusalem of Rev. 21:2; alpha and omega are in Rev. 21:6).

Amerigo Ormea leads us through a range of concepts attaching to fantasy, showing it to be an imprecise term. At one extreme is his sense of idealism, as illustrated by the spirit of party workers during World War II: "it was only now, when years had gone by, that he could begin to see it, to make an image of it, a myth" (p. 13; "soltanto adesso, a distanza di anni, egli poteva, cominciare a vederlo, a farsene un'immagine, un mito," p. 21). Myth is a good word for a fantasy with a collective nature: Amerigo and his fellow members share a vision of the perfected communist state. Another, and quite paradoxical, sense of fantasy is the exhibit of Cottolengo itself, undeniably "real," but fantastic in its distortions of health, sanity, and the norms of reality. As Amerigo studies this challenge of alternity, he slowly comes to understand the orders of love, spirit, and "the secret fire without which cities are not founded" (p. 72; "il fuoco segreto senza il quale le città non si fondano," p. 95). In other words, the fantasies of the nuns, the inmates, and, we suppose, the dwarfs and giantesses seen in the final epiphanic vision all are functional fantasies that make the institution work, and work perhaps even better than the "normal" dominant Italian society. Finally, Amerigo has a visual illustration of perfection, so that the fantasy seems to come equally from his idealistic, internal sense and from the concrete, external reality as he perceives it. This final vision is of "a city that had never been seen" (p. 72; "una città mai vista," p. 95); this is no collective mythology but Amerigo's idiosyncratic, gratuitous glimpse. Like his namesake Vespucci, he discovers, even creates the new land by his quest, by his vision. This vision, however, is hard to interpret. Is it a turning point in the watcher's life? Will it influence his relationship with Lia, her fetus? Will it change his sense of politics? Is this a day that will form a pivot in his life? We do not know. But his mind has been changed with his insights about love—that seems clear—and he seems to have a new understanding of the possibility of the dignity of the deformed, and the power of the city that can make all persons function, every person a *homo faber*.

All three of our narrators struggle against the obstacles of external reality. All three find a crisis in their own mental responses to reality; all three find no acceptable models of responses from other characters: they cannot borrow someone else's approach. So the inner life, which must bear them up, reaches a kind of crisis. The narrator of "Ant" fears that he has lost his capacity for fantasy; the narrator of "Smog" does not know how his ability to write can relate to his indefinite ideals on the one hand, or his definite obsession with dirt on the other; and Amerigo Ormea finds his utopian idealism unable to make sense of the mystical, Christian city of deformity and love at Cottolengo. In their final epiphanies, however, all three find new avenues for both their perceptions of reality and their evaluations of it. Their senses of value, image, connection are reawakened; their abilities to fantasize take new jumps forward. The external conflicts are still unresolved, but the new visions of the sea, the laundering suburb, the evening hour at the asylum refresh and reaffirm our narrators. As we leave them they are capable of an ameliorative vision in the face of insoluble obstacles; they have the capacity for fantasy of affirmation, despite ants, dirt, and physical and political deformity. The three stories, primarily realistic, illustrate nonetheless how fantasy may serve as a resource for survival.

In each story the desire of the main characters is to deal with the obstacles and oppressions of the mundane, whether symbolized in ant, dirt, or asylum. Each character ransacks his rational armament to explain, to solve, or to outwit the status quo. In each case, rational thought is either inadequate or irrelevant because of its lack of imagination, of breadth of consciousness, or of congruence with reality. Paradoxically, then, rationalism becomes a fantasy, a self-isolating system of explanation that, finally, explains nothing but illustrates the desire of the rationalist to limit the world to one order. In each case the presenting problem is transcended, so that the solutions each protagonist sought— to kill ants, to outwit dirt and a propaganda machine, to bring about a political order—are simply not in harmony with the full complexity of the world, where both mystery and grace reside in nature and in the love of humanity. The three epiphanic visions pull the larger fantasy into another direction, one attractive to readers in the affirmation of a virtually romantic vision of wholeness, clarity, mutual dependence, and love. That the proportions of the narrative are at least 95 percent the dilemmas of the rational protagonists and a scant 5 percent the final vision saves the stories from sentimentality and disappointing neatness: each male character is left on the brink of new choices, and the visions offer renewals through wider fantasies that may make more interesting, more adequate, more imaginative choices possible.

8

Cosmicomics: Fantasy and Science

Each of the twelve stories of *Cosmicomics* (1964)[1] begins with a scientific citation describing a phenomenon of evolution, such as the origin of matter, the first light of the sun, or the end of the dinosaurs. Then our narrator, one Qfwfq, takes over: he agrees with the citation but continues to extend the scientific model with his own personal reminiscences. What is fantastic about him is that he has lived, in one form or another, from the beginning of time to the present; his consciousness is one we may recognize as human, and it allows him to see both the past and the present simultaneously. Since our ways of thinking about primeval time are given to us by science, the collection of *Cosmicomics* allows us to consider the relationship of fantasy and science. The word "science," of course, comes from the Latin *scientia,* derived from *scire,* "to know." But science is a highly specialized way of knowing, based on a rigorous and conventional method of selecting data, tests, and rational analysis, and it assumes an ultimate order (to follow Whitehead's *Science and the Modern World,* especially chapter 1).[2] Furthermore there are other ways of knowing that science largely ignores—myth, artistic interpretation, religion, mysticism, transcendentalism, and so forth. But philosophers of science such as Whitehead and, more recently, J. Bronowski,[3] remind us that science works in terms of hypotheses to be tested, reformulated, and retested. By exploring the hypothetical nature of both fantasy and science, *Cosmicomics* suggests that they have more in common than we may have realized.

Paradoxically the scientific frame is very important in establishing the fantasy. Rhetorical authority comes from our respect for science, statistics, and technical terms, even the very names of scientists—word magic of a sort. Furthermore, because we are unable to propose alternative hypotheses, we gladly welcome the informal voice of Qfwfq, who frees us from our dependence upon a scientific view we may only partially understand. We accept the scientific description as authoritative, but we also hope Qfwfq's account will be more available to us.[4] Qfwfq speaks as an eyewitness (although not always one with eyes as such), giving a more personal authority to the narrative. In general, we are more interested in the reactions of a person on the scene than in the secondhand report of a scholar who writes in technical language with a formidable apparatus of documentation; moreover, the mass media have intensified the convention of the eyewitness and our dependence upon it. In contrast to the impersonal, formal diction of science, Qfwfq's reportage is much more lively, direct, personal. In sharing our point of view he is more than a Horatio figure; he is a Virgil leading us through a world that he knows well. There are many differences, of course, between Dante's guide and ours, but they both have the authority of experience and understanding of a fantastic realm that they make real for us. In the following discussion of the creation of the fantastic in *Cosmicomics,* I want to consider Qfwfq's rhetorical prowess; then I will discuss how the characters (including Qfwfq) people these strange realms, humanizing them and relating them to ours. Last I will consider how the stories themselves help to structure the fantasy.

Keeping in mind how important sensory data are to fantasy, that we need to see, to feel, to smell the events in our minds, we may look briefly at the sensory appeal of Qfwfq's language, especially his use of simile. In the opening of "The Distance of the Moon" ("La distanza della luna"), for example, we find a vivid use of visual images, colors, formal and informal similes:

> We had her on top of us all the time, that enormous Moon: when she was full—nights as bright as day, but with a butter-colored light—it looked as if she were going to crush us; when she was new, she rolled around the sky like a black umbrella blown by the wind; and when she was waxing, she came forward with her horns so low she seemed about to stick into the peak of a promontory and get caught there. (P. 3)

> L'avevamo sempre addosso, la Luna, smisurata: quand'era il plenilunio—notti chiare come di giorno, ma d'una luce color burro—, pareva che ci schiacciasse; quand'era lunanuova rotolava per il cielo come un nero ombrello portato dal vento; e a lunacrescente veniva avanti a corna cosí basse che pareva lí lí per infilzare la cresta d'un promontorio e restarci ancorata. (P. 9)

Rich in words of color and shape, this passage is carefully organized according to the three phases of the moon Qfwfq describes, each with a distinctive image. While the new moon is described with the simile of the umbrella, the first and last phases are described with the Italian "pareva" ("looked as if," "seemed"), presenting the "as if" world through what would seem to be logical extensions of the moon's size, shape, and direction. The style is lively, personal. The vocabulary is uncomplicated, and the verbs are active and dramatic. We immediately realize that we are listening to an accomplished speaker, one who "has been there," one who can effectively assemble words to present his experience. Qfwfq creates his own rhetorical authority *ex nihilo* by the skill of his speech. The extent to which he succeeds—and this is a bold gamble by Calvino—is the extent to which we as readers join in the narrative enterprise.

The next example is a scene more difficult to make credible, the description of the formation of a hydrogen atom. Qfwfq has just explained that space is more curved in some places than in others: "These niches are where, every two hundred and fifty million years, there is a slight tinkling sound and a shiny hydrogen atom is formed like a pearl between the valves of an oyster" (p. 66; "È in queste nicchie che, con un lieve tintinnio, ogni duecentocinquanta milioni d'anni, si forma, come la perla tra le valve dell'ostrica, un lucente atomo d'idrogeno," p. 80). Qfwfq appeals to sight and sound as well as offering the simile of an oyster's pearl, which connotes different values than would, say, a comparison with a maggot in a wound. Occasionally Qfwfq develops the image, aware of its connotations: "The Galaxy turned like an omelet in its heated pan, itself both frying pan and golden egg; and I was frying, with it, in my impatience" (p. 38; "la Galassia si voltava come una frittata nella sua padella infuocata, essa stessa padella friggente e dorato pesceduovo; ed io friggevo con lei dall'impazienza," p. 49). This delightfully absurd image reflects both Qfwfq's impatience and his self-consciousness in describing it. As we might expect, there is a strong sense of color in the stories about the beginnings of light and color, "At Daybreak" ("Sul far del giorno"), especially page 26 (p. 35), and "Without Colors" ("Senza colori"), especially page 55 (p. 68).

Qfwfq is also impressive in his encyclopedic use of detail; his wide vocabulary—when he uses it—suggests his knowledge of many things. There are some wonderful catalogues, for example, this description of the ingredients of moon-milk: "It was composed chiefly of vegetal juices, tadpoles, bitumen, lentils, honey, starch crystals, sturgeon eggs, molds, pollens, gelatinous matter, worms, resins, pepper, mineral salts, combustion residue" (p. 6; "Era composto essenzialmente di: succhi vegetali, girini di rana, bitume, lenticchie, miele d'api, cristalli d'amido, uova di storione, muffe, pollini, sostanze gelatinose, vermi, resine, pepe, sali minerali, materiale di combustione," p. 12). The joke about salt and pepper, usually mentioned in lists of ingredients for foods, is typical of Qfwfq's humor. When we might expect an attitude of awe or fear appropriate to such explorations of the primeval unknown, Qfwfq gives us a mood of light familiarity which encompasses both the present and ages past.

This levity has annoyed at least one writer, Michael Feingold, who titled his review of *Cosmicomics* "Doing the Universe Wrong."[5] Part of Feingold's difficulty is that he is trying to force the tales into the subgenre of science fiction and blaming Calvino for changing, even mocking some of its conventions. Feingold calls the tales "good jokes on the cosmos" through which we realize "that the universe may be a gigantic joke, endlessly repeating and reperpetrating itself" (p. 36). By looking at the tales, I think we can refute the charge on two grounds. First, in many of the tales, like "The Distance of the Moon," the humor is not irreverent but familiar; Qfwfq is not joking about a mere universe but his home. Second, in the tales that seem less optimistic, such as "The Spiral" ("La spirale"), the humor attacks not so much the universe as the presumptive inhabitants who impose their petty wants on their surroundings. Perhaps we envy Qfwfq's easy familiarity, his presumption. But has he not earned it? We may take, for example, the bravura section 2 of "The Spiral" as an example of his knowledge and ability to synthesize. Qfwfq is here a mollusk, looking onto land to find a train, an ice-cream wagon, a truck, and a peasant, from which he evokes the changes as well as the continuities of life, ancient and modern, through details, historical awareness, and a freewheeling sense of association. The enormously long but graceful sentences are most ambitious in their range of subjects, but they are tender in Qfwfq's expression of love not only for the Dutch girls specifically, but for everything he names and finds linked to everything else.

Besides a deft use of images, especially sensory ones, Qfwfq has a keen sense for conversational speech, which he puts in the mouths of his animal (or abstract) colleagues. Sometimes Calvino focuses on the tension of likenesses and differences between men and their prehistorical counterparts. For example, Qfwfq describes what it was like to be a dinosaur: "if you were a Dinosaur in those days, you were sure you were in the right, and you made everyone *look up* to you" (p. 97; Weaver's translation adds the pun on height, here italicized; "allora a essere dinosauro si aveva la coscienza d'essere nel giusto, e ci si faceva rispettare," p. 115). Character speech works well for Qfwfq. He describes and quotes his uncle, the fish: "Perhaps his authority stemmed from the fact that he was a leftover from the past, from his way of using old figures of speech, like: 'Lower your fins there, youngster!,' whose meaning we didn't grasp very clearly" (p. 73; "Forse la sua autorità gli veniva proprio dall'essere un avanzo del passato, dall'usare vecchi modi di dire, tipo: —E cala un po' le pinne, bravo!—di cui noi non comprendevamo neppur piú bene il significato," p. 89). Jokes on physical disparity seem to work well in general, as when Qfwfq as a mollusk considers in his fantasies scratching his armpit, crossing his legs, or growing a mustache (p. 141; p. 170).

This sort of speech is important in creating our sense of the characters. Whether they take the form of animals or even creatures whose visual shape is not clear need not bother us, since we can still feel we know them through their speech. Thus in "At Daybreak" ("Sul far del giorno") we do not know what the characters look like, but we do know that Signor Hnw, who was to become a horse later, is at one point on all fours, and we can recognize common family troubles from the dialogue, of age versus youth, mothers chasing children, how to get rid of unwanted guests, and other such topics of domestic comedy. Again, the power of language is important, both to suggest personality (even in these strange beings) and, in so doing, to make the tales accessible to the reader's collaboration.

Furthermore, these characters are of prime importance in peopling these distant and strange settings, bringing human perception, reactions, and evaluations to these fantastic scenes. By their descriptions and reactions, Qfwfq and his friends take us back to the scene; by their human speech and social behavior they bring the scene forward to us. When the jump seems too great, our nervousness is reflected in humor: we laugh at a mollusk dreaming of growing a mustache. But after this initial discomfort, we may settle into an understanding of the continuity of all time, all space, all life.

The last element to discuss as a means of creating the fantastic are the actual stories, the narrative structures of the twelve tales. There are two emphases: the etiological stories that present origins (e.g., of light, matter, the moon's position) and the more psychological stories that show characters in fairly static conditions searching for understanding and control of their environment. (These groupings are not, of course, absolute, since there is some overlapping.) The etiological tales treat both specific origins of light in "At Daybreak" and more cosmic processes, as in the expansion of the universe described in "All at One Point" ("Tutto in un punto"), but neither of these is a "pourquoi tale," as folklorists call a story that tells why the crow is black or why the rabbit has a short tail. With the possible exception of "Games without End" ("Giochi senza fine") and "The Spiral" ("La spirale"), the stories do not tell *why* something happened, but *what it was like* when it did happen. There are at least two fantastic elements: that Qfwfq and his humanoid crew should have been present and that the event should happen so quickly, as a discrete event that one could see occurring dramatically, rather than over a period of thousands of years, as science would describe it. Thus in "Without Colors" we imagine what the world must have been without colors and how spectacular the first colors must have been; the story is complicated by a reworking of the Orpheus and Eurydice myth, as Ayl prefers the subtle world of grays to the new startling hues. In terms of ordinary physics, it could not have happened that way since if there were light for grays and whites, there would have been light to be reflected by colored objects; perhaps the model is a photographic one, the black and white films in contrast to the color films? Similarly in "At Daybreak," we learn not so much why sunlight began but what it would have been like not to see and then to see light for the first time. The scientific citation gives a nominal reason, the thickening of matter in general, but the characters experience both processes unaware of any causal connection. In "The Aquatic Uncle" ("Lo zio acquatico") and "The Dinosaurs" ("I dinosauri"), the problem of origin becomes more complex, since we see ends of traditions in contrast with new ones. In the first story Qfwfq loses his reptilian girlfriend Lll (Lilith?) to his old fish uncle, as she becomes more interested in the evolutionary rear guard. In the latter story, Qfwfq plays the role of the older species, learning its joys and sorrows. Similarly "The Distance of the Moon" shows the relations of the earth and moon, as an etiological tale that gives a mythic view of what the moon is like more than it explains why the moon drifted away. The last sentence describing the moon is possible thanks to a rich interplay of values that are finally transferred and rooted in the moon, values of sexuality, mystery, secrecy, and dreamy purity. The interplay of animality and abstraction is reminiscent of *The Nonexistent Knight,* and we find again a triangle of lovers, not in the usual configuration of two loving one, but in series, X loving Y who loves Z who loves a mystery. The values and desires become more and more complicated as the story moves from the fantastic local color of milk-gathering on the moon. The stay there is an exile for Qfwfq but a transcendence or even an apotheosis for Mrs. Vhd Vhd as she, even more successfully than Gurduloo ever could, becomes the moon, the object of the Deaf One's desires.

The other two stories that are both etiological and epic are "All at One Point" and "Games without End." From a scientific point of view, as Calvino points out,[6] the pair show Qfwfq's interest in hypotheses, since they exemplify two different hypotheses about the origin of the cosmos; is Qfwfq a little too willing to remember *wie es eigentlich gewesen ist?* Furthermore, each has an entirely different mood. "All at One Point" begins in high domestic comedy and ends in worship of Mrs. Ph(i)Nk$_0$, who is a sort of Mother Earth.[7] The fantasy portrays a group of beings who lived all at one point, expanded with the universe, and met again, or imagined doing so. Indeed Mrs. Ph(i)Nk$_0$ makes a grand statement: "Oh, if I only had some room, how I'd like to make noodles for you boys!" (p. 46; "Ragazzi, avessi un po' di spazio, come mi piacerebbe farvi le tagliatelle!" p. 59). This statement not only allows the boys to imagine a world in which such a deed would be possible (a rich, forward-looking anachronism), but she seems to initiate the very concept of space and "properly speaking space itself, and time" in "a true outburst of general love" (p. 47; p. 60). As Qfwfq sees it in retrospect, her dream and the dreams she inspired were the models for the world and the universe, and the mood is both jovial and generous. The other story, "Games without End," shows playing to be the origin of the universe, on both an atomic and a galactic level, as Qfwfq and his playmate Pfwfp compete. Their play has no aim except to pass time and to spite each other. The fantasy lies in the exaggeration of the game, escalating it until the players are trapped in it, racing before and behind each other as in a hall of mirrors. The game loses its simplicity and pleasure, of course, as the cosmic system, once established, takes control. The players have created, from their point of view, a sort of Frankenstein's monster.

The last grouping of stories we can make could have started with "Games without End," since the theme they have in common is the search for personal control of environment. Often with limited action, these stories explore characters' hypotheses as they seek understanding and control. In both "A Sign in Space" ("Un segno nello spazio") and "The Light-Years" ("Gli anni-luce") Qfwfq tries to create something, to extend himself as a maker in control of part of his environment. In the first story, however, through another game of competition, signs become so numerous that the world becomes confused, and space becomes defined in terms of signs, not vice versa, as Qfwfq had originally intended. In the latter story, Qfwfq is not the initiator, but a somewhat paranoid responder to another sign-maker; his concern here becomes his reputation within the cosmos, which he feels he must correct. His discovery, however, is that the universe is expanding so intricately that his power to change his "image" is diminishing to nothing: he can wait in peace for the final judgment, since he can do no more. This sort of abstraction begins to dominate the tales, here and especially in the sequels in *t zero;* it is rich, sometimes hard to read, and often available to several interpretations. We will notice as well the predominance of games as models in the later works, especially in *The Castle of Crossed Destinies.*

"How Much Shall We Bet?" ("Quanto scommettiamo") is also a competition and game story, as two characters try to control the future through bets of the most hypothetical sort. One of the funniest of the stories, this tale pits the daring Qfwfq against the cautious and exacting Dean (k)yK; the two characters are, respectively, the spirits of hypothesis or fantasy and of realism personified. Qfwfq bets for fun, as a game, but loses himself in his "passion for gambling" into the "most marginal and aleatory" events (p. 90; p. 109). He realizes that he is creating forms and models, racing toward a future that will bring his desires to confusion. The brilliant parody of the last pages finds Qfwfq and Dean (k)yK working for a research foundation, the Dean claiming his wins, Qfwfq dreaming of the past when things were simpler.

"The Form of Space" ("La forma dello spazio") has even less of a story; there is a long series of hypotheses, some frantic action, and more hypotheses, with little real change. It becomes a reflection upon the infinite possibilities of space. The narrative drive comes from a nominal, mundane triangle of stereotyped characters (the voluptuous Ursula H'x, the carefully uniformed Lieutenant Fenimore, and Qfwfq) and the fantasies Qfwfq projects onto this static world. He even reflects on the reflections, playing with the letters as he writes them much as did Sister Theodora. Once again the thoughts of a character take precedence over the physical action.

Still in this group, but embracing the others as well through its complexity is "The Spiral," which closes the volume. The story (if it may be called that) moves through four stages, two in the first division and one in each of the following divisions. First Qfwfq as a mollusk reminisces about the freedom of the good old days, in some delightful lines. He concludes, in his conversational way:

When you're young, all evolution lies before you, every road is open to you, and at the same time you can enjoy the fact of being there on the rock, flat mollusk-pulp, damp and happy. If you compare yourself with the limitations that came afterwards, if you think of how having one form excludes other forms, of the monotonous routine where you finally feel trapped, well, I don't mind saying life was beautiful in those days. (P. 142)

Quando uno è giovane, ha davanti a sé l'evoluzione intera con tutte le vie aperte, e nello stesso tempo può godersi il fatto d'esser lí sullo scoglio, polpa di mollusco piatta e umida e beata. Se si paragona con le limitazioni venute dopo, se si pensa a quello che l'avere una forma fa escludere di altre forme, al tran-tran senza imprevisti in cui a un certo punto ci si finisce per sentire imbottigliato, ebbene, posso dire che allora era un bel vivere. (Pp. 170–71)

Qfwfq clearly realizes the richness of freedom that allows fantasies that are no more than fantasies. (But the story also tests the notion because they can be fulfilled and then be limiting, as we will see in a moment.)

If there is excitement in doing nothing there is also excitement in change, especially when females begin to appear: "The water transmitted a special vibration, a kind of brrrum brrrum brrrum" (p. 143; "L'acqua trasmetteva una vibrazione speciale, come un frin frin frin," p. 172). The second stage of the story begins here with the limitation of Qfwfq's freedom in general, but an expansion of it in a specific direction. So he turns his fantasies to females, imagining the many possible forms they might have. He feels, however, that he himself must be distinct, and so he hopes to make a shell, much as Qfwfq the sign-maker had left his mark in "A Sign in Space."

The next section is the brilliant description already mentioned of Qfwfq's view of the shore with its rich detail and historical continuity. He reflects: "*I see all this and I feel no amazement because making the shell implied also making the honey in the wax comb and the coal [etc.] . . . and so I feel as if, in making the shell, I had also made the rest*" (p. 148; "*vedo tutto questo a non provo nessuna meraviglia perché il fare la conchiglia implicava anche fare il miele nel favo di cera e il carbone [etc.] . . . e cosí nel fare la conchiglia mi pare d'aver fatto anche il resto,*" p. 178). Not that we have an explanation from physical chemistry or the like; we have an idea of what might have been his feeling as he decided to extend himself through making something, and we have a commentary on the creative process in general. In the last section, Qfwfq reflects on how this proliferation of making might be understood or even controlled. In making an image that could be apprehended visually, he had had faith that eyes would come to exist *as a consequence,* to perceive what was produced to be seen, by a sophisticated complication of Lamarckian evolution. But to his chagrin it was not his girlfriends that developed eyes, but others, who had not even had the idea—or so he thinks; his prejudices against non-mollusks become quite clear at the end. If he does not gain control visually himself over his surroundings, however, he feels he lives in the eyes of others that he made possible and in a wider conceptual world he helped create. In this abstract realization he loses his pride and gains a sense of his due place in vast surroundings. "The Spiral" thereby, offers a more comprehensive conclusion to Qfwfq's dilemma of facing an ever more complex world. His rich mental fantasy both frees and limits him as he maturely assesses the range of his hypotheses.

The psychological appeal of *Cosmicomics* is complex. We find delight in the freedom of the stories as they range through the widest orders of space and time, humanizing them for us. The humanization is rich, thanks to the variety of characters, the jokes comparing prehistorical and modern times, and the search for order and individuation in the midst of a proliferating universe. Insofar as Qfwfq finds order, coherence, and understanding, the book offers us the ordinary fantasy of affirmation; insofar as Qfwfq has to shrug his shoulders and try to continue to be free in a changing cosmos, the book tends toward a wider, amoral fantasy of affirmation, which plays with design for its own sake, not for a Weltanschauung that might order experience. We find this latter appeal in the abstract scientific quotations, the games with characters' names that look like mathematical formulas, and Qfwfq's adventures in the making of signs, symbols, and models, especially in "How Much Shall We Bet?" when he bets simply for fun, not to express himself or to conquer something. Indeed he personifies the free desire to play with forms, alternatives, futures, until his nemesis Dean (k)yK begins to call him to account.

We do not have the same sorts of hero and enemy we find in Frye's version of romance; there are contests between Qfwfq and other characters, both named (Pfwfp, Kgwgk, Dean (k)yK, Zahn, even Uncle N'ba N'ga) and unnamed (the sign-maker or sign-makers in "The Light-Years"), but they are not villains according to a given social order. Indeed they would seem to have rights at least equal to Qfwfq's. Often a tale ends with a stand-off as the universe becomes ever more complex, without the marriages and social reintegrations typical of romance. More useful, therefore, would be to see the conflict as between the enemy of ignorance, confusion, fear and the hero of understanding, trust, availability to change (*disponibilité*). We travel with Qfwfq into the fantastic past richly described and humanly interpreted, and much of our wish fulfillment comes from the personal, guided tour he gives us of the origins of our universe. He makes the strange seem familiar, as an eyewitness in the past, as a contemporary familiar with scientific theories, and as a gifted storyteller. He is a natural raconteur, poised, deft, and witty. He is also very human in his pride, lust, and hope. His gift of language allows him both satire in good fun and evocations of natural phenomena that are vivid, sensuous, rich. The fantasy of affirmation provides praise for the breadth and richness of nature and hope that there is, if not an ultimate order, at least understanding available to us. At its most intense, it celebrates the loving presence of Mrs. Phi(n)k_0, who would make noodles for the boys if only she had room.

We have plenty of potential villains in the nameless pranksters who flash signs across the cosmos like Big Brother, in the slick Lieutenant Fenimore, and even in Dean (k)yK, a perverse old man from the commedia dell'arte. But they never gain control over Qfwfq's world, and Qfwfq always survives. The greater evil, rather, is the loss of self in the increasingly confused world. The tales exorcise this evil in various ways, through a narrative twist that acts it out, as in the end of "The Dinosaurs" when Qfwfq catches a train and loses himself in the crowd; through humor, as in "How Much Shall We Bet?"; through a dramatic acceptance of the dark, lustful, animal side of man, as in "The Distance of the Moon"; or through a more abstract understanding that leads toward hope, as in "The Light-Years," "The Spiral," and even perhaps "A Sign in

Space." The admission of human animality, and the more general breaking of taboos and proprieties are further sources for fantasy of denial. The mollusk realizes the difficulties of love life in the open ocean, and Qfwfq muses on the sexual implications of the compressed world of "All at One Point" and the linear world of "The Form of Space." A few characters are wonderfully mysterious in their love for the dark, like Ayl in "Without Colors" and the sister G'd(w)^n (Gudrun?) in "At Daybreak"; the Deaf One in "The Distance of the Moon" is another example of a strange and secretive turn to the mind. Thus we have some glimpses of the dark, unfathomable side of our world and psyche to complement the skillful explanations and insights that Qfwfq gives us.

In the epigraphs to the stories, we review scientific theories in concise summaries of our conventional ideas about the origins of certain phenomena, before Qfwfq gives us his elaboration of how it was at the beginning. I do not think it is forcing matters to suggest that the stories follow a mythic pattern such as Eliade describes in seeking insights into things through exploration of their origins. Especially in the second group of stories, we follow Qfwfq's efforts to gain control over portions of his environment, and in the others, more generally, he is constantly trying to evaluate, to define, to understand what is new and his (and others') reactions. Further, in their very format the stories become a form of ritual as they repeat the same strategy of a scientific introduction and a personalized exploration of the past. The scientific citation represents our conventional and most authoritative mode of thinking. Within this structure Qfwfq operates with the associational freedom of the dream: his stories rarely have plots; he corrects himself; he remembers things at the last moment. The fantasy of freedom within all space and all time, with a handful of humanlike consciousnesses allows the stories to humanize the strange, to make familiar the unknown. Qfwfq's style of speech and complexity of character give him a conversational sort of authority that avoids overly neat control, by either artistic or social norms. After all, the predominant values of the book are not social but cosmic, and the values of that system are not conventional but open.

9

t zero: **Fantasy and Abstraction**

In previous chapters we have followed the mediations of fantasy by more ordinary ways of thinking. One way, the grotesque, is a specialized form of artistic stylization. Two others, history and science, are formal disciplines of thought. "The mundane" is not so much a form of thought as a particular stimulus that the characters interpreted according to their individual fantasies, and self-creation is a rather general and idealistic notion. In Calvino's works there is a general movement toward abstraction, toward the increasing refinement and internalization of fantasy so that we keep drawing closer to the calculations of the characters within fantastic environments. In *t zero* (1967)[1] the environments are sometimes specifically fantastic, sometimes mundane but interpreted as fantastic or expanded to fantastic dimensions by the interpreting character. (In *The Castle of Crossed Destinies* and *Invisible Cities,* this strategy reaches the ultimate: there is virtually no environment at all and the characters create just about everything). In *t zero,* a collection of stories, we find fantasy based once again on scientific styles of thought, often more strictly mathematical models. These are all first-person narratives, but narrative or even character is less important than the abstract thought and form of the stories. Our friend Qfwfq continues for half the book, but he is less personable than the voice from *Cosmicomics,* more cerebral, more arcane. These narrators act or react little; they think a lot, testing their world with formula, calculation, abstraction. This volume includes some of Calvino's most experimental narratives, including some that may try a reader's patience; as a book, however, the theme and variation of fantasy intertwined with abstraction provide much critical interest.

Generally, we take formulas to be the ultimate in concise expression of truth, as they sum up laws, principles, relations according to algebraic signs, as in $D = rt$, $A = \frac{1}{2}bh$, or $E = mc^2$. On the other hand, formulas of speech or writing ("Dear sir") may become so conventional as to lose the components' meanings. Homeric formulas such as "grey-eyed Athene" or "brilliant Odysseus" describe a characteristic attribute of a character, but the primary use of these formulas was not so much to offer new information as to fulfill metrical demands.[2] In both algebraic and verbal formulas we have a conventional grouping of symbols to represent an essential meaning of a generally agreed upon truth. What we often forget, however, is that formulas may exclude as much as they include, because of their selectivity within certain frames of reference (e.g., Euclidean geometry), simplifying problems to a limited set of variables.[3] Accordingly, we may emphasize two ways in which formulas work in the stories of *t zero*. First, the narrators use stylistic formulas as a kind of shorthand to present their stories, for example, cartoon strips and the accompanying conventions. Such formulas are efficient in establishing the fantasy quickly, but with some loss of depth. (Abstraction is in some senses a dis-incarnation.) The second use of formula is the effort by the narrators to understand a complex situation around them, often with the result that their logical, abstract thought fails to explain the fantastic milieu.

The volume comprises three sets of stories. The first, "More of Qfwfq," continues the format of *Cosmicomics,* exploring cosmic phenomena on a still more speculative and fantastic level. The "Priscilla" stories continue with Qfwfq nominally as a narrator, but we lose his personality in the complicated speculations about reproduction on the cellular level. The last group, called "t zero" after the title story, abandons Qfwfq altogether (unless the Q of "t zero" is a last form) in favor of a most cerebral and literary sort of mind, which confronts four unusual and dramatic situations. It seems to me a moot point whether this sort of mind is differentiated into separate characters, since thought takes precedence over personality in these highly abstract stories.

In discussing the creation of the fantastic, we will consider the stories by these groups, using the format of *Cosmicomics* for comparison. The "More of Qfwfq" stories share many of the same devices: the use of a scientific statement dramatically enacted with many appeals to the senses, the reactions of human-like characters, the stories of origins. The emphasis here, however, is on fewer characters who react less socially and more according to personal formulas. Two of the four stories, "The Soft Moon" ("La molle luna") and "The Origin of the Birds" ("L'origine degli uccelli"), are still etiological, but it is the formulaic assessment of the narrator that receives the emphasis, not the actual creation. The other two stories, "Crystals" ("I cristalli") and "Blood, Sea" ("Il sangue, il mare"), are even more hypothetical. Throughout, many of the devices of *Cosmicomics* are intensified and abstracted, possibly to their theoretical extremes.

In "The Soft Moon" we find the usual scientific citation and narrative of how it happened, as Qfwfq remembers. The story, however, exploits more specifically two techniques: disagreement between the characters as they evaluate the novelty and the comparison of the old and the modern worlds. We have seen other characters, like Granny Bb'b and the aquatic uncle, disagree with others more acceptant of change, but in this story the disagreement is expanded to a continuous dialogue between Qfwfq and Sybil, who are for all practical purposes the only characters present. Sybil, a scientist, readily accepts the moon's approach toward the earth: "the phenomenon was foreseen" (p. 5; "è un fenomeno previsto," p. 11), she coolly says to the frightened Qfwfq, who thinks the soft moon is disgusting (like Roquentin of *La Nausée?*). Her scientific formulas give her precise expectations of how the moon should behave. When it, however, fails to follow them, Qfwfq sees a new, unsettling side of her nature, somewhat animal, and we are left to speculate upon the causes as she evidently loses her self-respect, becoming fat and lazy. Qfwfq, on the other hand, does not have such a strict conceptual framework; he distrusts systems and the notion of perfection. At the end, for example, he rejects the idea that there are pure materials on the earth. His system, insofar as he has one, is in accepting the order of his business world, his Madison Avenue of aeons ago. This double time perspective is the second technique from *Cosmicomics* that Calvino stretches here to further extremes. Thus the earth had, some millions of years ago, a business world like ours, in a parody of the Golden Age trope. This fantasy allows Qfwfq to reject the modern order as a pale copy of the good old days, his formulaic standard for how things should be, a formula not of numbers but of more general social conventions. The story is bittersweet, a parody of explanations and expectations, but also one of the saddest in the book. At the end, neither character feels open to the future; neither has grown to accept fantastic occurrences that do not fit his or her preconceived models.

"The Origin of the Birds" is similarly an etiological story following the style of *Cosmicomics,* but the variation this time is not the characters' limitations but the ingenious exploitations of the frame of the story. Qfwfq tells us at the beginning, following the customary scientific reference, that the story can be told better with comic strips than with ordinary sentences. This is apparently true, because poor old Qfwfq, this time, cannot remember everything with his usual total recall, and, indeed, he has learned that the totality of knowledge is beyond the human mind. The comic strips, with all their conventions, are a means of allowing the reader to help make up the story and to allow Qfwfq to hide his ignorance. There are many pop art jokes on how dizziness might be indicated by a spiral, how balloons include characters' speech, how captions summarize action, as well as the interjections "bang!" (in cubic letters), "Flash!" and "Eureka!" Of the many such conventions (and there are at least half a dozen more), I want to discuss the interjections as formulas, how they reduce a complex action to a conventional symbol. Thus "bang!" represents the collision of two worlds, reducing a fantastic, complex incident to the same word we might use for the popping of a balloon. Qfwfq realizes this limitation of his comic strip conventions and constantly exhorts us not to read too closely but to get the general picture and to fill it in ourselves, or even to make up intervening adventures or alternative lines of action if we do not like the ones he suggests: "If you don't like this story you can think up another one: the important thing is to have me arrive there" (p. 24; "Se questa non vi piace

potete immaginarvi un'altra storia: l'importante è farmi arrivare là," p. 30).
Qfwfq self-consciously makes the reader a confederate in the creation of the
fantasy.

The next use of interjections is to illustrate Qfwfq's insight: "An explosion
marked with the word 'Flash!' or else 'Eureka!' in capital letters" (p. 26; "Un
lampo contrassegnato dalla scritta 'Flash!' oppure 'Eureka!' a lettere maiu-
scole," p. 31). The formulas are so alike that Qfwfq feels he can give us a
choice! On the one hand he is making fun of the epiphany he is having, but
on the other he is rejecting the cartoon parody by suggesting how inexact it is.
With this mediating irony he continues to describe his instant of total knowledge in which he sees the union of his world of things as they are and the birds'
world of things as they might be, all in one complete system. This realization
itself unites the two worlds for Qfwfq, despite the attempts of the birds to tear
them apart (there may be a play here on Aristophanes' comedy *The Birds*).
Qfwfq has seen the real and the what-might-have-been-real, realism and fantasy
united, but only for an instant, since it is too much for him and the other
characters (presumably including the reader) to maintain. The birds destroy the
frame of the story, much as Alice finally wrecks Wonderland; they tear up the
pages of the comic strips. Qfwfq forgets what really happened, doubting
whether today's birds are the same as the original ones. The last strip of cartoons suggested is made out of photographs zeroing in (by zoom lens or en-
largement) on a bird's eye, its vision annihilating ours.

The fantasy of this story—the Gilgamesh-like trips to birdland, the
Ariosto-like trips through the air, and the brief instant of total knowledge—is
richly and humorously complicated by the frame of comic strips. Comic strip
conventions serve the fantasy in two ways. First, we can recognize them
quickly, the balloons for speech, the legend, the colors, the diagonals, and we
can expect a stylized world of exaggeration, fast action, even violence, as in
the many comic strips of adventure and science fiction, both American and
European. Second, because of our strong sense of the medium, we are startled
when Qfwfq starts to depart from it, parodying the conventions: Old U(h)
draws diagonals in a panel, a bird lays an egg on the intersection; it breaks and
the next panel is all smeared yellow with yolk. Thus the conventional comic
strip frame becomes as real as any other part of the scene. Similarly, Qfwfq's
return to the land of the birds by means of gluing a bird to his panel so that
it is dragged along thereby pushes comic strip formulas a step past the ways in
which we are used to seeing them. As a result, the mood is a mixture of
hilarity, exaggerated action, irony, and whimsy. There are other shifts of mood
as old U(h) changes his view of the birds from rejection to worship and divina-
tion and Qfwfq changes from acceptance to doubt, but the strongest effect is
the author's ingenious exploitation of the highly conventional frame.

The last two stories of the first section are less complex in their creation
of fantasy. They also move away from the general procedure of *Cosmicomics*.

"Crystals" speculates on how the world might have been, all crystallized; this hypothesis is the formula for perfection for the Qfwfq of this story, who hated the Heraclitean flux of the earlier world and who took the first crystal as a step toward total crystallization. His girlfriend Vug (quite a name, in itself),[4] continuing the dialectic of many of these stories, takes the opposite view, that it is the imperfections that are more interesting. The two characters continue their playful arguments, in the past and in the present, when they meet looking in the windows of Tiffany's: he likes rubies because of their pure form; she admires the color due to chemical impurity. At last, in her Manhattan apartment, he realizes that the structural formula of crystals can be interpreted both ways, but hers is the more interesting: "The victory of the crystals (and of Vug) has been the same thing as their defeat (and mine)" (p. 38; "La vittoria dei cristalli (e di Vug) è stata la stessa cosa della loro sconfitta (e della mia)," p. 45). The fantasy is gentler, more conversational than in most of *Cosmicomics,* but it is also more abstract.

"Blood, Sea" has even less action and breadth in time and space, except in the mind of a most cerebral Qfwfq, who constantly reflects upon the chemical similarity of our blood and the sea. But this is both a humorous and an ironic story, for Qfwfq is traveling in a Volkswagen, trapped with two companions he does not care for, especially one Signor Cècere, who is now driving, and a third, female companion, Zylphia, whom he does like. His repugnance for Signor Cècere and desire for Zylphia become elaborately reinterpreted through his blood-sea equation, in long, wandering sentences suggestive of the continuity and flux of the ocean. His extensive mental ramblings, however, cannot free him from his position; he fantasizes about sexual freedom with Zylphia, about killing Signor Cècere, and about the modern, mechanical world as a part of all time, but he gains no real freedom. Instead, he is killed in a mundane traffic accident in a scene comparable to the gratuitous disasters of American naturalism (such as the boat wreck that opens *The Sea Wolf* or the car accident in *The Great Gatsby*). His elaborate metaphor is ironically fulfilled when the car plunges down a precipice into the sea: "the sea of common blood which floods over the crumpled metal isn't the blood-sea of our origin but only the infinitesimal detail of the outside, of the insignificant and arid outside, a number in the statistics of accidents over the weekend" (p. 51; "il mare di sangue comune che allaga la lamiera pesta non è il sangue-mare delle origini ma solo un infinitesimo dettaglio del fuori, dell'insignificante e arido fuori, un numero per la statistica dei sinistri nelle giornate di weekend," pp. 59–60). Qfwfq's formula of blood and sea is thus a failure, and another, much less rich than his (the accident figures), replaces it. And thus while there is nothing fantastic about four travelers in a Volkswagen, the fantasy lies in Qfwfq's mind as he not only hypothesizes his blood-sea formula but also interprets the words and actions of others. Yet however ingenious, however poetically suggestive his fantasy is, it cannot free him from the car or from the wreck. Neither he nor any of the other characters gains the sort of freedom or insight we have been finding in the earlier stories. "Blood, Sea" shows a darker, more ironic side to Calvino's fantasy, akin to some of the realistic stories. The Qfwfq who has, in different forms, been our guide through so many stories is killed in a most unfantastic way. Or perhaps, given the conventions, this is the most fantastic aspect?

The second group of stories, "Priscilla," is akin to "The Spiral" of *Cosmicomics* in its complex summation of the stories that precede it. In "Priscilla" the three stories follow seven impressive citations, not only from modern scientists, but from Galileo and such writers as Bossuet, Bataille, and Sartre. Obviously the conceptual framework is considerably wider this time, since several of the positions disagree about whether life continues or how we should accept change. Furthermore, the customary citations from physical chemistry and genetics have been joined by observations from theology and philosophy. The stories, to use the word in its widest sense, are the extended thoughts of a most intelligent speaker, designated as Qfwfq in the first story, but not mentioned again by name. In the first Priscilla story, "Mitosis," he (or it) speaks to us from a cellular level. The fantasy is the guided tour not only of his Lilliputian physical state, but also of his mental state, his urge to divide, his hypothetical thoughts about physical love, even when he is a nonsexed creature. Both fantasies coincide in the biological formulas of genetics: "As language I had all those specks or twigs called chromosomes, and therefore all I had to do was repeat those specks or twigs and I was repeating myself" (p. 68; "Io come linguaggio avevo tutti quei bruscolini o stecchini detti cromosomi, quindi bastava ripetere quei bruscolini o stecchini per ripetere me stesso," p. 75). Both fascinated and trapped by language, he comments on his limited viewpoint, observing that "me" was the only word (formula) he knew (p. 63; p. 71) and spinning long elaborate sentences. He tries to expand his world and describes his desires to extend himself, by means of his chromosomes, although obviously the verbal formulas will suffice. With an accelerated pace, such as Calvino often uses, Qfwfq finally expands himself to the role of a living person (we assume) in Paris. The long dormancy of potential, of abstract formula is suddenly realized in a series of new formulas (clothing, address) that we accept as factual, realistic. This twist is similar to "Blood, Sea" and pivots around an attractive female character, but the moods are completely different; instead of the oppressive irony of the other story, we find here a lighter intimacy in a narrator who finally shifts levels drastically.

The second Priscilla story, "Meiosis," offers a cell's-eye view of the second kind of cellular division, the sexual process, which is more advanced evolutionarily. Qfwfq, if we may still call the narrator by that name, has fallen in love with Priscilla, explaining it by a biochemical formula: their chains of nucleic acids and proteins have somehow become mutually attracted. Such explanations continue at length, defining both the speaker and Priscilla according to the formulas of genetics, biochemistry, and microbiology, which Calvino carries off with considerable aplomb. The final joke is that Priscilla (and presumably the narrator) is a camel; the formulas that we assumed referred to humans are wide enough to include other mammals! The fantasy has exploited this ambiguity, forcing us to recognize our similarity with animals, something our culture tends to ignore.

The last Priscilla story, "Death," pushes the desire for theoretical expansion through formulas to its extreme, the wish to live forever. More diversified than ever, our speaker finds a universal urge for self-perpetuation, culminating in the human's use of language, in its broadest sense, including words, ideograms, morphemes, numbers, punch cards, magnetic tapes, tattoos, social norms, advertisements, and napalm bombs (p. 91; pp. 98–99). Thus survival is not through biological existence but through the formulas of language, and the narrator abandons the page he is writing so that "a written I and a written Priscilla" (p. 92; "un io scritto e una Priscilla scritta," p. 99) can meet each other in new forms.

Taken together, the Priscilla stories are the most technical, the most philosophically ambitious of this volume (and perhaps of Calvino's entire corpus). As experimental narratives these stories work more with formula, mood, and irony than with character and action. The fantasy becomes extremely abstract, losing not so much the sensual appeal as the appeal of the human interpreter. Qfwfq turns into a computer, when we are perhaps hoping for a Granny Bb'b. But there is also a range of humor from the juxtaposition of disparate elements to the quick changes in pace, as we noticed. Especially in the last two stories, Qfwfq finds that language, the ultimate formula, is the surest means for survival. This conclusion is remarkably close to the end of Borges' story of "The Immortal," who, like Qfwfq, has lived through great expanses of time.[5]

Abstraction does not leave us in the last four stories, the "t zero" section, but we have much stronger and more dramatic frames. In each, the narrator is a specialist in hypothesis. As in many of the stories of this volume, the fantasy is in the mind of the narrator as he creates and tests hypotheses. While these hypotheses are reminiscent of the German's thoughts under duress in "The Crow," there is an increased level of abstraction, even to the point of self-parody. The narrator of "t zero," for example, has a mathematical turn of mind, indicating the absolute moment of truth as t (for time) sub zero (t_0) as part of a sequence of times. He designates himself as "Q," perhaps the last ghost of Qfwfq. His elaborate speculations stop the dramatic action: a lion has leaped at him; he has shot an arrow at the lion—what will be the outcome? Space and time are loci of potential, and the narrator suspends time, expanding it with his own hypotheses, applying, as he says, languages to it. He observes that he could apply all possible languages in order to live extensively in this instant-universe: "I must get used to conceiving my speech simultaneously in all possible languages if I want to live my universe-instant extensively" (p. 108; "bisogna che mi abitui a pensare il mio discorso contemporaneamente in tutte le lingue possibili se voglio vivere estensivamente il mio istante-universo," p. 116). This formulation accurately sums up much of the fantasy in these stories: the narrator seeks to live hypothetically beyond his ordinary space-time existence by projecting ideas in as many formulas as possible. Paradoxically, however, the moment retains its own purity beyond all this formulation. Thus the irony is that the lion and the arrow will meet where they will meet regardless of the narrator's brilliant thoughts. His fantasies cannot change the physics, but they can give his mind something to do, give some comfort, some recreation, some positive feeling instead of helplessness.

"The Chase" ("L'inseguimento") operates similarly, with a ratiocinative narrator and a dramatic situation in suspense: in the midst of a traffic jam he is followed by an enemy with a gun. The situation is less immediately dramatic than the problem of the lion and the arrow, but then there is less suspension of time, since the lanes of traffic advance, giving the narrator new material for his hypotheses (indeed the word "hypothesis" occurs several times). The resolution, however, becomes unexpectedly complicated, as the narrator turns out also to be a pursuer of a potential victim, and we embark on a sort of hall-of-mirrors symmetry reminiscent of Gide's fascination with the *en abîme* figure. In this case the narrator shoots his enemy, escapes his follower, and joins a new traffic flow, where neither the pursuers nor the pursued can be identified. Even more than in "Games without End," the characters are incorporated into a complicated system. In "The Chase" it is never given why the men are enemies: the Aristotelian senses of plot of a character's motivation are not important here. Instead we focus on the narrator's thoughts as we explore various possibilities. The final action is both gratuitous and, ultimately, inconclusive. The design, the formula of the followed and the follower, is paramount even in its final redefinition.

Similarly in "The Night Driver ("Il guidatore notturno") we have again a traffic problem, but with more action and more choice for action on the part of the narrator. This time, however, there are no other characters on the scene, and the narrator hypothesizes what his girlfriend and his rival for the girl might be doing on the road he is traveling. Yet the characters and the issues are strangely abstract. Letters represent the characters (Y and Z—"I" is presumably X) and towns, and emotions are generalized to love, hate, and jealousy, without, for example, any details of the quarrel that started X on his drive. The final complication is the use of the telephone as a medium for exchange of information, overshadowing even physical presence: such as X's final realization, as he turns around to return home thinking of the problem as an abstract problem in tactics, not interpersonal relations.

"The Count of Monte Cristo" ("Il conte di Montecristo") presents us with opposing models: Dantès hypothesizes that the topography of the Château d'If is so complex that he will never escape; while the Abbé Faria, on the other hand, believes that escape is possible. The good Abbé throws himself into his tunneling with such a resolve that he loses his sense of gravity, sticking his head into Dantès's cell upside-down: his fantasy has overcome ordinary physical laws. For his part, Dantès's explorations are all mental and of increasing complexity: the outside is his past, and there is no escaping that, but then the future would be inside, in the drawings of the fortress and of the island of Monte Cristo—which resemble each other. Thus the abstractions of the inside and the outside of the prison and the cave become reversible. These models are further complicated by the figure of Napoleon, whom Faria would liberate, and *his* island, Elba. The final complication is the introduction of the author, Alexandre Dumas, whom Dantès sees as a similar dealer in hypotheses, since he sorts through the plot outlines his helpers bring him, creating a series of more or less consistent possibilities, in the same manner that Faria and Dantès consider the possibility of escape. To dramatize and make concrete this abstraction, Calvino has Faria dig through a wall to discover Dumas at his writing desk! However neat his own model, Dantès speculates, escape will be possible *only if* the real fortress does *not* coincide with his hypotheses. Readers of the original novel know that such is the case; indeed Dantès mentions as a possibility a précis of how the novel continues. Whether anything "really" happens, literarily speaking, depends on the reader; such indeterminacy parallels Dr. Trelawney in *The Cloven Viscount,* who is borrowed from one framework and used in another, who exists finally in the realm of readers' hypotheses. In Calvino's story, at any rate, it seems clear that Dantès's formulaic thought, pushed to abstract extremes, will be of little practical use in an escape attempt.

Despite the individual differences between the stories of *t zero,* particularly the last four, what may we suggest that they have in common in creating their fantasy by using formulas? First, much more than in any of the earlier stories, there is the primacy of the narrator, through whose thoughts we experience everything, from his basic perceptions to his most abstract hypotheses. The fantasy comes largely from a mind at work trying to reconcile perception with preconceived formula. There are, commonly, two resolutions: (1) the narrator escapes into an exaggerated form of his thoughts, a design of image and formula, as in "The Origin of the Birds," the three Priscilla stories, "The Chase," and "The Night Driver," or (2) the narrator realizes that his speculations are inadequate, that the world is more complicated and unpredictable than his formulas allowed, as in (with variations) "The Soft Moon," "Crystals," "Blood, Sea," and, especially, "t zero." "The Count of Monte Cristo" combines both resolutions, creating an extravagant combination of literary and topological abstractions, but leaving the narrator unsure of what is actually possible. In all stories, and especially in the Priscilla group, the narrator seeks to control a situation by explaining it in rational terms and by applying his careful, confident thought. Especially in the "More of Qfwfq" and the "t zero" stories, he finds that the concrete phenomena reassert their complexity over his simplified formulas. The specific, the visual, the concrete, and the mysterious—all important elements of fantasy—reassert their importance over formula. In the Priscilla stories, where thought remains paramount, there is a lack of narrative drive except with the trick endings. In "The Chase" and "The Night Driver" the design takes over, limiting the richness of the fantasy. With the increased emphasis on abstraction and design, these stories limit the manipulation of desire. The psychological appeal is therefore different from the earlier, freer narratives. As the cerebral narrators seek intellectual control of their surroundings they deny themselves freedom of their own desires, but they are often wise enough to change their desires to match the complexity of the data they receive. They change their fantasies and gain new and less ambitious insights, even through jokes or abstract designs.

In the "More of Qfwfq" and the Priscilla stories we still have the fantasy of affirmation similar to what we found in *Cosmicomics*, e.g., the humanizing of a complex phenomenon, making it familiar, enjoyable. But such experiences are complicated by the narrator's driving urge for mental control through formulation, so that there may be the same appeal of wonder or even the sublime in "Crystals," but there is also the narrator's gentle tragedy in having to change or even abandon his reductive thought. Similarly, there is an appeal to a guided tour of a cell by a cogent voice, and we may feel we understand cellular biology as never before, but the voice subverts itself either to doubt or to a narrative joke that shifts the frame unexpectedly from the cellular to the animal point of view. There is order up to a point, indeed an oppressive order of long sentences and little action, but the final order denies much of the rationalism that went before, as in the discovery that Qfwfq is speaking to us as a camel throughout "Meiosis." The appeal, besides the situation comedy, is thus in part the reassertion of a natural order over the academic voice of the, ultimately, impotent spokesman.

In each of the four stories of the final section, "t zero," the narrator realizes that his ratiocinations are useless. The thinker of "t zero" knows his thoughts will have no bearing on the outcome of the action. The narrators of "The Chase" and "The Night Driver" are content to join the abstract patterns of action suggested by their thoughts with little hope of control, understanding, or escape (although "The Chase" has further complications). The narrator of "The Count of Monte Cristo" is not sure what his thoughts are worth, although he tries so many that he lists among them his future freedom, as envisioned by Dumas. In general, the stories suggest there may be hypothetical freedom in such thinking, but it never lasts long, since it is ultimately denied.

With a stronger emphasis on such denial, we find a more ironic evaluation of thought, as in "Blood, Sea." Again a rational speaker seeks to explain many things in terms of a formula, but he is impotent, finally to be destroyed in a mundane traffic accident. The fantasy of denial is the destruction of this super-rational chatterbox whose fancy (or fantastic) thinking solves nothing. With such limitations on the fantasy, the appeal of these stories is less in terms of patterns of desire than in the reordering of values, which we can discuss mythically.

In *Cosmicomics* we found the mythic truth in the search for understanding of origins, Qfwfq reporting to us how it was in the beginning. The Qfwfq of *t zero* continues this reportage, but as it becomes more abstract it seems less specific, less poetically rich. Later even Qfwfq disappears, replaced by nameless, abstract minds, more or less human, but not personable like Qfwfq. As increasing abstraction becomes insufficient in explaining or motivating action, the mythic truth becomes, in simplest terms, the recognition that reason is inadequate. The complexity of the world foils the ambitious thinking of our rational narrators. We may think of the end of Paul Valéry's *Monsieur Teste:* "Fin intellectuelle. Marche funèbre de la pensée."[6]

Nor is the story the source of order, as it is generally in myth. The plot is secondary to mental action, and the action is simple. Long, intricate reflections fail to reach a positive conclusion. As this formula is repeated in the stories, we find a repeating pattern: the failure of abstraction and a new emphasis on the ingenious manipulations of the author who is behind it all. With the failure of the narrator to advance action or thought, the guiding hand of the author is ever more apparent. The pieces are intellectual and artistic exercises, testing the limits of words, thought, and the reader's ability to recreate the fantasies of exaggerated thought. These stories are perhaps the most theoretically ambitious of Calvino's works to 1967, in their self-reflexive abstraction, with narrators continually reaching a defeat of their mental life. As we follow these characters through the Borgesian dilemmas, we find them increasingly limited in their mental freedom. As opposed to the earlier uses of fantasy, the fantasy in these stories is ultimately more limited by irony; a flight of fancy may give them momentary freedom, but it is ultimately inadequate as a model for a new style of existence. While this conclusion implicitly criticizes the complex thought of these cerebral characters, it also affirms the rich complexity of the world around them.

10

The Castle of Crossed Destinies:
Lost betwixt Sign and Myth

This chapter and the one following may be taken as a pair because they treat two books, *The Castle of Crossed Destinies* (*Il castello dei destini incrociati*) and *Invisible Cities* (*Le città invisibili*), that Calvino worked on alternately over several years. The first part of *The Castle* appeared in 1969; *Cities* appeared in 1972, and then *The Castle* reappeared, with a second section, *The Tavern of Crossed Destinies,* in 1973.[1] We know from Calvino's "Note"[2] to the full *The Castle* that he began this Tavern section before 1969 and that it continued to intrigue him through the time he was composing *Cities.* Theoretically and thematically, the books are complementary. Briefly: for *The Castle,* the manipulation of the tarot cards to tell stories leads us to consider the generation of meanings by fixed signs. The cards as concrete "bits" of information lead us inward to an interiority of thinking, a centripetal movement that suggests a compression of mental action, but also a sterility and, ultimately, a destruction. The frame of groups of lost travelers telling their stories is tragic, even infernal. By contrast, in *Cities,* the movement is outward, to the mental projection not of personal histories, but of entire social constructs, cities, which claim, at least in the abstract, large expanses of space. Here we move expansively, centrifugally, into sheer, fecund potential, an open field for the imagination. Finally, however, we seem to arrive at the same place by either book: whether the movement is inward or outward, the human mind both joys in its variety and sorrows in its limitations. Despite the Gothic enclosure of *The Castle,* there is a multitude of meanings and possibilities; despite the freedom of *Cities,* there is still the focus of the frame, two persons talking—and getting nowhere. Marco Polo and Kublai Khan find that their expanding thoughts become too wide, too "thin," and that, if there is any truth to their game, it is in the discovery of their own minds. For them we might say that "the way out is the way in," while for *The Castle,* "the way in is the way out."

In discussing earlier novels by Calvino we could often speak of a dialectic of fantasy and a discipline of thought such as history for *The Baron* or science for *Comicomics.* For *The Castle,* the intellectual tradition Calvino is playing with is the twentieth-century interest in discontinuous information. The nineteenth century was often interested in continuities: Darwinian evolution, Hegelian dialectic, Marxian dialectical materialism, romantic views of history, and even the naturalism of Emile Zola and the American crew, Frank Norris, Jack London, and Theodore Dreiser. In the twentieth century, Einstein's theory of relativity emphasizes similar conversions and continuities. Buckminster Fuller's neoromantic notion of synergy once again stresses continuity, cohesion, cooperation. But there is another intellectual tradition, as old as Democritus, that of discrete bits of things that have their own autonomy and often seem more important than the webs we may perceive as tying them together. Now we see many variations: Russian formalism; Vladimir Propp's morphologies; the French structuralists; the phenomenological tradition; the binary codings of computers and the whole technological, mathematical world of matrices, grids, optical displays, magnetic tapes, readouts, flowcharts and other codes of information, data, "bits," and, in general, discrete items of knowledge.

The paradox becomes: we are pleased to have definite things to work with but puzzled when they have no meaning outside their context. Or to put it differently: if you continuously divide and conquer, what do you have left but a Pyrrhic victory? (The search for the ultimate building blocks in atoms has revealed many subatomic particles, among them quarks, whose number and characteristics, such as "charm," continue to grow; there is apparently no rock bottom.) The interiority of fixed signs in particular has neatness, precision, and exactitude, but there is also a kind of suffocation, an extinction within the labyrinth. The tragic vision is death by trivialization; in more optimistic moments, there is the hope that a deck may be reshuffled, so that there is continuous or "steady-state" creation of knowledge, of play, of the universe itself as all counters are remixed, relocated, revitalized by new contexts. But even such a continuity seems empty, diffuse, a product of entropy and anomie.

Perhaps the best place to start with *The Castle* is a discussion of concreteness. The 24 stories of the book are told by means of tarot cards. In the Einaudi edition (1973) the cards are pictured in the margin so that the reader may compare the narrative descriptions of the cards with the cards themselves. The Harcourt Brace Jovanovich translation (1976) not only has the engravings in the margin but eight color plates of eight cards in full size (87mm. × 175mm.; 3⅜ in. × 6¹³⁄₁₆ in.). But it is the original Ricci edition of 1969 that most sumptuously presents us the cards as objects, the book itself as an object: this folio volume (24cm. × 35.7cm.; 9½ in. × 14 in.) in printed on Fabriano paper, bound in silk, then boxed. Calvino's story *Il castello dei destini incrociati* is printed in large type (12-point Bodoni) with generous margins, stretching it to some 60 pages. After the first page, the story is always on the left-hand page, while the facing pages are given over to reproductions of the fifteenth-century tarot deck, the Visconti deck, which is housed today in two museums, the Pierpont Morgan Library in New York and the Accademia Carrara in Bergamo, Italy. (Also known as the Visconti-Sforza tarot, the deck has been described in detail by Gertrude Moakley.)[3] There are a few missing cards and a baker's dozen are owned by a Colleoni family. As editor, Franco M. Ricci was proud to "reunite" the deck in his book, to show it as complete as possible. These cards are printed full size, in five colors (the three primaries plus black and gold) on a glossy stock, then tipped-in to the book (i.e., hand-glued, each one). There are also much smaller engravings of the cards that allow us to follow the stories as the cards are laid down in lines. None of this luxury comes cheap, of course; my copy, purchased in 1971, cost 42,000 lire, then about 40 dollars. Ricci also published an English edition in 1976.

The sheer physical presentation of the cards is awesome and literarily provocative: what are these discrete objects, what are their meanings, how may they be played with? Calvino reports in his "Nota" to the Einaudi edition that he had started with a deck from Marseilles, such as you can still buy in France today, and that he played with the deck to produce stories, the first of which was "The Waverer's Tale" (the first in *The Tavern*). The cards seemed to him "a machine for constructing stories" (p. 126; "una macchina narrativa combinatoria," p. 124), and he became involved in pattern after design after permutation, finally publishing the volume of *The Castle* and *The Tavern* to be free of them.

It is important to understand how Calvino uses the cards. First of all, he does not use the elaborate traditions of tarot lore as described by, for example, Mouni Sadhu in his *Tarot: A Contemporary Course of the Quintessence of Hermetic Occultism*.[4] Phenomenologically speaking, the cards have been "bracketed out" of their own tradition and taken as pure, naive, or discrete icons; to put it differently, Calvino has deconstructed the deck. What associations Calvino wishes to accrete to them come from his own manipulations, his own fiat. As the tarots are stripped of most of the usual baggage, the choices of Calvino as author become greater and more important to the creation of the fantasy. His long love for Ariosto, for example, prompts him to observe that the Visconti deck, produced a century before *Orlando furioso,* "could have well represented the visual world in which the ariostoesque fantasy was formed."[5] Calvino is generous in his "Nota" in describing his own imaginative process with the cards. Not only does he describe the many ways he laid the cards out, but he gives a bit of theoretical background that is crucial. The idea of using the cards as "una macchina narrativa combinatoria" came to him, he reports, from Paolo Fabbri's report on "Il racconto della cartomanzia e il linguaggio degli emblemi" ("The Relation of Cartomancy and the Language of Emblems") which, in turn, drew on two Russian theories of cartomancy, one by M. I. Lekomceva and B. A. Uspenskij, the other by B. F. Egorov.[6] The former article is a semiotic approach: the cards constitute a generative mechanism for sentences. The fortuneteller knows the cards, but the subject having the fortune told knows the subject's life and prospects. Each uses the signs (the cards) differently, although the teller tries to assemble clues, hints, reactions on the part of the subject and incorporate these into the fortune as it is told. Thus the same cards represent two spheres of information and the players, both teller and subject, resort to hypotheses to bridge the two worlds. For Lekomceva and Uspenskij, these two worlds and their dialectic make up a realm of infinite freedom. In commenting on this article, B. F. Egorov takes the opposite tack. He rejects the open game model and suggests that fortune-telling is highly predetermined by rules, systems, expectations, and the format of laying out the cards, especially (by the Petersburg-Leningrad system) the central square of cards, "the heart." But while the order is very tight, the meanings generated by the cards within the order are virtually infinite: the grammar is set, but the words may be interchanged ad libitum, perhaps on the order of 12×10^{22} combinations for a tarot deck. Egorov recalls the work of G. Polti, *Les 36 Situations dramatiques* (Paris, 1894) as a pioneering (if ingenuous) attempt to see the patterns possible in plots and, of course, V. J. Propp, *Morphology of Folk Tales* (Leningrad, 1928) as a more sophisticated attempt to create a dictionary of motifs that make up all tales by various combinations. Egorov doubts that a Mendeleev's table can be constructed, but hopes that mathematical approches to literature will give rigor, insight, and thoroughness.

Calvino is obviously most intrigued. He has gone to some trouble to reflect on these ideas and has introduced them into the "Nota." He then demurs slightly in a portion missing from the Harcourt Brace Jovanovich version:

> But I cannot say that my work profits from the methodological contribution of this research. From these, I have retained above all the idea that the significance of every single card depends on the place that it has in the succession of cards that precede and follow it; taking off from this idea, I moved with autonomy, according to the internal requirement of my text. (My translation)
>
> Ma non posso dire che il mio lavoro si valga dell'apporto metodologico di queste ricerche. Di esse ho ritenuto soprattutto l'idea che il significato d'ogni singola carta dipende dal posto che essa ha nella successione di carte che la precedono e la seguono; partendo da questa idea, mi sono mosso in maniera autonoma, secondo le esigenze interne al mio testo. (P. 124).

In terms of the articles just reviewed, Calvino wants the freedom of the first one (Lekomceva and Uspenskij) to generate meanings but the rigor of the second (Egorov) to structure the arrangement of the tales: "I felt that the game had a meaning only if governed by ironclad rules; an established framework of construction was required, conditioning the insertion of one story in the others. Without it, the whole thing was gratuitous" (p. 127; "sentivo che il gioco aveva senso solo se impostato secondo certe ferree regole; ci voleva una necessità generale di costruzione che condizionasse l'incastro d'ogni storia nelle altre, se no tutto era gratuito," p. 126). He goes on to say that "not all stories I succeeded in composing visually produced good results when I set myself to writing them down. There were some that sparked no impulse in the writing, and I had to eliminate them because they would have lowered the tension of the style" (p. 127; "non tutte le storie che riuscivo a comporre visualmente mettendo in fila le carte davano un buon risultato quando mi mettevo a scriverle; ce n'erano di quelle che non comunicavano alcuno scatto alla scrittura e che dovevo eliminare perché avrebbero abbassato la tenuta del testo," p. 126).

Not all combinations of literary elements, obviously, make good literature. To discriminate the random from the excellent, we may refer to another essay by Calvino. In his "Notes toward a definition of the narrative form as a combinative process,"[7] Calvino speculates on the origins of folk tales and the interplay of discrete elements and larger formats of literary construction. Calvino argues that folk tales are not debased or vulgarized versions of myth (like Frye's displaced myths) or even that myth and folk tale coexisted in some kind of counterbalancing dialectic. Rather, he feels, folk tales came first, trying the whole range of combinations of elements, and those tales that by chance, by luck, by intuition, best spoke to the subconscious needs of a people not only survived but revealed a secret truth. What began in play ended in ritual, religion, and taboo. Perhaps it is this sort of mythic check that Calvino put on the many tarot stories, to find the ones with the proper tension, sparking the right impulse to pass his critical scrutiny.

We cannot, of course, second-guess Calvino's creative process, but we can make our own mythic check into the power of these strange tales. The stories and their design are clearly ingenuous. These are works of an exacting, even fiendish imagination, but questions arise. What does all this add up to? What do we have at the end for a theme, for a conclusion? How are we supposed to feel as a result of reading these cards in fantastic narratives? I think that there are two answers: (1) The book is in many ways antimythic, parodying, compressing, and flattening any transcending urge; when I used the word "fiendish" above, I was not joking. Fantasy of denial is resplendent in this book, to the point of a kind of antiliterature. (2) I find the book an enormous set of jokes, black humor of a sort, but carefully shaped on literary elements. Samuel Beckett comes to mind as a parallel, the artist who explores the absurd, the dreary, the grotesque with such care, such skill, such love that the final result is a curious affirmation of language, art, and being itself. My path to these conclusions will run like this: a look at the frame and the stories as literary devices; a discussion of the desires and thoughts brought out in hearers and readers (in short the hermeneutical exercises both within and beyond the book); and finally the divergence between the characters' fantasies and the readers'. My assessments sometimes overlap with other critics', sometimes diverge. Perhaps the strangest of all his books, this one has elicited diverse opinions.[8]

The narrator passes from a thick forest, through a dark courtyard, into the castle's hall, where all is calm and elegant. But he also feels an impression of randomness, or disorder, as if all the guests were transients. Thus the opening four paragraphs establish the narrator's will to interpret and his facility in alternative, and often opposite, explanations. The mood is, of course, mixed: attractive and seductive on the one hand, forlorn and chaotic on the other. Before reentering the narrative, our narrator reflects that the "two contradictory impressions" (p. 4; "le due impressioni contrastanti,") could both explain the building in which the characters are gathered: either a castle lapsed to become an inn, or a tavern somehow was taken over by courtly folk. Thus explanation leads to mystery, and truth becomes extremely relative, even whimsical. The frame tales for *The Castle of Crossed Destinies* and *The Tavern of Crossed Destinies* are linked by this dual explanation, both entry points to the worlds of the cards through a gathering of the now mute characters, although from different social levels (which, finally, merge).

There is a further Dantean link that binds the two openings, as elements from each of the two famous opening tercets are used in the two openings, respectively, of *The Castle* and *The Tavern:*

> In the middle of the path of our life
> I found myself in a dark wood
> where the direct route had been lost.
> Ah, how hard it is to tell how it was
> this wild forest, rough and harsh,
> its very memory renews my fear!
>
> (My literal translation)

> Nel mezzo del cammin di nostra vita
> mi ritrovai per una selva oscura
> che la diritta via era smarrita.
> Ah quanto a dir qual era è cosa dura
> esta selva selvaggia e aspra e forte
> che nel pensier rinova la paura!
>
> *Inferno* I, 1–6

Clearly *The Castle* opening, "In the midst of a thick forest" (p. 3; "In mezzo a un fitto bosco") reminds us of the first tercet. In the frame for *The Tavern,* it is the second paragraph that parallels the second tercet: "How can I tell about it now that I have lost my power of speech, words, perhaps also memory, how can I tell what was there outside" (p. 52; "Come faccio a raccontare adesso che ho perduto la parola, le parole, forse pure la memoria, come faccio a ricordare cosa c'era lí fuori").

The cards are, of course the answer, but before we hasten on to discuss them, there is one more point, again prompted by Dante, to make about the frame and, therefore, the entire ambience of both books: its infernal nature. We shall return to this theme: the books are an underworld, a prison, a Gothic enclosure of repression, misfortune, tragedy, and (the last word of the narrative) disaster (p. 120). In each frame, the narrator is caught in his (her?) journey by night, alone, cut off from the regular world, bereft of the ability to speak, and, perhaps worst of all, cut off from the potential of the future: "we were as if drained of all future, suspended in a journey that had not ended nor was to end" (p. 6; "d'ogni avvenire sembravamo svuotati, sospesi in un viaggio né terminato né da terminare"). In *The Tavern* it is an entire group cut off, evidently at once, as if the Canterbury pilgrims had been captured and forced to tell their stories, or, the narrators of the *Decameron* are still holed up somewhere; but those two great works still have an open feeling, a potential for worth and goodness.

The infernal, inferior world of Calvino's cards is one cut off both from the future and from any sort of transcendence. The Devil figures as a character, but not God; in this world there cannot be any vertical scale of mythic affirmation. In *The Tavern's* opening we learn that the characters are "half-dead with fright" (p. 51; "mezzo morti dallo spavento"). The stories they want to tell with the cards are their past journeys, as if, in mythic terms, to gain control of how they arrived in this trap, but there is no promise of such salvation. In the last sentence of *The Castle,* it appears that the characters are doomed to tell tales over and over. In *The Tavern,* a common image is that the cards are as mirrors to the characters, indeed the characters have become cards, flattened, manipulated, stuck in the curious ontology of cardboard. They enter the tavern through the unfriendly world of clubs and swords, and the seductive world of coins and cups (p. 51), making clear the limitations of the four suits of the deck. But it is a world so grim and so playfully constructed as to be funny. Perhaps the greatest joke on the narrators of both frame tales is that it seems that they are unaware that they are in hell, or some version of it. In each book there are twelve tales, possibly a demonic reversal of the twelve apostles; the four suits may remind us of the four evangelists, but I am not going to push this line. The dominant mythos, in satiric form, is not the New Testament, but the Fisher King, especially in *The Tavern,* as we shall see below.

The individual tellers are flat characters, as flat as the cards that are their mirrors, and anything that accrues to them is given by the interpreting narrator. They are, more accurately, their stories, but the stories are so susceptible to interpretation, so tenuously linked to the cards, that, once again, the characters are constructs by the narrator and by us as we look over his shoulder. Each tells a story by starting with a card that resembles the "speaker."

For example, the guest who begins places the Knight of Cups, which he resembles, then follows with sixteen more cards that seem to tell his story. Then others follow, beginning at some point on the previous story: they see a card or two that reminds them of their story, which they then tell, reinterpreting, of course, the cards from previous stories. As the lines of cards go down, a large mandala is built for each book, shown on page 40 for *The Castle* and on page 98 for *The Tavern*. The frame narrator of *The Castle* has a very clear idea of what is happening:

In fact, the task of deciphering the stories one by one has made me neglect until now the most salient peculiarity of our way of narrating, which is that each story runs into another story, and as one guest is advancing his strip, another, from the other end, advances in the opposite direction, because the stories told from left to right or from bottom to top can also be read from right to left or from top to bottom, and vice versa, bearing in mind that the same cards, presented in a different order, often change their meaning, and the same tarot is used at the same time by narrators who set forth from the four cardinal points. (P. 41)

Infatti, il compito di decifrare le storie una per una m'ha fatto trascurare finora la peculiarità piú saliente del nostro modo di narrare, e cioè che ogni racconto corre incontro a un altro racconto e mentre un commensale avanza la sua striscia un altro dall'altro estremo avanza in senso opposto, perché le storie raccontate da sinistra a destra o dal basso in alto possono pure essere lette da destra a sinistra o dall'alto in basso, e viceversa, tenendo conto che le stesse carte presentandosi in un diverso ordine spesso cambiano significato, e il medesimo tarocco serve nello stesso tempo a narratori che partono dai quattro punti cardinali. (P. 41)

In *The Castle,* the first six stories are all 17 cards long, in two lines; the seven remaining tales start similarly from the positions of narrators on the edge of the great design, but the number of cards used varies from 11 to 22, and the strict linear order is abandoned for some discontinuous strings of cards (i.e., cards taken from different portions of the diagram). In *The Tavern,* all tales are discontinuously told, at least in terms of the design on page 98 (it is ambiguous whether the telling is linear, then scrambled). *The Tavern* differs also in the numbers of cards used—lavish amounts—31 in the first tale alone. By either method, the regular or the free form, all stories have the same tragic nature and, of course, use the same deck.

The tragedies are cheerfully routine, the stuff of folk tale, melodrama, ghost story, chapbook: characters die, go mad, become lost, go into hiding, are damned. These are archetypes of separation, in Frye's sense of tragedy; the question of literary merit becomes complex, however, since an archetype can be the source of a cliché or a masterpiece. The third tale of *The Castle,* "The Tale of the Doomed Bride" ("Storia della sposa dannata"), is typical. A warrior with melancholy eyes has, it seems, left one lady and taken another for his tourney queen. The latter lady rewards him (the reason is somewhat unclear) with herself, but Saint Peter (the Major Arcanum of The Pope) see the lady's voluptuous abandon and denies heaven to her forever. The warrior turns to his paramour to find her figured as Death itself, and the frame narrator (not the warrior) interprets the rest of the cards: "from the forest had come the betrothed whom the deceased bride-to-be had so feared," and Beelzebub himself carries the corpse away "into the bowels of the earth" (p. 24; "dal bosco era uscito il fidanzato tanto temuto dalla promessa sposa defunta," "giú dritto sottoterra").

Calvino plays with the question of narrative similarities by retelling the tales of Oedipus, Orlando, Parsifal, Lear, Faust, and Hamlet in similar idioms to the tales of the ingrate, grave robber, warrior, and so on—all of which begin to appear interchangeable, at least in terms of the elements, the cards. This interchangeability is, of course, the great game, following Vladimir Propp's *Mor-*

phology of the Folktale, Stith Thompson's *Motif Index to Folk Literature,* or even approaches from structural anthropology, which would make the elements universally available to a wide variety of combinations. Naturally, the great tales of Oedipus, Hamlet, and Parsifal do not appear as literary masterpieces, but in wildly compromised and truncated versions. Calvino carefully overplays his hand by combining the stories of Faust and Parsifal, "Two Stories of Seeking and Losing" ("Due storie in cui si cerca e ci si perde") and scrambling the three Shakespearean stories of Hamlet, Lear, and Macbeth into a pastiche—or a travesty, really, in the original sense of the word—"Three Tales of Madness and Destruction" ("Tre storie di follia e distruzione"). The Shakespearean scramble is particularly hilarious and overblown: we lose all sense of the stories as tragedies for the individual characters, since the characters have no specific gravity, no psyche, no personality with which we might have empathy. The tragedy becomes something more circumstantial and funny, much as playing with cards becomes a trap, even a neurosis:

> Instead, for the young man ahead of him the *Fool* is merely the role he has set himself to play, the better to work out a revenge plot and to conceal his spirit, distraught by the revelation of the guilty deeds of his mother, Gertrude, and his uncle. If this is neurosis, there is a method in it, and in every method, neurosis. (We know this well, glued to our game of tarots.) (P. 115)

> Invece, per il giovane di prima *Il Matto* altro non è che la parte ch'egli stesso s'è imposto, per meglio studiare un piano di vendetta e nascondere l'animo sconvolto dalla rivelazione delle colpe della madre Gertrude e dello zio. Se la sua è nevrosi, in ogni nevrosi c'è del metodo e in ogni metodo, nevrosi. (Ben lo sappiamo noi inchiodati a questo gioco di tarocchi). (Pp. 115–16)

The Hamletian method in madness and neurosis leads us into the thematic heart of this book, the meaning of meaning and the confusing role of desire. Obviously, these are highly hermeneutical tales. There are at least three levels of interpretation going on. The first level is the interpretation by the characters in the story, notably the narrator, who guides us along possible interpretations; whether the other characters are in agreement, the other viewers or the current teller, we do not know. As the narrator puts it, "I have no idea how many of us managed to decipher the tale somehow. . . . The narrator's powers of communication were scant, perhaps because his genius was more inclined to the severity of abstractions than to the obviousness of images" (p. 21; "Non so quanti di noi fossero riusciti a decifrare in qualche modo la storia. . . . La comunicativa del narratore era scarsa, forse perché il suo ingegno era piú portato al rigore dell'astrazione che all'evidenza delle immagini"). The narrator's comment leads us to the second level of interpretation, the original interpretations by Calvino himself as he toyed with the cards while writing the story; throughout, it is his dogged concentration and invention that keep the tales coming, that interlink them ingeniously, that generate the many possibilities that the narrator relays to us. The final and obvious enough third level of interpretation is that we as readers first read the story on the surface level, taking the cues as the narrator gives them. Then, if we choose to accept further complexities of the game, we look at how the stories interconnect, how Calvino has laid it all out, and so on. All levels of interpretation are caught in the dilemma hinted above: "the severity of abstractions" even if based on the specific, concrete cards. In the cards we seem to have something definite, but the recontextualization of each of them by the different narrators changes their meanings. Near the end Faust and Parsifal reflect upon the paradox we have been following, the tension between definiteness and polysemy:

> "The world does not exist," Faust concludes when the pendulum reaches the other extreme, "there is not an all, given all at once: there is a finite number of elements whose combinations are multiplied to billions of billions, and only a few of these find a form and a meaning and make their presence felt amid a meaningless, shapeless dust cloud; like the seventy-eight cards of the tarot deck in whose juxtapositions sequences of stories appear and are then immediately undone."
>
> Whereas this would be the (still temporary) conclusion of Parsifal: "The kernel of the world is empty, the beginning of what moves in the universe is the space of nothingness, around absence is constructed what exists, at the bottom of the Grail is the Tao," and he points to the empty rectangle surrounded by the tarots. (P. 97)

> —Il mondo non esiste,—Faust conclude quando il pendolo raggiunge l'altro estremo,— non c'è un tutto dato tutto in una volta: c'è un numero finito d'elementi le cui combinazioni si moltiplicano a miliardi di miliardi, e di queste solo poche trovano una forma e un senso e s'impongono in mezzo a un pulviscolo senza senso e senza forma; come le settantotto carte del mazzo di tarocchi nei cui accostamenti appaiono sequenze di storie che subito si disfano.
>
> Mentra questa sarebbe la conclusione (sempre provvisoria) di Parsifal:—Il nocciolo del mondo è vuoto, il principio di ciò che si muove nell'universo è lo spazio del niente, attorno all'assenza si costruisce ciò che c'è, in fondo al gral c'è il tao,—e indica il rettangolo vuoto circondato dai tarocchi. (P. 97)

Faust and Parsifal remind us of the theoretical poles of Lekomceva and Uspenskij, the highly abstract paradox of signs without referents, so that the signs can be multiplied into a profusion of meanings in an overwhelming process; and of Egorov, flux versus the more austere classical (or Eastern) view that there is an inner purity and order around which we may build a reality.[9] Sorting out this thematic process is, however, less important than drawing a conclusion about Faust and Parsifal as intensifications of other characters, especially the narrator: their weight as characters exists almost solely through their interpretive thoughts (in the tradition of Agilulf, the nonexistent knight), and not so much in action or feeling.

There is a divergence between the readers and the characters that makes it difficult to follow the desires kindled in this strange book. The pasteboard figures are so simplified as to be little more than ciphers; the great figures of literature (Lear, Hamlet, Faust, Oedipus, Parsifal) are rendered so one-dimensional as to lose their stature, thus making a tragic fall impossible in ordinary terms. Since these cartoon figures are not complex enough to display emotions that might involve us, we must view them in a more detached fashion. Even the narrator cannot (or does not) do much to intervene, to shape our reactions to the characters. As the characters are distanced, they seem like animals put in a pit to fight while the crowd cheers and whistles; there is something morbid about watching these characters go to their doom one after another without involving our empathy or compassion. We find not tragedy but some ingenious form of melodrama, akin to the television soap opera or the European fotoromanzo (comic books of photographs of persons in continuous trouble, especially romantic difficulties).

In no other book has Calvino experimented so drastically with the notion of character or so willfully driven a wedge between the characters and us. Our desires seem, somehow, transcendent, as gods or fates watching the narrator, who watches the players or tellers. It is hard, indeed, to tell what we want: entertainment, ingenuity, ever more clever variations upon the cartomantic hermeneutics. We feel a fantasy of denial in the basic infernal enclosure, the mute characters, and the variations on tragic themes. The famous characters (Oedipus, Faust, Hamlet) become parodies of the originals, giving us a strange, combined pleasure of both recognition and distortion, like a trick mirror at the carnival. Even the second book, *The Tavern of Crossed Destinies,* is a parody of the first, *The Castle of Crossed Destinies,* and Calvino jokes, in his "Note" about the possibility of still a third, "The Motel of Crossed Destinies"! If the reader can hang on for the ride, the fantasy of affirmation then deals with various forms of the author's wit: cleverness; craftsmanship, deftness in the tales, satire, and parody; gamesmanship; apparently endless variations on a theme; and even some fatalistic endurance that seems to say, "I can keep this up almost indefinitely; can you read to the end with me?"

Earlier in this chapter we referred to the myth of the Fisher King as a source of meaning in this book. I am not arguing that the myth is the key, a skeleton, an armature to explain the book; for one thing, the myth is often satirically used. The form of thinking that seems most central to this book is not myth at all, but the terrible problem we have been pursuing, hermeneutics, the discovery of truth amidst disparate and decontextualized signs. Thus any suggestion of a pervasive myth must be understood as something like a life buoy always a little out of reach of the drowning reader. Calvino himself draws our attention to the story of the Fisher King several times. In "The Waverer's Tale" ("Storia dell'indeciso," p. 62) we find a reference with a light touch to the use of a tarot card in "The Waste Land" of Eliot. In "Two Tales of Seeking and Losing" ("Due storie in cui si cerca e ci si perde") we find a series of references to King Arthur, Parsifal, the Fisher King, and the Grail (pp. 90–97; pp. 89–97). Again, the references are not "straight," in the sense of invoking the mythos of quest and healing of the medieval myth, but more "crooked," in the sense that Calvino touches on the familiar story and bends it to his own purposes. He mixes it with the Faust story, so that both men end up in the tavern retracing their routes and exchanging their nihilistic comments already examined in this discussion. The wastelands of their myths are still wastelands, and the sterile, paradoxical, koan-like literary world of *The Castle* (and, of course, *The Tavern*) remains "an ambiguous miracle" (to borrow a phrase from *Invisible Cities*, p. 65; p. 71). The question that has plagued the critics of Eliot's poem remains here: does it rain? Amidst the infernal, the discrete, the detached, is there some sense of transcendence, connection, fertility?

In terms of some sort of phenomenology of reading, we readers are the quester, both Faust and Parsifal, seeking a wholeness, a redemption. We are cast in the role of Perceval, the loquacious boor who does not ask the crucial question of the Fisher King, so as to heal him, the one who is mute, much as the travelers at the castle and tavern are speechless. The plenitude of meanings cannot be brought to an order other than the mandala of cards; the sterility of the game may command our respect for its ingenuity but not, I think, our compassion and a depth of interest. Indeed, the twentieth century seems to have cast off the myths of millennia before of wholeness, regeneration, expiation, external return. Signs, bits, bytes, information we have in excess, in this book and in our times, but what is the sense of it all, what is a myth that would give meaning? If there is an answer, it is not a new one: in modern times, each person shall be his or her own mythographer, for better or for worse. Such is the burden of Joseph Campbell's argument in *Masks of God,* and he goes back to *Tristan and Iseult* to demonstrate the egoism of the lovers. Calvino follows a different track, but promotes the same theme, in "Story of the Writer" ("Racconto dello scrittore").

"Surely my own story is also contained in this pattern of cards, my past, present, and future, but I can no longer distinguish it from the others" (p. 46; "Certamente anche la mia storia è contenuta in questo intreccio di carte, passato presente futuro, ma io non so piú distinguerla dalle altre"), writes our narrator at the end of *The Castle* and lets it go at that. In *The Tavern,* however, he is considerably more aggressive, presenting himself as the King of Clubs, who holds a large implement, surely a pen. "As far as I know, the black line that comes from the tip of that cheap scepter is precisely the path that has led me here" (p. 99; "Per quel che so, è proprio il filo nero che esce da quella punta di scettro da poche lire la strada che m'ha portato fin qui"). Every man his own mythographer! And who are the patron saints? Freud (obliquely styled as Sigismund of Vindobona—the old Celtic name whence Vienna) and Stendhal (the Egotist of Grenoble). This pair provides the unconscious of the dream world with the conscious literary shaping of the self, so much that Henri Beyle's (Stendhal's) autobiography is called *La Vie d'Henri Brulard,* as if Henri Brulard were a different person from the author. Another set of standard Christian saints follow, Jerome and George, again inner and outer men, sage and warrior, but the categories merge, melding the voice of the narrator with the stories of Justine and Oedipus, until all is solved literarily: "Thus I have set everything to rights. On the page, at least. Inside me, all remains as before" (p. 111; "Così ho messo tutto a posto. Sulla pagina, almeno. Dentro di me tutto resta come prima"). The literary enterprise may have its own integrity and coherence, but it is not, in this strange book, one relating directly to personal destinies of self, character, psychology, or even reality, which the narrator twits: "(as they now say) 'real life'" (p. 104); "(come ora dicono) 'vissuto,'" p. 103).

At the end of each book the playing cards are shuffled, to be dealt again in the same horizontal space. Indeed the horizontality of the book is part of its claustrophobic nature. The characters are flat, both in their literal origins, the cardboard tarots, and in Forster's sense of having one or at most two motivating urges. They live in a thin realm of laterality where signs can link on a plane, but there is little hope for a transcending, a vertical mythos. There is nothing of the sense of illimitable three-dimensional space that we shall see in *Invisible Cities*. On a spiritual scale, there is an attempt to extend the realm of consciousness and action "downward," into the realm of the Devil, but he too is just another card. The fiendish or devilish nature of the book is but a feint, a basso ostinato that does not have its own dominion. The writer in *The Tavern* makes an effort to palm himself off as the Devil, but I believe that he convinces neither us nor himself. Nor is there anything in the opposite, "upward," or transcendental direction, toward angels, gods, God.

This is a world unredeemed by gods or myths, with the only hope of salvation and wholeness in the eyes and mind of the reader. As Perceval-Parzival-Parsifal, a rash Welsh bumpkin, we are the last best hope, in mythological terms, of saving the world of this book; it must be the readers who quest, respond, ponder, providing a verbal complement to the enigmatic mandalas of the cards. In our reflections and musings we find the patterns of literary worth in these subtle and ingenious Rorschachs; *we* become the heroes for a book that is a wasteland where heroes do not dwell. This theme of the heroism of reading becomes a focus of Calvino's book, *If on a winter's night a traveller* (*Se una notte d'inverno un viaggiatore*). Is the reader, like the characters of *The Castle* and *The Tavern*, lost between sign and myth? Only the reader knows!

11

Invisible Cities: **Fantasy as Mental Topography**

In his famous *Travels* (ca. 1300) Marco Polo described, often in sumptuous detail, many of the cities he had visited. In Calvino's volume,[1] Marco Polo has been making such reports to the emperor of the Tartars, Kublai Khan. Polo's reports, however, have shifted from the factual to the fantastic, a series of descriptions of "invisible" cities. Polo, the Khan, and we as readers are all participants in a series of fantasies writ large: cities, possibly the largest and most social of human constructs, are efficient symbols for creating a kind of mental topography. They are highly visual; they are large and concrete, so that we may move within them; they seem to comprehend the whole of human experience in encyclopedic fashion, and they enter into a dialectic with humanity: men shape cities, and cities shape men. Calvino's invisible cities, more plastic than material, serve as an infinitely malleable poetic dramatization of the mind, both as projections from the Khan and Polo and as images that, in part, create those two men and, of course, shape the reader's experience. To discuss how this book charts cityscapes of the mind, first I want to examine the spatial structure of the book; second, I want to examine some of the uses of space as a locus for fantasy and the process of, so to speak, concretizing desire; and finally, I want to look at the highly self-conscious conversations between Kublai and Polo as they seek to understand the process they are performing. I think "performing" is the right word for two reasons: Calvino carefully manipulates these characters almost like circus animals to comment on the action, something like Fielding's introductory chapters to the books of *Tom Jones,* and, they appear in an elaborate *form* or frame of the book, again at the highly calculated beck and call of the author.

Calvino's structure is very rigid, as if to create an abstract, spatial organization for the great conceptual freedom of the fantasy. There are several implications, but let us lay out the structure first: The book is divided into nine sections; each opens and closes with a portion of the frame, the conversation of Kublai and Polo. The bulk of each section is a set of descriptions of cities. Sections 1 and 9 have the frame plus 10 cities; sections 2 through 8 have the frame plus five cities, totaling 55 cities and eighteen frame pieces. These numbers do not seem to have inherent meanings; indeed Calvino has avoided some of the traditional numerologies of the threes, nines, or tens of Dante, or the threes, fours, sevens, and twelves of Spenser. Five and eleven (there are eleven kinds of cities) are sturdy prime numbers; sections 1 and 9 have twice the number of cities of the others, as if to stand as a solid frame around the smaller sections, 2 through 8—but I cannot establish any further symbolic overtones: the mathematical divisions seem pure in their arbitrariness, an abstract game that exists for its own sake.

As to the order in which the cities are deployed, there is an elaborate counting game. In each of the eleven categories of cities (Cities and memory, Cities and desire, Cities and signs, and so on) there are five cities. We may illustrate how these are arranged by labeling each category with a letter, and repeating it as it recurs.[2] Section 1, for example (disregarding the frame) has cities like this: a a b a b c a b c d. If we rewrite this progression vertically, we may emphasize an order throughout the cities:

```
        a
        a  b
        a  b  c                    Section 1
        a  b  c  d
        -----------------------------------
        a  b  c  d  e              Section 2
        -----------------------------------
           b  c  d  e  f           Section 3
        -----------------------------------
              c  d  e  f  g        Section 4
        -----------------------------------
                 d  e  f  g  h     Section 5
        -----------------------------------
                    e  f  g  h  i  Section 6
        -----------------------------------
                       f  g  h  i  j   Section 7
        -----------------------------------
                          g  h  i  j  k  Section 8
        -----------------------------------
                          h  i  j  k
                             i  j  k
                                j  k     Section 9
                                   k
```

We start in section 1 with Cities and memory (a), and then start over (a)—as if trying to remember?—and proceed to add the first of the Cities and desire (b)—an echo of "The Waste Land," "mixing / Memory and desire"? (ll. 2–3)—until the first four categories (abcd) are launched; at this point ten cities have been started, and Calvino starts a new section. Section 2 completes the Cities and memory group, adding the fifth (a) and begins the Trading cities group (e); similarly sections 3 through 8 each finish and initiate a group, so that the principle of fives is maintained both vertically for each category and horizontally for each section. By the last section, section 9, we are counting down the final categories, finding the last group to be (suitably enough) Hidden cities (k). My diagram, viewed as a whole, is a double wedge, with a tapered beginning as we work our way into the game; a stable center, sections 2 through 8, where the game of serial progressions maintains itself, presumably indefinitely; and a final tapering in section 9, where Calvino has chosen to end the game by starting no new categories. Thus the cities exhaust themselves, according to the principle of fives. Section 9 comes out a mirror image of section 1, in a chiasmus of pattern (but not subject). Again, I feel the arbitrariness is paramount; I do not find any thematic reasons for the number of cities or the order in which they occur (except for the ones about which I speculated briefly: the first two, *memory* and *desire,* and the last, *hidden*). There are some sections that seem to have recurring themes: 1, emptiness; 3, women and sex; 4, movement; 6, Venice. These are not controlling or determining motifs, as far as I can tell—certainly nothing like the criteria Joyce established (if we follow Gilbert) for the eighteen sections of *Ulysses.* Pattern, not theme, is paramount.

There is another numerical oddity: within each section, the numbers of the cities create a countdown toward the never mentioned, but always implied number zero. Take section 2, where we find the fifth instance of Cities and memory, the fourth of Cities and desire, the third of Cities and signs, the second of Thin cities, and the first of Trading cities. Each of the center sections 2 through 8 follows this countdown, always ending with the frame, which seems a sort of surrogate for the ever implied zero. That the table of contents should indicate the frame sections with five dots (. . . . .) suggests three notions: the expandable and indefinite nature of ellipses (. . .), the pattern of five cities (as if here reduced to purist abstraction—what is smaller than a dot?), and the uncountable nature of the frame, which carries no numbers like those of the cities. In a final irony, this system of counting down is itself negated in the final section, so that the system self-destructs:

$$
\begin{array}{c}
5\ 4\ 3\ 2\ 1 \\
5\ 4\ 3\ 2 \\
5\ 4\ 3 \\
5\ 4 \\
5
\end{array}
$$

to take the numbers alone. Is there any comfort in the five dots that come along with machine-gun regularity? Do the five dots show the survival of the structure or the ultimate sterility of a frame with no flesh? We shall return to such questions when we take up the conversations of Kublai and Polo.

By contrast to the mathematical strictness of the presentation, the prose poems of the cities themselves are widely scattered in all sorts of implied space. First, the categories themselves are mixed: *memory* and *desire* are clearly mental categories, but *thin* and *continuous* are physical traits; *signs* and *names* are similar, but *trade, eyes,* and *dead* bear little direct relation: Calvino has evidently given himself free hand. If Kublai and Polo, in their ordering, are following the rational, the orderly, and the linear, the cities seem to be associational, organic, and free-form. The Khan and Polo are men, emblems of a military-commercial empire, but the cities partake heavily of the feminine: they all have women's names and are energized largely by female characters. The invisible cities seem to be anima figures projected by the archetypal subconsciousness of the two men, to put it in Jungian terms. The men find themselves reduced to the rectilinear pattern of the chessboard, but the cities soar in unlimited space.

In turning to the "spatiality" of the cities, there are two theorists I should like to keep in mind. The first is Joseph Frank in his well-known essay, "Spatial Form in Modern Literature."[3] Frank is talking here about poetry, but he soon extends these comments to the novel:

> Esthetic form in modern poetry, then, is based on a space-logic that demands a complete re-orientation in the reader's attitude towards language. Since the primary reference of any word-group is to something inside the poem itself, language in modern poetry is really reflexive: the meaning-relationship is completed only by the simultaneous perception in space of word-groups which, when read consecutively in time, have no comprehensible relation to each other. (Pp. 229–30)

Frank concludes that temporality in modern, spatially conceived literature, has vanished: "the dimension of depth has vanished from history as it forms the content of these works; past and present are seen spatially, locked in a timeless unity which, while it may accentuate surface differences, eliminates any feeling of historical sequence by the very act of juxtaposition" (p. 633). It is easy to argue with Frank, because he overstates his case; for one lively attack, see Walter Sutton's "The Literary Image and the Reader: A Consideration of the Theory of Spatial Form."[4] Frank takes the Kantian categories of space and time as polar opposites, and uses the term "spatial" rather indefinitely to mean something like abstract, atemporal, and nonlinear. He does not take up the more physical aspects of space, such as three-dimensional space both in reality and in literary descriptions, and barely exploits the spatial realities of words on the page or of sections (as in *Invisible Cities*) of a book. Sutton protests that even the most "spatial" images are still perceived in the reader's own time, and we may add that the notion of a space-time continuum in twentieth-century physics further complicates the resources available to writer and reader, as space and time became reversible.

Frank can help us nonetheless to follow the emphasis (if not a stricture) that literature dealing with space may tend to do less with time. It seems possible that Calvino's emphasis on counting the cities and arranging them in serial fashion may be a temporal countermove to the heavy spatial dimension of the cities. Kublai and Polo may have been plucked out of ordinary historical time, but *Invisible Cities,* for all its spatiality, aggressively signals its own internal time by the formal arrangements we have detailed. We have a sort of "literary time" created by the many numbers to help "place" the invisible, fantastic cities.

Perhaps more useful are some notions from Gaston Bachelard, the ever diffuse, suggestive, and mystically nuanced Jungian philosopher. The first is his term "oneiric space," the title of an essay that begins, "What kind of space do our dreams inhabit?" in *The Right to Dream.*[5] Part of his answer is the following:

> The space in which we shall spend our nocturnal hours has no perspective, no distance. It is the immediate synthesis of things and ourselves. If we dream of an object, we enter that object as into a shell. Our oneiric space always has this coefficient. Sometimes in flying dreams we think we are very high up, but we are no more then than a little bit of flying matter. And the skies we soar through are wholly interior—skies of desire or hope or pride. (P. 172)

This is a key for *Invisible Cities:* the implied space of the cities is only metaphorically exterior; phenomenologically, it is totally interior, both in the projection of it by Calvino through Kublai and Polo and in the perception and recreation of it by the reader. Part of the excellence of the cities is in their suggestive renderings of those "skies of desire or hope or pride." We shall look at a few examples in a moment. But there is still another movement Bachelard suggests: "Stripped of all distant worlds and all telescopic experience, thrown back by the concentrated intimacy of night upon a primitive experience, man rediscovers in the depths of his sleep formative carnal space" (p. 174); Bachelard finds a renewal in dreams: "the core of our being possesses new strength. . . . Instead of a rounded space we have a space containing preferred, desired directions, axes of aggression" (p. 174).

I would like now to look at several of the cities to see how the spatial imagery reflects a topography of the mind. There are three uses of space I want to follow: space and desire, reversible or negative space, and space and pattern. (I might add that many other uses might be fruitfully worked out, so rich is this volume.)

Despina (Cities and desire, 5; pp. 17–18; pp. 25–26)[6] illustrates space and desire and reversibility. The name "Despina" reminds us of the flirtatious soubrette in Mozart's *Così fan tutte* and, possibly, *spina,* which means "thorn" in Italian—in sum, an attractive but ultimately disappointing city. The camel driver sees the city as a ship about to take leave port for romantic voyages; "he thinks of all the ports, the foreign merchandise the cranes unload on the docks, the taverns where crews of different flags break bottles over one another's heads, the lighted ground-floor windows, each with a woman combing her hair" ("pensa a tutti i porti, alle merci d'oltremare che le gru scaricano sui moli, alle osterie dove equipaggi di diversa bandiera si rompona bottiglie sulla testa, alle finestre illuminate a pianterreno, ognuna con una donna che si pettina"). The sailor, on the other hand, sees the city as a camel and images the caravans and oases and "palaces of thick, white-washed walls, tiled courts where girls are dancing barefoot, moving their arms, half-hidden by their veils, and half-revealed" ("palazzi dalle spesse mura di calce, dai cortili di piastrelle su cui ballano scalze le danzatrici, e muovono le braccia un po' nel velo e un po' fuori dal velo"). Calvino gives us something of "the grass is always greener on the other side of the fence," as each viewer projects his fantasies on the skyline of the city, perceiving the outline of a vessel or a camel, according to his desires, imagining desirable women within the buildings of the city. Like a mirror, or a Rorschach blot, the city reflects the viewer's desire and is variable, even reversible, according to the perspective from which it is viewed.

Then comes the kicker: "Each city receives its form from the desert it opposes; and so the camel driver and the sailor see Despina, a border city between two deserts." ("Ogni città riceve la sua forma dal deserto a cui si oppone; e cosí il cammelliere e il marinaio vedono Despina, città di confine tra due deserti"). Beyond mere reversibility, we have something chilling here, a negativity inherent in projecting desire: the sailor and camel driver *give form,* create the city because of the sterility of their existence so that the city, as created by them, exists between two deserts: thus the sailor and the camel driver seem destined to enter a desert on the other side of Despina, a mirage of desire, an empty fantasy that will disappoint the desires projected upon it. Each viewer "knows it is a city but he thinks of it as" ("sa che è una città ma la pensa come") a vessel or a camel, suggesting the kinetic nature of desire in fantasy, even with an accompaniment of realistic knowledge.

Despina will also serve to illustrate some general characteristics of the poetic descriptions of the cities: they are all short, highly evocative in image and other appeals to sense, but at the same time abstract in thematic concerns. They have a glossy, attractive style but difficult, even forbidding meanings: they seem like conundrums, mystical riddles, or koans. The descriptions themselves arouse our desires, but the philosophical problems are raised to acute paradoxes not to be solved. The very brevity of the sketches reinforces this dissonance: the poetic details are attractive and seductive, but the philosophical concerns are insoluble, leaving us dazzled and stunned as if by a quick blow. The texts for the cities range from about 140 to 800 words, averaging somewhere around 300 words: questions of perception, ethics, ontology, and causality are continuously being set but not developed, not even in a superficial sort of way. On one page we read that "There is no language without deceit" (p. 48; "Non c'è linguaggio senza inganno," p. 54) but on another, "Falsehood is never in words, it is in things" (p. 62; "La menzogna non è nel discorso, è nelle cose," p. 68). It is as if we are seduced into the fantastic landscapes only to find ourselves lost and disoriented conceptually—but right on schedule according to the book's carefully counted out structure.

The city of Chloe (Trading cities, 2; pp. 51–52; pp. 57–58) is especially vivid in showing desire in relationship to space. In this "great city" persons, all strangers, continuously imagine "a thousand things about one another; meetings which could take place between them, conversations, surprises, caresses, bites. But no one greets anyone; eyes look for a second, then dart away" ("mille cose uno dell'altro, gli incontri che potrebbero avvenire tra loro, le conversazioni, le sorprese, le carezze, i morsi. Ma nessuno saluta nessuno, gli sguardi s'incrociano per un secondo e poi si sfuggono"). These glances create a pattern "like lines that connect one figure with another and draw arrows, stars, triangles" ("come linee che collegano una figura all'altra e disegnano frecce, stelle, trianogoli") so that the desires, quite vivid in themselves exist nonetheless in a frozen limbo of potentiality: "A voluptuous vibration constantly stirs Chloe, the most chaste of cities" ("Una vibrazione lussuriosa muove continuamente Chloe, la piú casta delle città"). The sketch ends in praise of this petrified state of desires: "If men and women began to live their ephemeral dreams, every phantom would become a person with whom to begin a story of pursuits, pretenses . . . then the carousel of fantasies would stop" ("Se uomini e donne cominciassero a vivere i loro effimeri sogni, ogni fantasma diventerebbe una persona con cui cominciare una storia d'inseguimenti, di finzioni . . . e la giostra delle fantasie si fermerebbe"). The fantasies seem to belong to a safe carnival world where no dangers can occur because nothing happens; if the fantasies are acted upon in human relationships, disaster is the result. The "concretization" in this sketch is still abstract: the desires exist as geometric loci, as cerebral links following the eyes, but not as bodies touching. What a doleful conclusion!

Anastasia (Cities and desire, 2; p. 12; p. 20) plays it somewhat differently. It is a city of sensuous delights—semiprecious gems, food, and lively women—that awaken desires. The tactile objects attract the visitor, and the women, in a rich spatial image, invite strangers into the pool in the garden to chase them, a complete immersion into the flux of pleasure. But (again a countermovement) "the description of Anastasia awakens desires one at a time only to force you to stifle them" ("la descrizione di Anastasia non fa che risvegliare i desideri uno per volta per obbligarti a soffocarli"), so that "you can do nothing but inhabit this desire and be content" ("a te non resta che abitare questo desiderio ed esserne contento"). The city itself does all the enjoying, in an ultimate concretization of desire, leaving none for people! The persons are sucked dry, as it were, and the stonecutter finds that his "labor which gives form to desire takes from desire its form" ("fatica che dà forma al desiderio prende dal desiderio la sua forma"). The city becomes the projected mental topography, leaving the minds exhausted, unenjoying, enslaved. A variation of this pattern is the charming city of Armilla (Thin cities, 3; pp. 49–50; pp. 55–56), which is made up entirely of water pipes. Within the showers, tubs, and spouts, young women are bathing themselves sensuously. Marco Polo believes them to be nympths and naiads enjoying the new spatial possibilities; desire has been given form, but ordinary humans are, again, excluded. At least in Armilla humans may overhear the contented singing of the bathers.

In Fedora (also a City of desire, 4; p. 32; p. 39), we find desire concretized in a different way; a museum houses models of Fedora which, in times past, persons have envisioned for the perfect city. More than in Despina or Anastasia, persons in Fedora may connect according to their desires: each visitor to the museum chooses "the city that corresponds to his desires" ("la città che corrisponde ai suoi desideri") and imagines the joys of the space that the model implies, for example "the fun of sliding down the spiral, twisting minaret" (the translator has added the word "fun"; "scivolare lungo la spirale del minareto a chiocciola") that was never built. This psychokinetic image brings a celebration of bodies turning in space with a joy not found in Despina or Anastasia. Polo gives a recommendation to the Khan that Fedora and all the models must be included in the empire: "Not only because they are all equally real, but because all are only assumptions" ("Non perché tutte ugualmente reali, ma perché tutte solo presunte").

This statement lies at the heart of fantasy: fantasies are as real as perception, knowledge, and reality of any sort, and even reality, to follow something of a solipsistic line, is an assumption. Still, there is a bittersweet quality to the fantastic Fedoras, the models of perfection: they contain "what is imagined as possible and, a moment later, is possible no longer" ("ciò che è immaginato come possibile e un minuto dopo non lo è più"). Because the large, concrete city exists, the models cannot exist, except as images of fantasies, opportunities for viewers to connect their desires with the models, much as readers seek a rapport with a text. The arbitrariness of the viewers' selections and musings may remind us of someone trying on hats (do we detect such a pun in "Fedora"?).

In Chloe, the city where glances created designs, we saw one use of pattern in space. In Octavia (Thin cities, 5; p. 75; p. 81) we find another use. It is called "the spider-web city" ("città-ragnatela") and surely the name is a pun on the eight legs of spiders. Calvino makes an adroit use of spatial images here, mixing moods. On the one (joyful) hand, the city is a delight of design: it is suspended between two mountains by a net; from this net, everything hangs below. Calvino plays a lovely metaphysical game in his catalogue of hanging items: "rope ladders, hammocks, . . . baskets on strings, dumb-waiters, . . . trapezes and rings for children's games, cable cars, chandeliers, pots with trailing plants" ("scale di corda, amache, . . . cesti appesi a spaghi, montacarichi, . . . trapezi e anelli per i giochi, teleferiche, lampadari, vasi con piante dal fogliame pendulo"). What a marvelous collection of hanging items! We feel the delight of invention, unexpected connection, and the playfulness of this grandiose spatial game. But, on the other (gloomy) hand: the inhabitants "know the net will last only so long" ("Sanno che piú di tanto la rete non regge"). Calvino has chosen to make this counterpoint; he could also have chosen to show that the inhabitants, like spiders, renew the net and so shall hang forever. Rather, in three brief paragraphs, Calvino has established a lavish set of images, and two conflicting moods: desire, however concretized and celebrated, has a terminus of death.

The mental topography, like the variety of the mind, is multiform; Calvino has manipulated many kinds of desire, many kinds of space, mixing them in the individual cities, and juxtaposing them in groups of five. The cities have an aggregate effect, a procession of images, moods, effects that, in spite of their brevity, begin to take on an epic quality. Cities represent and shape desire, cities can change before our eyes, cities have mysterious resonances to metaphysical patterns that seem to come and go like mirages. With each city we drift into an oneiric space that illustrates and elicits desire, but that usually limits it by some sort of countermovement. Having noticed some of the general ways the cities illustrate a topography of the mind, I should like to look at three kinds of cities that seem especially rich: cities related to the sky, double cities, and cities that refashion themselves.

The cities relating to the sky are those for which there might be a divine, astral, or astrological sanction. As in his other works, Calvino proposes no religious possibilities of ultimate order: indeed the lack of religion, we might baldly suggest, is one reason for the solipsism, the scepticism, and the labyrinthine mental games of the later work. Eudoxia (Cities and the Sky, 1; pp. 96–97; pp. 103–4) is the city that resembles a carpet, something like James's famous pattern in the carpet. An oracle has suggested that the city "has the form the gods gave the starry sky" ("ha la forma che gli dei diedero al cielo stellato"), which was taken as a salubrious justification. "But you could, similarly, come to the opposite conclusion: that the true map of the universe is the city of Eudoxia" ("Ma allo stesso modo tu puoi trarne la conclusione opposta: che la vera mappa dell'universo sia la città d'Eudossia"), which is a mess! Thekla (Cities and the sky, 3; p. 127; p. 134) is also chaotic, apparently unplanned, certainly unfinished; it takes the stars for a blueprint. Perinthia (Cities and the sky, 4; pp. 144–45; pp. 150–51) sets the case even more harshly. The city was laid out according to astronomical calculations that would favor the harmony of the heavens and the earth. When the city filled with its first born, monsters and freaks abounded. Were the calculations wrong or is the order of the gods, in fact, monstrous? Here the desires of the mind have been betrayed entirely. Andria (Cities and the sky, 5; pp. 150–51; pp. 156–57) is similarly laid out to correspond to the motion of heavenly bodies, but here the result is favorable. The variation this time is that the interplay between heaven and earth is so causal that changes in the city seem to bring changes in the stars. By this neat bit of hyperbole, Calvino plays with the control cities may have not only over humans, but over the cosmos as well.

The reflection between heaven and earth represents a kind of polarity that we find in tighter quarters: the double cities. So far we have found many paradoxes, countermotions, and polarities that exploit Manichean dualities, theses and antitheses, and ironic oppositions. Calvino gains compression and efficiency in the kind of city that is itself double. There are easily eight that could be so described. Maurilia (Cities and memory, 5; pp. 30–31; pp. 37–38), for example, exists in the present, and via post cards, in the past. Zemrude (Cities and eyes, 2; p. 66; p. 72) has an upper and lower side, Beersheba (Cities and the sky, 2; pp. 111–12; pp. 117–18) has a corresponding heavenly city, and Marozia (Hidden cities, 3; pp. 154–55; pp. 160–61) is simultaneously two cities, that of the rat and that of the swallow. Laudomia (Cities and the dead, 5; pp. 140–41; pp. 147–49) is a double city of life and death.

There are three, however, that are worth a longer look: Eusapia, Valdrada, and Sophronia. Eusapia (Cities and the dead, 3; pp. 109–10; pp. 115–16) houses all its dead in an identical city constructed beneath the ground. This necropolis houses persons who continue the same activities as before as well as those who take the opportunity (so to speak) to be something else, such as "big-game hunters, mezzosopranos, bankers" ("cacciatori di leoni, mezzesoprano, banchieri"), and so forth. The couriers who take the dead down to the necropolis serve as messengers between the two cities; they are "a confraternity of hooded brothers" ("una confraternita di incappucciati") such as you can still see today in Italy, a fraternal organization that helps run ambulances for the sick or injured. To maintain the nobility of their service, members maintain anonymity by wearing hooded robes, a tradition reaching back to the bubonic plague of 1348. Calvino takes this bit of Italian tradition and works his jokes on it: "rumor has it that some of them are already dead but continue going up and down" ("lasciano credere che alcuni di loro siano già morti e continuino a andare su e giú")! The confraternity, in fact, brings up news of changes the dead have made below, and the city of the living feels it must keep up. Maybe the dead built the entire city of the living; maybe you cannot tell the difference between the living and the dead. The black humor is somewhat cheery; after all, "No city is more inclined than Eusapia to enjoy life and flee care" ("Non c'è città piú di Eusapia propensa a godere la vita e a sfuggire gli affanni"). The dead carry on as did the living and still have power to shape their space.

Valdrada (Cities and eyes, 1; pp. 53–54; pp. 59–60) has a different tone. A traveler sees two cities built on a lake, the earthly and the mirror image, which has an infernal completeness in showing all. The inhabitants know that their every action is mirrored below, judged, as it were. "The twin cities are not equal, because nothing that exists or happens in Valdrada is symmetrical: every face and gesture is answered, from the mirror, by a face and gesture inverted, point by point" ("Le due città gemelle non sono uguali, perché nulla di ciò che esiste o avviene a Valdrada è simmetrico: a ogni viso e gesto rispondono dallo specchio in un viso o gesto inverso punto per punto"). The inversion often changes value and generally seems to unsettle the inhabitants. This optical damnation locks them in a closed system where both freedom and privacy are denied: "The two Valdradas live for each other, their eyes interlocked; but there is no love between them" ("Le due Valdrade vivono l'una per l'altra, guardandosi negli occhi di continuo, ma non si amano"). Valdrada is one of the most ferocious and undesirable of the invisible cities.

A final double city is the delightful Sophronia (Thin cities, 4; p. 63; p. 69): in contrast to Valdrada, Sophronia's two halves create a good whole, in symbiosis. There is the circus half and the business half, and one of these is dismantled periodically and taken away on tour. Calvino's joke is quickly apparent: it is the business half that is taken apart and shipped away, while the carnival rides and booths are left behind in waiting. As in Eusapia with the necropolis, the point is not so much thematic conclusion as the effect of variations and surprises we may find in the permutations of spatial arrangements. The traveling business district is equally real, and the fantasy directs our attention to this charming hypothesis.

Finally, we may consider the cities that constantly recreate themselves. Clarice (Cities and names, 4; pp. 106–8; pp. 112–13) keeps recreating itself on the same site, while Ersilia (Trading cities, 4; p. 76; p. 82) moves as soon as it becomes too crowded with the strings that the inhabitants stretch between the houses to show relationships. Leonie (Continuous cities, 1; pp. 114–16; pp. 119–20) refashions itself in the sense that it recycles its materials, sending the old Leonie (garbage) out into the countryside; obviously this has a limited future, and there is an ecological theme, brought to a grotesque comedy: "In the nearby cities they are all ready, waiting with bulldozers to flatten the terrain [of Leonie], to push into the new territory, expand, and drive the new street cleaners still farther out" ("Già dalle città vicine sono pronti coi rulli compressori per spianare il suolo, estendersi nel nuovo territorio, ingrandire se stesse, allontanare i nuovi immondezzai"). If Leonie is the materialistic permutation, Berenice (Hidden cities, 5; pp. 161–63; pp. 166–67) gives a conceptual equivalent: a just city is hidden within the unjust city. But the seed of still another unjust city is hidden in the just city, so that "the real Berenice is a temporal succession of different cities" ("la vera Berenice è una successione nel tempo di città diverse"). Berenice is the last city in the book, and the closing lines of its description offer something of the potential all the cities have been exploring: "all the future Berenices are already present in this instant, wrapped one within the other, confined, crammed, inextricable" ("tutte le Berenici future sono già presenti in questo istante, avvolte l'una dentro l'altra, strette pigiate indistricabili"). The genre of the city is an open field, and as many invisible cities as we have already seen, in many shapes, spaces, moods, concepts, and desires, they imply many more.

There is one other recreating city that will serve as a transition to the dialogues of the Khan and Polo: Eutropia ("good turning"?) (Trading city, 3; pp. 64–65; pp. 70–71). This city has several residences, and all the inhabitants move together to a new set of buildings, taking up new families, jobs, and friends. "So their life is renewed from move to move," and "variety is guaranteed by the multiple assignments" ("Cosí la loro vita si rinnova di trasloco in trasloco" and "la varietà è assicurata dalle molteplici incombenze"). So far the fantasy sounds inviting. But then we learn that the life of the city stays the same, "shifting up and down on its empty chessboard" ("sponstandosi in su e in giú sulla sua scacchiera vuota"). The citizen "open alternate mouths in identical yawns" ("spalancano bocche alternate in uguali sbadigli"). The image of the chessboard will follow us through the dialogues of the Khan and Polo, a locus of great potential and elaborate, unvarying rules. The final line is a throwaway: "Mercury, god of the fickle, to whom the city is sacred, worked this ambiguous miracle" ("Mercurio, dio dei volubili, al quale la città è sacra, fece questo ambiguo miracolo"). Mercury, of course, is the messenger of the gods, and is associated with commerce, eloquence, cunning, and even theft: "fickleness" is not a god-sized notion. Calvino plays with the physical properties of mercury here, I suspect; it breaks apart readily and rejoins the same as before. The concept of ambiguity is as important as the order of the chessboard: we have followed many opposites, counterassertions, and doubles.

A "topography of desire" is, of course, a metaphor, since the cities themselves are abstracts, and any map of them is a still higher level of abstraction. The very question of whose fantasies are involved demands multiform answers, since the words on the page represent the intersection of various fantasizing minds: Calvino's, ours (and just think of the differences among readers!), and the characters', including Marco Polo himself. (Indeed the phenomenology of fantasy among literary characters would be a curious question to pursue.) Fears, hopes, lusts, desires are richly present in these pages, carefully ordered, and vividly set or incarnated into the many cities; the feminine qualities help "set" the desires, both through cities as social organizations and through the female characters (nymphs, for example) who sing the siren song, yielding a range of values from sexuality, incarnation, and interiority, to civilization itself. The total of all these images and fantasies is, however, strangely indeterminate, as if so wide a range of emotions and images results in a canceling out of the extremes, leaving a neutral result. There is no global map, only a sheaf of insets of hypothetical cities in an atlas whose order is either unknown or fanciful: Calvino's counting game with fives to order the cities is a numerical sequence that can be visualized in many ways. That the prose poems are so short leaves us with a series of *hits,* something like beautiful but brief fireworks, so short that we are tempted to reread immediately, stuck, for a moment, in the strange, random, discontinuous geography of the cities.

So far we have raised a number of questions involving the cities, how to interpret them, whether there is consistency of theme, the mixed mood of the descriptions, and so on. We might expect that the frame—the conversations of Kublai Khan and Marco Polo—might answer some of these. Instead, we find the problems and paradoxes further heightened. Henry Fielding and William Thackeray might use authorial comment to explain, to justify, to theorize, but we are no longer in an Enlightenment sort of narrative; instead we are in a post-Symboliste, phenomenological-existential realm of bare assertions, paradoxical counterassertions, and no conclusions. This is very nearly a book without characters: the cities are full of nameless "inhabitants," and the Khan and Polo are like disembodied oracles, something like the author's muses, who can give the book a highly self-conscious discussion of what the book is about. That all their sections are in italic type (both in English and Italian) further distances them from the cities and possibly from us, although I will consistently cite them in roman type for convenience.

As we might expect, the eighteen sections of the frame introduce and reflect upon the descriptions of the cities, as have the famous frames of the *Decameron,* the *One Thousand and One Nights,* and Ovid's *Metamorphoses.* The first section, for example, sets the spirit-matter duality: despite the decadence and entropy of the empire, the Khan sees "a pattern so subtle it could escape the termites' gnawing" (p. 6; "un disegno cosí sottile da sfuggire al morso delle termiti," p. 14), perhaps a pattern such as the principle of five we found for the cities? The closing frame to section 1 (pp. 21–23; pp. 29–30) suggests the range Polo has gone through, from a foreigner who knew no Eastern languages to the omniscient speaker of many (all, we might think) tongues. The notion of chessmen is introduced briefly, and the closing riddle tells us something about the hermeneutic of the book: Kublai asks, "On the day when I know all the emblems . . . shall I be able to possess my empire, at last?" ("Il giorno in cui conoscerò tutti gli emblemi . . . riuscirò a possedere il mio impero, finalmente?"). Polo replies: "Sire, do not believe it. On that day you will be an emblem among emblems" ("Sire, non lo credere: quel giorno sarai tu stesso emblema tra gli emblemi"). This tricky turn of phrase serves as a model for the interpretation of *Invisible Cities:* in interpreting them, we so project ourselves into the realm of emblems as to join them. Once we have become emblems, so to speak, we are no longer external to them enough to "possess" or interpret them. The emblems are but signs for reality, yet they gain a life of their own, even at the expense of reality: "Perhaps, Kublai thought, the empire is nothing but a zodiac of the mind's phantasms" ("Forse l'impero, pensò Kublai, non è altro che uno zodiaco di fantasmi della mente"). Perhaps more important than any external reality are the panoply of fantasies we project; we embody these fantasies, perceiving reality through them and perceiving the fantasies themselves. We *are* our fantasies; the world also is our fantasies. Such a closed system is a source of both comfort and despair.

The opening frame to section 2 (pp. 27–29; pp. 33–35) stresses the interchangeability of the real and hypothetical past; Polo seems a Wandering Jew driven to comment on all possibilities. His last remark echoes the grimness of such an effort: "Elsewhere is a negative mirror. The traveler recognizes the little that is his, discovering the much he has not had and will never have" ("L'altrove è uno specchio in negativo. Il viaggiatore riconosce il poco che è suo, scoprendo il molto che non ha avuto e non avrà"). The closing frame to this section (pp. 41–42; pp. 45–46) continues Polo's development in speech and gives another hint to interpretation. "But what enhanced for Kublai every event or piece of news reported by his inarticulate informer was the space that remained around it, a void not filled with words" ("Ma ciò che rendeva prezioso a Kublai ogni fatto o notizia riferita dal suo inarticolato informatore era lo spazio che restava loro intorno, un vuoto non riempito di parole"). The descriptions are open enough to invite the listener and reader in and beyond; we meditate on the evocative richness of the cities. Question: as Polo becomes more articulate, does this pleasure diminish? Is the critical, interpretive act (such as this chapter) an invader, a killer of poetic space? Or does interpretation give a wider base for the surrounding space?

The opening frame to section 3 (pp. 43–44; pp. 49–50) makes a bold move: Kublai is to join the game by describing cities and having Polo verify their existence. Thus the descriptions from then on are ambiguous in point of origin. Then we have a key passage: Polo asserts that cities must have "a connecting thread, an inner rule, a perspective, a discourse" ("un filo che li connetta, . . . una regola interna, una prospettiva, un discorso")—the sorts of order, presumably, we found in the organization of the book. But further, Polo continues, "With cities, it is as with dreams: everything imaginable can be dreamed, but even the most unexpected dream is a rebus that conceals a desire or, its reverse, a fear" ("È delle città come dei sogni: tutto l'immaginabile può essere sognato ma anche il sogno piú inatteso è un rebus che nasconde un desiderio, oppure il suo rovescio, una paura"). We may recall Gaston Bachelard's wholly interior "skies of desire or hope or pride." One of the inner patterns is the topography of desire that the images shape for us, and cities, in dialectic with men, serve both to answer questions and to ask them. We have now identified the major themes of the frame: patterns (especially of desire) within the vast range of material decadence and conceptual possibility, the evocation of language beyond itself, and the participative nature of interpretation, by which we ourselves become emblems, at a level more abstract and hypothetical than the level of fact. The following sections work many ingenious variations on these themes.

There are two important images that help summarize and conclude the frames—the chessboard and the atlas. The first reference we saw (p. 21; p. 29) used chessmen as a simile for objects Polo displayed before him, objects from his travels. We noticed near the middle of the book how the inhabitants of Eutropia (p. 64; p. 70) exchange places, shifting around on the empty chessboard of the city. These two somewhat latent images of the chessboard expand to a controlling metaphor in the opening and closing frames of section 8 (pp. 121–23, pp. 131–32; pp. 127–29, pp. 139–40). Polo again displays his wares before him and Kublai notices how the black and white tiles of the floor suggest a chessboard. He again hopes to discover an order to his empire; "He thought, 'If each city is like a game of chess, the day when I have learned the rules, I shall finally possess my empire, even if I shall never succeed in knowing all the cities it contains'" (p. 121; "Se ogni città è come una partita a scacchi, il giorno in cui arriverò a conoscerne le regole possiederò finalmente il mio impero, anche se mai riuscirò a conoscere tutte le città che contiene" p. 127). Then the trope is reversed: instead of reducing the cities to a chessboard, Kublai and Polo attempt to use the chessboard to imply or create cities. Polo need travel no more, and the two men sit, playing chess, Kublai looking all the while for an ultimate pattern but finding, alas, that all the empire "was reduced to a square of planed wood: nothingness. . . ." (ellipses in the original, closing the section; "si riduceva a un tassello di legno piallato: il nulla . . ."). This final paragraph is repeated at the opening of the next bit of frame, the one completing section 8, suggesting that all the cities of section 8 were projected from the chessboard. Kublai, all the while, is dazed by the concept of nothingness, but Polo, now prodigiously fluent, takes the chessboard as a point of departure to talk "about ebony forests, about rafts laden with logs . . . of docks, of women at the windows" (p. 132; "dei boschi d'ebano, delle zattere di tronchi . . . degli approdi, delle donne alle finestre," p. 140) as if to give the plenitudinous opposite to the Khan's reductionist despair. Calvino, as usual, keeps wide open the range of possibilities.

If the chessboard is an emblem of cities emphasizing pattern and space, the atlas is an emblem representing other patterns and worlds. The final two portions of the frame to section 9 discuss an atlas, which lists all cities. The book is magic in its detail and, finally, in its prophetic ability, describing cities not yet found. Polo, ever the optimistic chameleon, seems quite at home in the atlas, although he slyly ascribes his apparent nimbleness to his hearers, who hear what they want. (He suggests, somewhat coyly, the possibility that he be put in a Genoese jail with a writer of adventure stories, so that his tales might be set down—all of which is, of course, what happened to the historical Marco Polo.) The atlas ends at a point beyond form: the death of the city by urban sprawl, formless and cancerous, such as Los Angeles or Kyoto-Osaka. The atlas (we learn in the final section—pp. 164–65; pp. 169–70) also describes utopias and anti-utopias, cities of pure desire and fear, archetypal cities of

Bachelard's oneiric space. Kublai wants his guide to tell him how to reach a utopia; Polo replies that the journey to such a city is "discontinuous in space and time, now scattered, now more condensed" ("discontinuo nello spazio e nel tempo, ora piú rada ora piú densa") and that one must keep faith. "These fragments I have shored against my ruins" comes to mind ("The Waste Land," 1. 430). But there is a countermovement. Kublai fears the anti-utopias (Babylon, Yahooland, Brave New World) may be pulling us in.

Now comes the end and climax of this subtle but rich, beautiful, and powerful book: Polo says that the inferno is not coming but is here.

> There are two ways to escape suffering it. The first is easy for many: accept the inferno and become such a part of it that you can no longer see it. The second is risky and demands constant vigilance and apprehension: seek and learn to recognize who and what, in the midst of the inferno, are not inferno, then make them endure, give them space. (P. 165)

> Due modi ci sono per non soffrirne. Il primo riesce facile a molti: accettare l'inferno e diventarne parte fino al punto di non vederlo piú. Il secondo è rischioso ed esige attenzione e apprendimento continui: cercare e saper riconoscere chi è cosa, in mezzo all'inferno, non è inferno, e farlo durare, e dargli spazio. (P. 170)

These are the final words of the book. They serve not merely as a moral or motto, but a mainspring for *Invisible Cities:* in this book Calvino took his artistry to a new range of explorations, the fantasies of space that create vivid and full images representing the passions of the mind. He made the naiads of Armilla endure, the hanging city of Octavia take shape in our minds. He gave us patterns to inhabit as we entertain some of the classic problems of existing and thinking: what is reality; what is perception; what is desire; what is nothingness; what is plenitude; what is order?

We find no facile answers, yet we find an answer: to give these questions form in prose poems, to give them charm, to make them familiar is to tame and order them and bring them to beauty. But we need presume no oversimplification through answers; the questions themselves are now acceptable as part of the inferno and, possibly, part of the noninferno: man's heroic attempt to find an order that may not, ultimately, exist. The "pattern so subtle it could escape the termites' gnawing" is perhaps too subtle (or too multiform, too variable, or even too simple) for us to find, but *Invisible Cities* offers patterns that inform our searching poetic mandalas for our contemplation, deliberation, and pleasure. If we accept the invitation to visit the invisible cities, we may visit Bachelard's wholly interior "skies of desire or hope or pride." From this renewed contact with the inner self, Bachelard finds a renewal, new strength, a space with "desired directions, axes of aggression." Whether all readers of Calvino feel that, I cannot be sure; I find, at the very least, an awe and reverence for the powers of the human mind, both in the dazzling play of fantasy and in the sobering insights into its limitations.

If on a winter's night a traveller: **Fantasy and Reading**

Any of Calvino's books—perhaps any book at all—could be approached through a discussion of fantasy and reading, but *If on a winter's night a traveller* (1979)[1] seems most suitable to such an approach, since it chooses to explore, in some detail, the dynamics of reading. The main character of the book is actually called the "Reader" ("Lettore"): he never has a given name. Further, he is always called "you," thus creating an ambiguity between him as a character and us as readers, from the very first sentence: "You are about to begin reading Italo Calvino's new novel *If on a winter's night a traveller*" (p. 3; "Stai per cominciare a leggere il nuovo romanzo *Se una notte d'inverno un viaggiatore* di Italo Calvino," p. 3; in Italian, the intimacy is intensified by the use of *tu*, the familiar form.) Thus, Calvino has accepted the narrative challenge of the old cliché that "there is first-person fiction and third-person fiction, but never second-person fiction." Through the second-person point of view, he continuously explores the interactions of text and reader, whether it be you the "Reader" or you "we readers" (as I shall designate us, the literary audience external to the novel). A corollary of these interactions appears to be that all reading, regardless of the technical point of view employed, is in some sense "second-person fiction": fiction does not exist, literature is not literature unless someone—*you*—are reading it. We are considering an informal sort of phenomenology here, something like André Malraux's suggestion that art does not come into being unless it is looked at.

Calvino might have chosen a more strictly philosophical phenomenology, or structural linguistics, or deconstructive criticism, for that matter; he has often used sophisticated intellectual currents as important concepts in his fiction. Instead, this time he has taken a more humorous, more mystical, and (to my mind) more holistic view of literature. In *If on a winter's night* there are several discussions about literature, criticism, uses of literature: each time the tone is satirical of intellectual, reductive approaches. We have pulled away from the abstract, highly rational trajectory of *t zero, The Castle,* and to a lesser extent, *Invisible Cities,* books in which rationalism found its own extinction. In some ways *If on a winter's night* is even anti-intellectual, reminding us that the intellect is but one component of many in the pleasures of reading. In 1969, Calvino told me that he was thinking of writing something on the theory of fiction; it appears to me that ten years later he wrote a theory of fiction, not in the format of a critique, which would be *too* theoretical, but, more appropriately, in the very medium of fiction. *If on a winter's night* is a demonstration of how fiction works, how we read it, how the world is treated, and (to a lesser extent) how authors write. In the following discussion, we shall explore (1) the form of the literary stimulus that helps create the fantasy, notably its organization; (2) the particular passages that discuss the act of reading, emphasizing the manipulations of feelings; and (3) the passages that touch on literary theory itself.[2]

If on a winter's night seems at first to be another "jigsaw-puzzle" book, in the fashion of *The Castle* and *Invisible Cities:* we have ten stories within a frame, and the ten titles come together at the end to form a sentence, thus giving an impression, however superficial, of intersection. Each of the stories, however, is a fragment, much as the title is a fragment of a sentence, and the alternation of frame and tale breaks down at the end, when there is a twelfth portion of the frame. The fact of ten stories may remind us of the *Decameron,* which is built on tens, but that famous frame narrative is never mentioned. Instead the extravagant *One Thousand and One Nights* is both mentioned and used: asymmetry, proliferation of stories, and mystery are more important than order, completeness, and control. The jigsaw-puzzle style of *The Castle* and *Invisible Cities* is maintained only in form, not in spirit. In *If on a winter's night* we do not feel a push toward structural complexity for its own sake; there is complexity, to be sure, but of a more synthetic, more organic, more irrational nature.

Nine of the ten stories are written in the first person (in contrast to the "you" of the frame tales), drawing us in by projection; the first-person narrators are generally sketchily drawn, making our identification with them easy. Further, most of the stories are familiar as types, having conventions of popular literature: thrillers, spy stories, naturalistic novels, pornography. These conventions are used with a light touch: Calvino gives his novel fragments a satiric flavor.[3] The humor ranges from wit to downright slapstick buffoonery; "On the carpet of leaves illuminated by the moon" ("Sul tappeto di foglie illuminate dalla luna") will serve as an example. We first meet the title and author in Silas Flannery's diary, where he introduces the book to the Reader as a source for a plagiarism that has been passed off as Silas Flannery fiction. The Reader takes it to read on his trip to South America.

"On the carpet of leaves illuminated by the moon" is curious: it has a pseudo-oriental flavor that overlays a sly erotic comedy that may remind us of both *Lolita* and *Confessions of Felix Krull: Confidence Man;* our hardy male protagonist is interested in both the mother and daughter of a respectable Japanese family. The narrator is somewhat mannerist and solipsistic, perhaps something like a Yukio Mishima protagonist. This sentence illustrates his precious sensorium:

> Now, without losing anything of these pleasant general sensations, I would like to maintain distinct, not confusing it with the others, the individual image of each leaf from the moment it enters the visual field, and follow it in an aerial dance until it comes to rest on the blades of grass. (Pp. 200–201)

> Ora io, pur senza perdere nulla di queste gradevoli sensazioni complessive, avrei voluto mantenere distinta senza confonderla con le altre l'immagine individuale d'ogni foglia dal momento in cui entra nel campo visivo e seguirla nella sua danza aerea e nel suo posarsi sui fili d'erba. (Pp. 199–200)

But all this high-minded observation is undercut by his animal lust for mother and daughter, with whom he keeps colliding: we have both the humor of his hypocrisy—he is in short order exposed both in his intentions and in the flesh—and the humor of two levels of existence, the artistic and the animal. In a long sentence at the animal level, Calvino works the joke backward by inserting a note from the translator about the proper name of a tree: "one of the lady's hands, from among the branches of the *keiyakí* [*translator's note:* in Europe called Caucasian elm], had reached my member" (p. 206; "una mano della signora di tra i rami di keiakí (detto in Europa: olmo del Caucaso; *n.d.t.*) avera raggiunto il mio membro," p. 206).

"On the carpet" illustrates the self-consciousness of the novel fragments. They are purposefully overwritten, overplayed, often predictable, all to the effect that they remind us that much of literature is traditional, that much of it is on a popular level with little variation in its elements, and that, by contrast, the frame tale is both experimental and difficult to follow. The fragments, by being more normal, provide clear, memorable beads on the Reader's quirky string of adventures. All novel fragments share the artificiality of conventional, formulaic writing. In "Around an empty grave" ("Intorno a una fossa vuota"), for example, we hardly know whether to laugh or cry at the melodrama, which brings to mind resonances of Gabriel García Márquez, Borges, and perhaps Mariano Azuela. Of course "On the carpet" breaks off, this time because of "extraliterary" forces: the book is taken from the Reader by the customs personnel at Ataguitania!

In general, the fragments mimic literary traditions and cultural traditions, especially traditions of "lesser" and endangered cultures. Most of the nations represented by the authors are small, such as Poland, Belgium, and Ireland; most are cultural satellites to "mainstream" literary leaders. Two of them, Cimmeria and Cimbria, are even mythical: Calvino is playing with the Homeric Cimmerians (*Odyssey,* XI, 14), who were associated with invasive warfare until their defeat—either way, the traditional analogues have disappeared, and so have the authors Calvino is fabricating. We are entertaining, then, the question of suppressed, dying, or "minor" cultures that may produce art—whether it is rich or merely formulaic—that the world ignores. These countries are countries of alternity, to recall George Steiner's word, where the "other" is possible. The larger themes of war, spying, murder, betrayal, and so on, reinforce one of the emphases of the book: the discontinuity of human existence. This discontinuity is both dangerous and, somewhat sardonically, interesting, whimsical even to the point of humor.

The novel fragments are a kind of sampler of popular literature; they do not have a lot of intrinsic interest for two reasons: the characters and plots never gain much development (with the possible exception of "On the carpet"), and the quality of the stories is melodramatic, portentous, in fact pretentious, without the length to make good on the possibilities raised. We may reflect, in passing, that Calvino is somehow paying tribute to the story-making urge that fuels the world of popular literature—the detective novel, the Gothic, the spy story, the romance—and such an urge is the same, at base, as the urge that drives highbrow literature. Flaubert (and Calvino) never wrote the same book twice, but Agatha Christie, Zane Grey, and Isaac Asimov have all done so. Calvino's remark that folk stories and myths probably originated together (and not, following Frye, by a "displacement" from the myths to the folk stories) might be extended to the two strata of *If on a winter's night:* the fragments are one part of the world of literature, the more devious, more sophisticated frame tale another part. (Statistically speaking, popular culture outsells "serious" literature by leaps and bounds; the academy studies five percent or less of the literary world, while thousands of thousands of readers, listeners, viewers experience stories in books, oral presentations, video formats, and so on.) So if we pass, now, from the fragments to the frame, we do so not out of disdain for popular forms and Calvino's crafty burlesques, but as readers interested in the continuities of the frame tale.

The frame tale explores the nature of reading, both the direct, immediate pleasures, and possible responses by readers to literature. Few books are more explicit: Calvino, from page one of the text, tells us that reading is pleasurable: it is an activity of protected time, space, and consciousness: "having your feet up is the first condition for enjoying a read" (p. 3; "tenere i piedi sollevati è la prima condizione per godere della lettura," p. 4). Furthermore, it is an activity of "this youthful pleasure of expectation in a carefully circumscribed area like the field of books, where you can be lucky or unlucky, but the risk of disappointment isn't serious" (p. 4; "questo piacere giovanile dell'aspettativa in un settore ben circoscritto come quello dei libri, dove può andarti male o andarti bene, ma il rischio della delusione non è grave," p. 4).

Then follows a mock war of the books, a mildly Swiftian discussion of the ranks and divisions of books, all of which have to do with reading: books you meant to read, books you hope to read when in paperback, and so forth. You, the Reader, buy the book by Calvino, get it home, see how long it is. Checking the length (don't we all?) leads the discussion to a more serious point: in the modern fragmentation of time, books provide continuity (p. 8; p. 8). Finally, we begin to read: how will the author sound? This one is an author "who changes greatly from one book to the next" (p. 9; "che cambia molto da libro a libro," p. 9) writes Calvino of Calvino; that *is* his sound, that he is always different. Yet the book is always more important than the author: "But then you go on and you realize that the book is readable nevertheless, independently of what you expected of the author, it's the book in itself that arouses your curiosity" (p. 9; "Ma poi prosegui e t'accorgi che il libro si fa leggere comunque, indipendentemente da quel che t'aspettavi dall'autore, è il libro in sé che t'incuriosisce," p. 9). Thus we start with hope, tempered and modest, but enough to claim the time for reading; the adventure begins in hope and mystery as well: I cannot lose much, but I may gain a continuity of time that will help redeem my world.

Chapter 2, by contrast, explores some negative feelings. The book, *If on a winter's night,* turns out to be faulty, repeating a gathering of pages over and over. Even the most cooperative (and droll) efforts to understand a modern author might falter should he "display one of those virtuoso tricks so customary in modern writing, repeating a paragraph word for word" (p. 25; "sfoggiare uno dei soliti virtuosismi letterari moderni, ripetere un capoverso tal quale," p. 25). The book is physically deformed, thereby ruining the Reader's hope; he wanted "an abstract and absolute space and time in which you could move, following an exact, taut, trajectory" (p. 27; "d'uno spazio e d'un tempo astratti e assoluti in cui muoverti seguendo una traiettoria esatta e tesa," p. 27) but instead he finds himself at the mercy "of the fortuitous, the aleatory, the random, in things and in human actions—carelessness, approximation, imprecision, whether your own or others'" (p. 27; "dell'aleatorio, del probabilistico, nelle cose e nelle azioni umane, la sbadataggine, l'approssimatività, l'imprecisione tua o altrui," p. 27). The response he considers, to hurt the book, to reduce it to words, morphemes, atoms, to hurl it out of his house, city, planet, and galaxy, is described in a bravura paragraph that reaches both to the infinitesimal and to the infinite: the novel claims an epic format in molecular and cosmic scope. But there is a further theme: a consideration of what printing, interpretation, communication might be. Thus, upon meeting Ludmilla, the Reader wants her phone number in order to communicate with her. The new book, by one Bazakbal (Basketball?) will be "an instrument, a channel of communication, a rendezvous" (p. 32; "uno strumento, un canale di comunicazione, un luogo d'incontro," p. 32), in short a link, even in the tradition of the book of Lancelot as read by Tristan and Isolde, as recounted by Dante in Book V of the *Inferno*. The Reader foresees "the beginning of a possible story" (p. 32; "l'inizio d'una possibile storia," p. 32) between him and her.

Chapter 3 promotes the Freudian image of a blade exposing secrets, in describing the tactile, auditory, and visual pleasures of using a page cutter, an experience known more by Continental readers than by Americans. At this point the chapters become less private and more public. Still in chapter 3 we meet Ludmilla's sister Lotaria, who studies literature as political data, Irnerio, who does not read at all, and the comically named Professor Uzzi-Tuzii, who studies the cultural, historical setting of literature. As the good professor translates and explicates, it becomes clear (chapter 4) that "all interpretation is a use of violence and caprice against a text" (p. 69; "ogni interpretazione esercita sul testo una violenza e un arbitrio," p. 68). Interpretation of a text makes him reread the original: literature per se is always more important than critical commentary, in this novel. But the professor also understands books as a threshold to the beyond, and concludes with a lovely statement:

> "Reading . . . is always this: there is a thing that is there, a thing made of writing, a solid, material object, which cannot be changed, and through this thing we measure ourselves against something else that is not present, something else that belongs to the immaterial, invisible world, because it can only be thought, imagined, or because it was once and is no longer, past, lost, unattainable, in the land of the dead." (P. 72)

> —Leggere . . . è sempre questo: c'è una cosa che è lí, una cosa fatta di scrittura, un oggetto solido, materiale, che non si può cambiare, e attraverso questa cosa ci si confronta con qualcos'altro che non è presente, qualcos'altro che fa parte del mondo immateriale, invisibile, perché è solo pensabile, immaginabile, o perché c'è stato e non c'è piú, passato, perduto, irraggiungibile, nel paese dei morti. (P. 71)

For him, the fantastic dimension is linked to the passage of time; his beloved Cimmerian language is like the Basque, the Breton, the gypsy, as he points out. On the other hand, Ludmilla, who picks up his flow of words, is oriented toward the future "that is not present because it does not yet exist, something desired, feared, possible, or impossible. . . . Reading is going toward something that is about to be, and no one yet knows what it will be" (p. 72; "che non è presente perchè non c'è ancora, qualcosa di desiderato, di temuto, possibile o impossibile . . . leggere è andare incontro a qualcosa che sta per essere e ancora nessuno sa cosa sarà," p. 71).

Chapter 5 continues the polemical approach to reading introduced by Professors Uzzi-Tuzii and Galligani. Lotaria's seminar on the feminine revolution responded to the reading of fiction in various critical fashions: "The polymorphic-perverse sexuality," "The homologies of the signifying structures," "Deviations and institutions" (p. 91; "Il desiderio polimorfo-perverso," "Le omologie delle strutture significanti," "La devianza e le istituzioni," p. 91) and so on, leaving behind "pages lacerated by intellectual analyses" (p. 92; "pagine lacerate dalle analisi intellettuali," p. 92). From this satire of academic criticism, we leap to another end of the literary process, the production of it by a publishing house. Ever in search of a complete book, the Reader has gone to find the true story about these incomplete books, four of them now, that he has been trying to read. But the publishing house, instead of being a haven for an author, turns out to be a battleground for social forces: "The figure of the author has become plural" (p. 96; "La figura dell'autore è diventata plurima," p. 96). In this morass, the Reader wishes to affirm, "I'm a reader, only a reader, not an author" (p. 97; "Io sono un lettore, solo un lettore, non un autore," p. 97), but the soup becomes thicker as we enter the matter of the translator, Ermes Marana.

Ermes is of course Hermes, either the cunning and eloquent messenger of Greek mythology, or Hermes Trismegistus, the Greek phrase for the Egyptian god Thoth, the giver of alchemy and other occult sciences. Thus he is verbal, intermediary, and indeterminate. "Marana" may remind us of "marachella" ("fraud"), "maramaglia" ("riffraff"), even "marame" ("garbage"), or "marazzo" ("swamp"), and "rana" ("frog")—this character really hops about! Ermes Marana becomes a trickster figure, the devious-devising mouthpiece of stories translated, stolen, or otherwise plagiarized, who somehow roams the world. He becomes a universal urge of counterfeiting, very much like the boys of André Gide's *Les Faux-Monnayeurs* (*The Counterfeiters*), who create novelty without regard to morals.

As the Reader reads Marana's correspondence (chapter 6), he finds a further intensification of this concept: Marana claims to have found a "Father of Stories" ("Padre dei racconti"), an old Indian somewhere in South America, a blind and illiterate old man, who seems to be "the universal source of narrative material" (p. 117; "la fonte universale della materia narrativa," p. 117), something of a parody of Carlos Castaneda's Don Juan. But this emblem of vates, bard, sage is not fully explained (perhaps hallucinogenic mushrooms, perhaps . . .), and we have yet another and somewhat vague image of the multiplicity and even duplicity of the narrative enterprise. Marana, naturally, has taken the opportunity to tape-record the old man. At the other extreme is a further Marana contact, the OEPHLW (p. 118; p. 118)—an outfit that can generate literature electronically. Thus Marana goes from the primeval to the technological avant-garde, from the oral origins to the state-of-the-art techniques of word processing. Marana is Proteus, a passe-partout, an image of the complete malleability, the metamorphoses, and the surprises that are all part of the literary world. This is a world that may accept or reject social norms of morals, rationalism, politics, and so on. Literature can somehow take what it needs or remake anything into what it needs, if we follow, even at second hand, this wonderful figure Ermes Marana.

Now comes a crescendo of links, possibilities, and forces that will fuel the rest of the book: (1) Marana has spent time in a sultanate on the Persian Gulf, playing some version of *One Thousand and One Nights,* (2) he has founded a sect called the Organization of Apocryphal Power (OAP), (3) he has translated an Irish writer of thrillers, one Silas Flannery, who has also written a diary of the two wings of the OAP. The Archangel of Light side of the OAP wants to steal Flannery's diary for the truth it would contain, while the Archon of Shadow side wants his next novel, because "only counterfeiting, mystification, intentional falsehood can represent absolute value in a book, a truth not contaminated by the dominant pseudo truths" (p. 129; "solo la contraffazione, la mistificazione, la menzogna intenzionale possono rappresentare in un libro il valore assoluto, una verità non contaminata dalle pseudoverità imperanti," p. 129). Obviously the fantasy of reading, writing, political forces, and plain tomfoolery has taken a quantum leap. Calvino has chosen to boost the range, complexity, and whimsicality of the narration midstream. If we have managed to be seduced this far, just over half the book, perhaps a new barrage should not dissuade us.

Chapter 7 picks up at the simpler level of the Reader and Ludmilla, but soon gets to the complexity of Marana and Flannery. Ludmilla sends the Reader to her home while she is not there; his "reading" of her home helps him understand who she is, although the hermeneutics of a household are as difficult as those of a literary text, and he remains with many questions. Even when he and she, finally in bed, are "reading" each other's bodies, they may be reading their own fantastic projections more than the signs of the physical body:

> Meanwhile, in the satisfaction you receive from her way of reading you, from the textual quotations of your physical objectivity, you begin to harbor a doubt: that she is not reading you, single and whole as you are, but using you, using fragments of you detached from the context to construct for herself a ghostly partner, known to her alone, in the penumbra of her semiconsciousness, and what she is deciphering is this apocryphal visitor, not you. (p. 156)

> Intanto, nella soddisfazione che ricevi dal suo modo di leggerti, dalle citazioni testuali della tua oggettività fisica, s'insinua un dubbio: che lei non stia leggendo te uno e intero come sei, ma usandoti, usando frammenti di te staccati dal contesto per costruirsi un partner fantasmatico, conosciuto da lei sola, nella penombra della sua semicoscienza, e ciò che lei sta decifrando sia questo apocrifo visitatore dei suoi sogni, non te. (p. 156)

This is an old theme of fantasy: desire projects to meet an external stimulus, creating a fantastic vision in a dialectic between subject and object. Again, reading a text is like responding to a Rorschach blot; literature may be judged on its richness as a mirror to the reader, the viewer. For example, the Reader wants wholeness, to pursue all the fragments of the novel until a wholeness is reached. When he finally marries Ludmilla, there is one kind of wholeness, but he, as reader, as perceiver, is still a separate being, and, when they read together in bed, they are in their "parallel readings" (pp. 157, 260; "letture parallele," pp. 157, 263). The Reader's "crystallization" of love, to recall Stendhal's concept, comes in this chapter upon hearing that Ludmilla has been linked romantically to Ermes Marana and maybe to Silas Flannery! This precious bit of plotting brings out the requisite jealousy in him and reminds us that Calvino really is running the show. If the book has appeared episodic, self-indulgent, and whimsical, there is also a countermovement of control, intersection, and synergy. It is appropriate that this chapter of links and ties should come between "In a network of lines that enlace" and "In a network of lines that intersect" ("In una rete di linee che s'allacciano," "In una rete di linee che s'intersecano").

Chapter 8 is the only chapter not in the second person, since it is an extract of the aforementioned diary of Silas Flannery. In a novel about reading, publishing, criticism, the relation of literature and politics, and so on, this is the segment that provides much about the author's relationship to a text. In general, we are close to the Joycean author "paring his nails" in serene detachment from the art work: the implied literary aesthetic of this book seems to assume an *auteur caché*. Even the "insights" afforded by Silas Flannery are suspect, since he is of course a character and not a mouthpiece for Calvino; I cannot put my finger on why, but the very name "Silas Flannery" seems distressing, untrustworthy, equivocal, irresponsibly vague: maybe it is the lack of hard consonants, the falling meter, or the pun on flannel in English. Flannery, like many other characters in this book, is a gamesman, concerned with who is reading his work, what kind of authors there are, and plans for future books: "I keep circling around the idea of an interdependence between the unwritten world and the book I should write" (p. 172; "continuo a girare intorno all'idea d'un'interdipendenza tra il mondo non scritto e il libro che dovrei scrivere," p. 172). Thus, as the chapter closes, he is a perfect candidate to propose an outline for the very book we are reading, in a Gidean effect of internal reflection (*en abîme*).

Flannery also relates, hilariously enough, to both of the sisters in this chapter, rejecting the satirical literary analyses of Lotaria (electronic word counts of novels), and making an awkward pass at Ludmilla who, Pamela-like, fends him off with her wit and *Webster's International*. Ludmilla holds that an author exists *as author* on a different plane from personhood and sexuality. Thus we are back to the concept of the author as known through his works, not through his life or letters or interviews—a stance Calvino himself maintained.

The adventures in "Ataguitania" (chapter 9), for all their action and fun, do not add much to a theory of fiction, with one exception: at the Reader's sexual coupling with the woman Corinna-Gertrude-Ingrid-Alfonsina-Sheila-Alexandra-Lotaria, the text asks him what he is doing: "You're the absolute protagonist of this book, very well; but do you believe that gives you the right to have carnal relations with all the female characters?" (p. 219; "Sei il protagonista assoluto di questo libro, d'accordo, ma credi che ciò ti dia diritto d'aver rapporti carnali con tutti i personaggi femminili?" p. 220). The high comedy plays with the notion of the independence of characters, beyond the demands of story, sensibility, author. Psychosexually, the Reader appears to be exacting some kind of justice from or upon Lotaria, who is described thus: "this girl always acts with her head, what she thinks in theory she does in practice, to the ultimate consequences" (p. 219; "questa ragazza fa tutto con la testa, quel che pensa in teoria lo mette in pratica fino alle estreme conseguenze," p.

220). The Reader not only claims something of her body but gets her in trouble with her comrades. Theory, computers, machinelike thought have all been screwed! The Reader has claimed, it appears, his own freedom, pleasure, and justice. (After all, Ludmilla had her freedom with Marana, and who is to rule out Irnerio for that matter?)

Chapters 10 and 11 seem a pair, the former exploring a closed-down literary universe through censorship, the latter exploring a world that opens out through the library. The arguments of Arkadian Porphyritch for censorship are weak, of course, and rejected by the satiric tone of the chapter, but weak or not, they represent a somber reality that reading is not always a privilege open to everyone. Porphyritch seems to live in a world like Thomas Pynchon's *The Crying of Lot 49,* while the Reader, ever nearing his goal, is thinking of Ludmilla as some kind of Beatrice, a "radiant vision" leading us onwards.

And where else would literary paradise be if not in a library? "Reader, it is time for your tempest-tossed vessel to come to port. What harbor can receive you more securely than a great library?" (p. 253; "Lettore, è tempo che la tua sballottata navigazione trovi un approdo. Quale porto può accoglierti piú sicuro d'una grande biblioteca?" p. 255). With this traditional Petrarchan image, the chapter brings the Reader to his last hope of finding all ten novels complete. The titles are all listed, but the books, for one reason or another, are not there. Instead, there are seven readers at a table with the Reader, like some seven elders (or seven days of the week, cardinal virtues, or trinity plus quaternity, hence, for Jung, a perfect unit). Each speaks eloquently and thoroughly of the joys of reading (pp. 254–56; pp. 256–58). What we should notice is that although the readers' points of view differ, they do not exclude each other; literature is sufficiently rich to support centripetal or centrifugal reading, rereading, memory, anticipation. The Reader solidly wants a complete book, definitive within itself, to be read from start to finish: alas, he finds "everything has been going wrong for me: it seems to me that in the world there now exist only stories that remain suspended or get lost along the way" (p. 257; "tutto mi va per storto: mi sembra che ormai al mondo esistano solo storie che restano in sospeso e si perdono per strada," p. 259). But the other readers seem to find this demand for beginnings and endings, his desperate urge for closure, old-fashioned. Although the Reader may plead his case for literary unity, his simplicity and his flexibility seem naive, pressing us toward the sophistication of the other readers, who take narration as they find it.

When the sixth reader reads all the titles of the novel fragments together as a sentence, the book coalesces in a way we never expected, giving one kind of completeness to the design, if not another. The Reader cannot accept this "solution" at all and grabs eagerly for marriage, one of the endings explained by the seventh reader. So chapter 12, as brief as it is, releases the Reader into the arms of Ludmilla and into life at large. He finally sees that he is finishing the novel by Calvino, and not, say, planning another manic trip to find complete fragments. I infer that he is accepting the book as it is, and this is bearable against the base of reality, "the continuity of life, the inevitability of death" (p. 259; "la continuità della vita, l'inevitabilità della morte," p. 261), as the seventh reader put it. When the text ends for us, it ends for the Reader, and he is released to the rest of his life that we never learned about (his job, his income, his household). Stories themselves may no longer assume life and death, beginnings and ends, or continuities and causations, but the Reader makes his own claim on these. And, presumably, he keeps on reading.

Throughout, the Reader has followed his urge for closure, his desire for completion, wholeness, entirety; these he has defined as one whole book to be kept as a talisman against discontinuity. Reading is a guided fantasy into the most wide-ranging of possibilities, and the Reader wants this experience to be fully controlled from start to finish. When the novel fragments deny this expectation, he becomes a quester, a stubborn searcher for the Sangreal of a whole novel. Even at the holy of holies (the library) his search is denied, and the elders tell him he is a fool on the wrong mission. He realizes that literary wholeness may or may not be attainable. It appears that he finds that wholeness is temporary in either realm, literature or real life, and he abandons his immediate search for literary wholeness for a temporary wholeness in marriage to Ludmilla. But, of course, he keeps reading and *does wholly finish* the Calvino novel (however fragmentary it may be). We may infer that wholeness and fragmentation are relative and intermingling terms, that a fantasy of affirmation may have to mature to include fantasies of evil (or indeterminacy).

What does it all mean? Dare we ask? One of the clear messages of the book is that a predetermined literary approach (any reductionist critical scheme) or any personal agenda (that all books must be complete) will come to grief. Such a message may well remind us of Mark Twain's notice at the beginning of *Huckleberry Finn:*

NOTICE

Persons attempting to find a motive in this narrative will be prosecuted; persons attempting to find a moral will be banished; persons attempting to find a plot will be shot.

BY ORDER OF THE AUTHOR
Per G. G., CHIEF OF ORDNANCE

Perhaps we should take a hint from Robert M. Pirsig's *Zen and the Art of Motorcycle Maintenance* that *mu* is often the correct response to a question: we should unask the question and try a different approach. "What does it all mean," is not quite right: it means itself: *If on a winter's night* is equal to *If on a winter's night.* It need not mean anything beyond itself. But readers, aware of the dialectical nature of criticism and literature may, nonetheless, continue to explore meanings that we derive from our reading.

Let us ask, then, what is reading? It appears, from the novel, to be an interaction of an adventuring person with a text, in the conditions of relative freedom, luxury, and privacy; the reader, in escaping randomness, flux, and chaos, affirms, if only temporarily, the possibility of continuity and wholeness. In this affirmation all fiction is second-person: *you are the hero of your reading.* If, however, you come bound by a critical system or an expectation, you are likely to find only what you already know; the text will function as a Rorschach blot, mirroring back your predispositions. Perhaps all readers will find something of this Rorschach effect, but the more open readers will be guided into new feelings, new thoughts, new literary experience by allowing the text to work its magic. To understand the radical freedom of the literary world, we need the image of an author who writes a new book every time, who has no voice except the voice of change or who is an Ermes Marana or even the Father of Tales, a devious interpreter of the infinitude of literary possibilities. (The author may write for many reasons—some as nutty as Silas Flannery's—and the novel seems to suggest that these are not worth looking into, since the literature itself is more interesting.) Yet there is something elegiac in the way time and reading are shown in this book: we must find the protected time to read (and this may be easy or hard; in some places, where there is censorship, very hard), and reading may be interrupted by many causes. The Reader's hope that reading will give him some *perfect time* is not realized, although he gets to read a lot and, in the end, gets the girl.

If he does indeed finish the one book *If on a winter's night,* and if, then, he takes the hint from Ludmilla (as I read it) to make love, and if he has learned not to be demanding of literature and reality—if, in short, he has learned the lesson of Ecclesiastes that all is vanity and you might as well give it all up—then, still following Ecclesiastes, perhaps he can embrace pleasures, be they literary or marital, as moments of grace in the midst of chaos and inevitable death. But the book does not say. It stops, leaving the Reader to his continuing life, leaving us to our inferences and speculations.

If on a winter's night is Calvino's most erotic book.[4] The reader follows Ludmilla for two hundred pages, reads the eroticism of "On the carpet of leaves illuminated by the moon," finds himself in the arms of the metamorphosing Lotaria character, and finally marries Ludmilla. When the text asks him about his opportunism with Lotaria (p. 219; p. 220), it suggests that he has gained his own freedom and choice in the world of the novel, beyond the guiding hand of the author. Desire at a natural, biological level leads not to the tyranny of naturalism, but to a kind of moral order of the universe. The Reader decides to marry Ludmilla *fulmineamente,* as if struck by lightning—blasted by the enlightening powers of the cosmos that are both total and irrational. Besides eros, we find paradox. Continuity and discontinuity are intertwined, life and death are partners, much as the Wing of Light and the Wing of Shadow that must, to follow the metaphor, work together to make something fly. But there are no fully adequate metaphors, rational systems, or even structures in the book. Silas Flannery's diary breaks into the story of the Reader, the ten novel fragments and eleven frame chapters give way to an eleventh story inserted into the eleventh chapter, and the basic frame of ten fragments and eleven frame chapters is extended into a twelfth chapter, which does not match in size. Besides eros and paradox, the comic is richly here: the end of rationalism comes with a lot of play, jokes, wit, and laughter. The reading of literature is rich enough to enter a dialectic with theory, reason, and summation, but so rich that none of these is adequate. Closer in spirit to the power and depth of literature are eros, paradox, and humor.

13

Mr. Palomar: **Fantasy as Death**

Mr. Palomar, the last book published during Calvino's lifetime, explores the difficult mental life of its title character, who dies in the last sentence of the book; that Calvino himself should die shortly after writing the book is an ironic parallel, but not a point of critical significance.[1] What will concern us in this chapter is the highly ordered world of Mr. Palomar, a latter-day Agilulf (the nonexistent knight; see chapter 6) who timorously, tremulously, attempts to order the world, even the universe around him with his speculating, meditating, but always analytic mind. The result of this idiosyncratic point of view is a series of somewhat claustrophobic prose pieces, high on thought, low on emotional content, often melancholic in tone. Throughout we find variations on a twentieth-century theme, the alienation of the man whose thinking seeks order, meaning, purity, and control in a universe that is random, contingent, complex, and—in the repeated word of the book—"labile" (a good Italian word of a Latin root, meaning about to fall, or unstable; this word is also used in *Invisible Cities*). In chemistry, for example, compounds are labile, about to fall into other forms. In Mr. Palomar's world, both his thought and his being (which are roughly the same thing) are continuously labile; he lives, almost suicidally, on the margins of his mortality, his death.

There are 27 short prose pieces in this volume, with their own idiosyncratic attempt at order, reminiscent of the number games in *Invisible Cities*. In *Cities,* however, the numbers were abstract; their complicated structure appeared to exist for its own sake. In *Palomar,* by contrast, the numbers of the 27 pieces are allegorized in a note in the index. (The American edition follows the European convention of putting the table of contents at the end of the book; thus it seems likely that many American readers may read the tales without knowing "the key" to the number system; would not reading the book without the key be a different literary experience from reading it with the key?) The code for the three numbers goes like this:

1. Visual experience, usually of objects; descriptive text
2. Cultural experience; visual data and language; narrative text
3. Speculative experience about self (especially mental self) and the world, even the cosmos; meditative text

(I find it useful to remember these as: 1, see; 2, signify, and 3, meditate.)

These areas, Calvino writes, are throughout the book but emphasized according to the number coding. Thus the third story, "The sword of the sun" ("La spada del sole"), is coded in the table of contents (but not in the text) as 1.1.3, suggesting that visual experience will dominate, but there will be some speculation about the mind and nature. By working all combinations of the three modes in the three positions we get $3 \times 3 \times 3$ or 27 combinations. Furthermore, there is a matching organization by content, so that the first nine stories are "Mr. Palomar's Vacation" ("Le vacanze di Palomar"), and within these there are three subdivisions (Beach, Garden, and Sky, to use short titles), in which there are, again, three stories, each with its own title. Calvino presents a formidable array, and the three modes make sense for each story, if, that is, the reader is willing to look up the numbers and puzzle out the levels of the code for a story.

This very act seems to me to change the literary experience of the stories, requiring an abstraction and critical distance that change the primary literary perception. On the positive side, we might say that the decoding of the three numbers might enrich a reader's understanding of the story, its subjects, its general rhetorical mode, and its particular emphasis on the relation of the mind and reality; the performance of such an operation makes the stories "read bigger." On the negative side, we might say that the decoding is an abstract function that takes us away from the immediacy of the stories, a kind of "instructions for reader" that may seem too directive, almost oppressive or claustrophobic, so that our literary responses are limited, controlled, or even muted. As in *The Castle,* a highly structured, highly mediated narrative limits the freedom both of the reader and of the characters. As we read, we can, of course, choose to use the numbers as guides or ignore them; in critical discussion, we should not ignore a scheme that the author clearly worked out as part of the structure and theme. The title character, Palomar, has, of course, no choice but to live within the confines of this rigorous scheme.

In *The Viscount, The Baron,* and *The Nonexistent Knight,* we had books named after their characters, but only as heraldic titles. The only book clearly titled for a character is *Marcovaldo* (1965; 1983), in which this comic, sad-sack figure attempts to survive in the difficult world of the city; this children's book has some parallels with *Mr. Palomar,* clearly a book only for adults. In the phrase "Mr. Palomar," we have both an honorific and a family name. Palomar has no honorific at all in the Italian book title (and only "Mr." in English), certainly no title of aristocracy. Nor does he have a Christian name at any point in the book. Perhaps he is "one of us," an Everyman, a modern personage in an impersonal, urban society. The family name is more specific and suggestive; if we do not think of the Mount Palomar observatory (and Europeans might not), the book itself makes the connection clear early in "The eye and the planets" ("L'occhio e i pianeti"): "he bears the same name as a famous observatory" ("porta lo stesso nome d'un famoso osservatorio").

So what is our character? An observer, a keen one, one with a scientific outlook; an inquirer who believes that the world, even the universe, makes sense, or should make sense; a man who is willing to scrutinize things even through the mediating mechanism of a telescope, literally, or of a cognitive scheme, figuratively. Emblematic of such mediated scrutiny is the jacket illustration "Draftsman with Reclining Woman," by Dürer, which Calvino undoubtedly selected. In this engraving, the draftsman, whose eye is fixed in place by a vertical rod, peers intently through a window with a grid of squares (perhaps 6 × 6) to see a reclining, half-nude woman. His pen is alert to take down her sumptuous curves on yet another grid, which is on his drawing surface, directly below his drawing implement (a pen, perhaps). This engraving is analogous both to the 3 × 3 scheme we discussed above and to the tendency in Palomar to rely on structural or conceptual schemes to direct his perceptions of reality. In two stories he attempts to simplify reality by isolating a square to look at ("Reading a wave" and "The infinite lawn"; "Lettura di un'onda" and "Il prato infinito"). Palomar is not only deductive, however, since many of his speculations move "upward," inductively, from data perceived to be an abstraction or a formula which he then attempts to apply back to reality. (I suspect the same might be said for Calvino's methods of composition, that some stories were written before the scheme of 27 slots was worked out.)

In Spanish (which Calvino knew), "palomar" carries several meanings: one is the family name as used here, but there are deeper puns.[2] The first is the meaning of "dove cote" ("paloma" meaning dove), the structure in which doves roost; such a structure is built with horizontals and verticals so that, in English, we speak of "pigeonholing something," much as James Murray sorted out thousands of strips of paper for his *Oxford English Dictionary* in a dove cote. This meaning fits, of course, with the grids discussed above, adding a spatial dimension: Palomar may be said to pigeonhole aspects of reality into the rectilinear (i.e., not organic, not flexible, not Einsteinian) categories of his mind. A further set of meanings comes from dividing the word into "palo" ("stake") and "mar" ("sea"), which suggest a collision of a single stiff pole (like the pole at the eye of Dürer's draftsman) and a fluid, ample, infinity of an ocean (like the woman in the engraving). The most clear narrative on this imagery would be "The sword of the sun," but many stories touch on this basic dilemma of straight versus curved, singularity versus plenitude, order versus chaos, constancy versus change, control versus mystery. In each case, Mr. Palomar takes the former, reductionist, part.

So who is this man? Although we look over his shoulder for more than a hundred pages, he is actually rather ill-defined. He lives in an apartment in Rome. He has an unnamed wife. A daughter is mentioned once. He does some sort of work, presumably at a professional level (white-collar worker or freelance writer, say), but that is not specified. He has some friends but spends little time with them (except on the phone, for brief messages, according to "The

Invasion of the Starlings" ("L'invasione degli storni"). He loves food. He has vacationed at the seashore. That is about as much external information as we can gather; he is, at this level, a generic character, a cultured, urban figure—a modern, Continental Everyman.

Internally, however, his individuality is intense; he is a person hidden to an external viewer. In just the fourth paragraph of the book we learn:

> A nervous man who lives in a frenzied and congested world, Mr. Palomar tends to reduce his relations with the outside world; and, to defend himself against the general neurasthenia, he tries to keep his sensations under control insofar as possible. (p. 4)

> Uomo nervoso che vive in un mondo frenetico e congestionato, il signor Palomar tende a ridurre le proprie relazioni col mondo esterno e per difendersi dalla nevrastenia generale cerca quanto piú può di tenere le sue sensazioni sotto controllo. (p.6)

Mr. Palomar isolates himself from the world and tries to control his sensations, sensations which, nonetheless, overwhelm him as he attempts to sort them out. Thus while on vacation at the beach (the first three stories), (1) he tries to make a model to simplify looking at waves, and he fails; (2) he walks by a topless young woman four times, trying to reach the proper understanding for how to perceive this sight, but he scares her away; and (3) he battles with the solipsistic and perspectival problems of viewing the sun as reflected on the water, and concludes that the world will get along without him, after his death. Does this sound like a vacation? Mr. Palomar lives in an ascetic world shot through with his mental machinations. He does not seek sensuous pleasure or even lassitude but rather persues mental struggles, which he usually loses. Too obtuse for the usual fantasies of desire, he lives an internal life of little joy. In viewing the tortoises mating ("The loves of the tortoises"; "Gli amori delle tartarughe"), he cannot imagine their sensations; he feels that their shells must decrease their sensations so that "The poverty of their sensorial stimuli perhaps drives them to a concentrated, intense mental life, leads them to a crystalline inner awareness" ("La penuria di stimoli sensoriali forse le obbliga a una vita mentale concentrata, intensa, le porta a una conoscenza interiore cristallina"). After mating, however, the tortoises seem capable, like the sword of the sun, of going on with their own life: "They go back under the jasmine. He gives her a nip or two on the leg, always in the same place" ("Tornano sotto il gelsomino. Lui le morde un po' una zampa, sempre nello stesso punto"). Calvino uses the text to turn irony against our ratiocinative protagonist; Palomar may not know how the tortoises should make love, but *they* surely know.

In three other instances the ironic betrayal of Mr. Palomar is much less subtle. The first, already mentioned, is the huffy irritation of the sunbather, who departs the scene. The next two are more alarming, as Calvino embarrasses Palomar through public ridicule. The first is in "The Contemplation of the stars" ("La contemplazione delle stelle"), in which Palomar struggles with his star charts and their relationship to the heavenly bodies (model against reality). Palomar's current hope for purity is to remove himself from earth to the heavens:

> Is this exact geometry of the sidereal spaces, which Mr. Palomar has so often felt the need to turn to, in order to detach himself from the earth, that place of superfluous complications and confused approximations? (P. 46)

> E questa l'esatta geometria degli spazi siderei, cui tante volte il signor Palomar ha sentito il bisogno di rivolgersi, per staccarsi dalla Terra, luogo delle complicazioni superflue e delle approssimazioni confuse? (P. 47)

So he studies the stars, worried that they may not really exist but are projections of his own optics (the solipsist dilemma) and that they no longer symbolize the order the ancients saw in them. Turning in his chair, fussing with his flashlight and charts, craning his neck, he suddenly looks around him to see: "a few paces from him a little crowd has gathered, observing his movement like the convulsions of a madman" (p. 48; "a pochi passi da lui s'è formata una piccola folla che sta sorvegliando le sue mosse come le confusioni d'un demente," p. 49). The story ends abruptly there, leaving our antihero a laughingstock, a ludicrous figure to be ridiculed by random passersby!

Mr. Palomar is similarly embarrassed in "The cheese museum" ("Il museo dei formaggi"), this time by the serving girl primarily, but, conceptually, by the society at large. He has been enjoying his study of the cheeses in the store and their rich social context (this is a 2.2.2 story) so that the store seems to him like the Louvre itself. Like Agilulf, he is reducing the cheeses to geometric structures in his notebook with calculations of their dimensions:

> "*Monsieur! Hoo there! Monsieur!*" A young cheese-girl, dressed in pink, is standing in front of him while he is occupied with his notebook. It is his turn, he is next; in the line behind him, everyone is observing his incongruous behavior, heads are being shaken with those half-ironic, half-exasperated looks with which the inhabitants of the big cities consider the ever-increasing number of the mentally retarded wandering about the streets. (P. 74)

> —*Monsieur! Houhou! Monsieur!*—Una giovana formaggiaia vestita di rosa è davanti a lui, assorto nel suo taccuino. È il suo turno, tocca a lui, nella fila dietro di lui tutti stanno osservando il suo incongruo comportamento e scuotono il capo con l'aria tra ironica e spazientita con cui gli abitanti delle grandi città considerano il numero sempre crescente dei deboli di mente in giro per le strade. (P. 76)

He forgets the fancy order he was going to place and orders something common, "as if the automatons of mass civilization were waiting only for this moment of uncertainty on his part in order to seize him again and have him at their mercy" (p. 75; "come se gli automatismi della civiltà di massa non aspettassero che quel suo momento d'incertezza per riafferrarlo in loro balía," p. 76). Thus ends the story, again a betrayal of Palomar, the man who is at one level a clown because of his exacting mental life, at another a kind of a lunatic who, because he cannot function in society, is both ridiculed and manipulated by it. Thus he has little freedom, and, at least in these three "ambush" stories, he dies a sort of a social death because of his absent-minded mental gymnastics.

These three ambush passages are disturbing: the character loses integrity and any semblance of heroism. Each time, he is excluded from society, cut off from an attractive woman in one case and in two other cases from society at large, which questions whether he is mentally fit. In a world where the character's mental process is virtually everything, such an indictment is serious! Socially, he is dead: unable to serve as a male attractive to a woman, unable to watch the stars in an unusual setting, unable to buy cheese in a mundane setting. He is cut off, hooted at, taken for crazy. In a book that presents various sorts of symbolic death, this social death is one of the more troubling.

Another sense of death is with us in Palomar's emotional realm. Recalling his viewing of the mating tortoises and his notion that their shells must make them feel less and think more, we may wonder whether this notion is not more applicable to him than to them: as he becomes walled off from successful social relations, his mental life becomes more rational and less emotional in relating to daily stimuli. In most of the stories, he is distant, calculating, observing and processing, not involved and reacting with a full range of emotional response. In "The gecko's belly" ("La pancia del geco"), for example, he dispassionately watches, in wonderful detail, a gecko eat a butterfly. Is he inspired by the delicacy of the creatures, the accuracy of the gecko's tongue? No, instead, he thinks in allegories: that the gecko represents his youth and that the butterfly is a Eurydice; the text suggests that the immobility of the gecko and Palomar are similar.

One of the few times that Palomar is aroused at a sensuous level is in "Mr. Palomar does the shopping" ("Palomar fa la spesa"), but there is an ironic countermove: we have already seen the betrayal in the cheese shop. In "Two pounds of goose fat" ("Un chilo a mezzo di grasso d'oca"), he begins his only extended fantasy of memory, desire, imagery, and association as he looks at the meats and delicacies of a *charcuterie* in Paris. He contemplates the jars of goose fat, and they awaken in him "an immediate fantasy not so much of appetite as of eros: from a mountain of goose fat a female figure surfaces, smears white over her rosy skin" ("un'instantanea fantasticheria non tanto della gola quanto dell'eros: da una montagna di grasso d'oca affiora una figura femminile, si spalma di bianco la pelle rosa") and so on. But Palomar sees the desire neither in the other shoppers nor, finally, in himself, and he comes to the unusual notion that the "pantagruelic glory" ("gloria pantagruelica") exists not in the persons there but in the foodstuffs themselves. A seriocomic comment at the end pushes him further away: "Perhaps, for all the sincerity of his love of galantines, galantines do not love him. They sense that his gaze transforms every food into a document of the history of civilization, a museum exhibit" ("Forse per quanto sinceramente egli ami le galantine, le galantine non lo amano. Sentono che il suo squardo trasforma ogni vivanda in un documento della storia della civiltà, in un oggetto da museo").

Only in "Marble and blood" does Palomar have emotions that continue throughout the vignette, but this time the emotions oppose each other, joy versus fear, and so on. The highly descriptive prose makes the meat attractive, but Palomar begins to worry about killing in order to eat. So we leave him "neither fish nor fowl" according to the cliché, neither fully affirming nor denying. It may seem an ungrateful charge for a critic to raise, but I feel that Palomar is emotionally dead. For a point of contrast, look at Palomar's Mexican friend in "Serpents and skulls" ("Serpenti e teschi"), who not only has ideas about a given art work, but has the enthusiasm to share his ideas. Palomar interprets and interprets, but there is no passion in his ideas.

If society and emotion do not vitalize this character, there is one last hope, the ideas that he constantly spins out and pursues. He is exceptionally alive mentally, of course, seeking explanations, mental controls, models that will somehow account for the reality he perceives. Such activity is, basically, the main subject of the whole: there is virtually no action, very little dialogue, and not even much of the "story" suggested in the strategy 2 of the table of contents. A few examples will suffice: the attempts, already mentioned, to reduce the sea and his lawn to a rectangle that he can control; his attempt to group the birds' songs into categories (p. 23; p. 25); his hope to take possession of a planet (p. 42; p. 43); his drawings of cheese (p. 74; p. 76); and his deep hope that the reptiles represent some deeper order of the world (p. 86; p. 87). All of these efforts fail, in mental deaths of sorts. Even the effort of efforts ("The model of models"; "Il modello dei modelli") fails, leaving Palomar with a series of paradoxes. He has asked himself several times whether the world can get along without him. In the very last section ("Learning to be dead"; "Come imparare a essere morto"), he feels that death means not being able to change, a state he is willing to entertain. Without metamorphosis, there is no progression, to paraphrase William Blake. By the end of the section—which has its own essayistic complexity of a narrative voice speaking over Palomar's head— Palomar decides to describe his own life instead of thinking about death. "At that moment he dies" ("In quel momento muore"). What irony: release him from thinking about death and then wipe him out! Clearly, thinking has not been the road to life, and even the Ciceronian-Montaignean attempt to learn how to die has been a failure.

If we pause a moment to recall the 1.2.3. scheme of the book, we can see that Palomar is an observer who sees (code 1), a character who interprets symbols in cultural contexts (code 2), and a speculator (code 3) who entertains various meditations. None of these vitalizes him, empowers him, raises him to action. Nor are there other numbers, a code 4 to represent love, a code 5 for action, a code 6 for spiritual insight, a code 7 for emotion.

If Palomar is an Agilulf, there is no earthy Gurduloo, no love-struck

Raimbaut, no vital Bradamante to charge up this book from another perspective. Palomar, our man with his eye on a stick as in the Dürer drawing, is a spectator and speculator for whom fantasy, if it can be said to exist at all in this emotion-starved, passion-deleted world, has been reduced to a single strand of rationalization, and even this is without redemption. The first two sections of the book have as subjects "Vacation" and "City." The third section is not parallel: "Silences." Palomar slowly fades out, becomes more abstract as the 3-code of speculation and meditation takes over from observation and cultural analysis.

Why does this gloomy vision have any appeal? There are three reasons, I think. First, Calvino makes Palomar an interesting observer; when through his eyes we see geckos, cheese, a nude female chest, we have our own sensations extended and we find insights into these subjects and how humans may view them. Palomar is fantastic in his heightened consciousness, a specialized version of proclivities innate in all of us; we can safely explore this projection of ourselves to see the limits, without commiting ourselves to the risk. At some levels, we affirm Palomar's participant-observer status in life. Second, however, is a countermovement that allows us to reject Palomar as an unworkable way of living; the book is packed with irony against Palomar, and I think that Gore Vidal is wrong in equating Calvino with Palomar.[3] Calvino created Palomar, and it is most likely that he used some of his own thoughts in extending Palomar's ideas, but the authorial voice of the book repels Palomar through ironic events, satire of Palomar's obsessive thinking and arrogance, and the social isolation that makes him unattractive to us. Palomar, for me, functions as a scapegoat, a demonstration of the extremes of life so mental that it becomes untenable. At this level, the fantasy is one of denial. Third is the epic range of this slim book; it is pleasing in the efficiency of the short pieces and in the extraordinary variety of subjects (much as *Invisible Cities* used the short pieces). Palomar looks at the gecko close-up, the planets far away; he watches the sea, sky, lawn, birds, and various animals in the zoo. He looks at the domestic and the cosmic. He has traveled to Mexico, Japan, the Near East. He studies exhibits of town and country. Palomar gives the impression of a passepartout, a character who has experienced variety, something that we can respect in a wanderer or quester, but we do not love him, because he travels as a lens with a calculating mind attached, but little emotional or spiritual resonance.

Thematically, then, the book is much like *The Nonexistent Knight*, a rejection of self-limiting thought. *Mr. Palomar* appeals to a smaller audience than *The Nonexistent Knight* because of its more limited use of characters, events, and passions, yet the lessons (if we dare draw such) are parallel: too much thinking leads to self-annihilation, because of the futility of explaining a complex universe on the one hand but also the "opportunity cost," in the economists' phrase, of the roads not taken: if you only look and think, when will you feel, share, marvel, or act?

Fantasy, reduced to such a narrow spectrum of thought, with the loss of sensation, emotion, association, imagination, is perhaps not even fantasy any more; the final fantasy, that he is dead, is inadequate to deal with death, and death comes gratuitously to carry him away from his mental gymnastics. Palomar's brand of fantasy is so limited that in a way he has been dead all along, and his final demise ends not only the narrative but a series of variations on a theme that has probably gone on long enough.

14

Conclusion: This Ambiguous Miracle

Calvino wrote long and wrote well. He wrote short fiction, short novels, and fiction that is not easily classified; he wrote essays, gave lectures, and granted interviews; he also did translations, editions, and collections of folk tales. He was, in the traditional phrase, a man of letters, in the sense that literature permeated his life, but he was not the comfortable man of letters who wrote classic, conventional books. Rather he was a restless, questing author—we might almost say obsessed—as in the composition of the tarot card stories, which he said he published in order, finally, to be free of them. As a scholar and a bibliophile, he collected and styled *Italian Folktales*. As an intellectual, avantgarde writer, he wrote the stories of *t zero*. Since his career was of seemingly endless invention, unusual variety and, always, literary intensity, to classify him can only be an act of approximation. I propose four descriptive terms as a way to begin to assess his role in twentieth-century letters: experimenter, craftsman, student, and renewer.

First, we may call Calvino an experimenter. Not only did he move away from traditional forms, themes, and styles, but he even moved within his own corpus from book to book, especially after the middle 1950s; from that point each book was a new departure, with the possible exception of *t zero*, which started off as a continuation of *Cosmicomics* but kept evolving. The point of view experiments with Qfwfq, the use of the tarot cards in *The Castle*, the prose poems of *Invisible Cities*, the mixture of moods and realities in *If on a winter's night*, the descriptions of *Mr. Palomar*—all these ambitious literary efforts show a writer of great ability and unflagging interest in trying new forms, new effects. For some critics, the tarot card tales pushed the experiment too far; others may not like *Mr. Palomar* as much as, say, the trilogy. But it is important to allow experimenters room to fail, so that the aesthetic breakthrough alone may be considered a success in expanding the possibilities of fiction, even if a particular work does not last. Yet even the harshest critics do not concur that any single work was a complete failure, and I believe that most of Calvino's output (and certainly all the works I have discussed under the elastic rubric of fantasy) will last.

Second, I propose that Calvino be remembered as a craftsman par excellence, a writer who was, yes, a virtuoso, but no facile performer: Calvino was a highly self-conscious writer who wrote and rewrote, writing polished Tuscan sentences and balanced paragraphs, mixing melodrama, humor, and realistic description as he chose. Any writer may have great ambitions and aims, but only a persistent drafter and self-editor can bring the literary dream successfully to the printed page: thus Calvino's success as an experimenter owes in large part to his craftsmanship, and I believe the evidence of his writing and rewriting (as in his description of writing *The Castle*) will be inspiring to writers in future years. What appears as spontaneous fantasy is a result of rewriting, considering alternatives, and trying various combinations to result in a scene in *Invisible Cities,* sly mimicry in *If on a winter's night,* or droll social criticism in *Cosmicomics.*

Third, we may remember Calvino as a student of fiction. Not only did he write and rewrite, but his artistic efforts were in a continuous dialectic with his study of fiction and related philosophical, linguistic, and other cultural currents. As an editor for Einaudi, as a dweller of Rome, Paris, then Rome, and as a wide reader, Calvino kept his mind occupied with intellectual and artistic stimuli of a wide range. From his earliest university studies (in English literature, with a thesis on Conrad) to his later travels as a celebrated writer, Calvino was in touch with many ideas, thinkers, and texts that he then used in his own writing. He generally "bent" the ideas he absorbed to his own aesthetic purposes, so that source hunting is probably not the best way to deal with his work.

Fourth, and partially implied already, we may consider Calvino as a renewer of fiction as a genre. He is not alone in the twentieth century, of course, since Kafka, Borges, García Márquez, Stanislaw Lem, and many others may come to mind. All of these have moved beyond realism or, more important, found ways to mix realism with various sorts of alternity (Steiner's word). When readers may have tired of the varieties of social realism, when it may have seemed that even the surrealists, minimalists, midnight novelists, fiction collectivists, and on and on had exhausted the possibilities of literature, there was Calvino, trying one thing after another. Indeed something a little scary about the thoroughness of his experiments is that he sometimes created and perfected a form so that he himself saw no further possibilities (as in the Qfwfq stories). Who would want to follow directly in his path to write further tarot card stories? How is one to continue *Invisible Cities?* The consequence of this dilemma, I think, is that his influence will be indirect, not direct.

I want to consider briefly another dilemma, the relationship of fiction to the social world. John Gatt-Rutter has complained that Calvino lost his early commitment to social justice and that the forays into fantasy were a betrayal of earlier, worthy ideals.[1] For example, Gatt-Rutter calls *Invisible Cities* "an exquisite failure." Gatt-Rutter seeks a specific political program in the person of the author behind each work. Calvino, of course, sought to distance himself as an author, so that the literary activity stands on its own, but the deeper philosophical point is that Calvino found the world increasingly complex, and not susceptible to political programs that would solve things. Gatt-Rutter claims that "Calvino has never really been aware of the power of play" (p. 339), a claim that I would not know how to support or deny. It seems to me that Calvino's work (not the man) is extraordinarily playful, and that it may—just may—have political expediency in the expanding of our imaginations, but it is under no obligation to do so. Nor do I feel that Calvino has fallen into determinism or diffidence. Closer to the mark is a comment by Teresa de Lauretis, that "human activity is at once 'doing' and 'saying,' praxis and poiesis" so that his art demonstrates freedom of mind and action.[2] Calvino himself was aware of his move away from politics, but he believed that the careful investigation of literature was a way of finding new syntheses of understanding. Thus he spoke, in his 1983 James lecture,[3] of "the great authors whose voices seemed to reach me from the summit of an absolute experience. What they succeeded in conveying to us was an approach to experience, not an arrival; this kept intact all the seductions of desire. That may be the way great authors give us that precise feeling of knowledge that we cannot find anywhere else" (p. 39).

Calvino was intensely aware of the injustices of the world, the materialism, the misuse of power, the egoism, the greed, the betrayals of trust, the sexual tyranny, but he never let this understanding of experience wear him down to stoicism or cynicism. Rather, as Olga Ragusa points out in her 1983 assessment, his work is generally marked by "the usual ebullience, the youthful, life-affirming joyfulness we are accustomed to find in Calvino's coming to grips with diversity and open-endedness."[4] For Gore Vidal, in his 1985 tribute "Remembering Italo Calvino,"[5] Calvino was an acute observer of politics, but not a politician. Vidal, in his 1974 piece and in the 1985 piece, saw that Calvino had the gift to create unities, the oneness of writer and reader, or writer, reader, and world.

Thus we come to the subtitle of this chapter, "this ambiguous miracle." The phrase comes from *Invisible Cities* and describes Eutropia (Trading cities, 3): "Mercury, god of the fickle, to whom the city is sacred, worked this ambiguous miracle." Like Mercury, Calvino is a quicksilver master of metamorphosis, both of the materials he treats and of the forms in which he casts them anew. Like the fickle Eutropians, we readers cast about here and there for authors who will delight us, dedicating our "city" to whatever "supernatural" writer we may happen upon. What is miraculous about the city of Eutropia (in brief) is that all the participants may change roles. I would propose a similar miracle for readership of Calvino's work: in reading his extraordinary stories we enter the metamorphoses of his literary art and send our consciousnesses in unusual directions. (Even the sense of miracle as a looking with wonder applies.) The more difficult point comes with the word "ambiguous," but a distinction made in the *Oxford English Dictionary* may help us: whether the word is used objectively about something (like a story), or personally about a person, such as Calvino. Clearly, we would want to apply the word to the corpus, so that the word does not mean wavering or equivocal, but, simply, moving here and there. Calvino's work is rich, complex, and holds many simultaneous meanings within it; it is common that his critics disagree in interpretations. I think such richness is a strength and a suggestive simulacrum for a world that is also rich and complex. Only a parallel construct of rich ambiguity could begin to claim adequacy.

How, finally, can we "place" Calvino? Naturally we must be fully aware that we have only the story up to his death and not beyond; we do not know how literary forms will evolve, how future audiences will read him, what sorts of influence he may have. Thus the following comments can only be offered as tentative speculations. First, I think Calvino will be remembered as one of Italy's greatest writers: a developer, like Boccaccio, of Italy's prose and narrative; a visionary like Dante; a storyteller and stylist like Alessandro Manzoni; a wit and social critic like Italo Svevo. Second, I think Calvino will be one of the great twentieth-century masters, along with Proust, Mann, Kafka, Camus, Sartre, Grass, and others. Third, I think Calvino will be seen as one of those "extraterritorial" (the term is George Steiner's) writers, like James Joyce, Samuel Beckett, and Vladimir Nabokov. While each wrote lovingly and specifically of his own culture, he also wrote at a level available to a worldwide audience. Each of these, Calvino included, lived in different places, traveled widely, both in the obvious geographic sense and in the metaphoric sense described by Keats: "Much have I travell'd in the realms of gold."

Calvino's corpus—a rich and ambiguous miracle—will stand to entertain and enlighten readers, extend and confuse critics, and challenge and inspire future writers. The variety of his work is so extensive that there is probably something for every serious reader: if you cannot bear *The Castle,* pick up *Invisible Cities*. The last word of this assessment, however, should counterbalance the word "serious." There are at least two other dimensions in Calvino: humor and awe. As a nonreligious writer, he did not invoke religious dimensions, but he saw wonder in the microscopic worlds of *t zero* and the cosmic space and time of *Cosmicomics*. Calvino invited us to see the butterfly in the gecko's stomach, the nymphs and naiads bathing in the water streams of Armilla, the antics of the nonexistent knight, and a young boy's fantastic ability to shoot moving targets. The metamorphoses of his writing offer us the opportunity to shift the shapes of our minds, to delight and extend our imaginations, and to understand anew the possibilities of imagery, character, and narrative. For such we may offer thanks.

Notes

Chapter 1

1. Albert Howard Carter, III, "Calvino's 'Ultimo viene il corvo': Riflery as Realistic AND Fantastic," *Italian Quarterly* 22.84 (Spring 1981), 61–67.

2. Rosemary Jackson, *Fantasy: The Literature of Subversion* (London: Methuen, 1981).

3. Italo Calvino, *Racconti fantastici dell'ottocento,* 2 vols. (Milano: Mondadori, 1983).

4. Tzvetan Todorov, *Introduction à la littérature fantastique* (Paris: Seuil, 1970). Eric S. Rabkin, *The Fantastic in Literature* (Princeton: Princeton Univ. Press, 1976).

5. Northrop Frye, *Anatomy of Criticism* (Princeton: Princeton Univ. Press, 1957). Mircea Eliade, *Myth and Reality,* trans. Willard R. Trask (New York: Harper & Row, 1963). George Steiner, *After Babel: Aspects of Language and Translation* (London: Oxford Univ. Press, 1975).

6. Albert Howard Carter, "Continuity and Particularity; or the Pleasures of Recognition and the Pleasures of Discovery," in *Problems of International Literary Understanding,* ed. Karl Ragnar Gierow, Nobel Symposium 6 (Stockholm: Almquist and Wiksell, 1968).

Chapter 2

1. One of the best descriptions of Calvino's life and works is in the "Nota introduttiva" to *Gli amori difficili* (Torino: Einaudi, 1958, 1970), especially pp. v–ix; this material (surely written by Calvino himself as an editor at Einaudi) is one of the best revelations of "straight" autobiography. One of the best critical overviews of his life and works is Giovanni Falaschi's "Italo Calvino," *Belfagor* 27 (1972) 530–58; extending the story further is Olga Ragusa's "Italo Calvino: The Repeated Conquest of Contemporaneity," *World Literature Today* 57.2 (Spring 1983), 195–201. For other studies, see note 10, below.

2. *The Castle of Crossed Destinies,* trans. William Weaver (New York: Harcourt Brace Jovanovich, 1967), 123–29. Unfortunately the English version is somewhat cut from the original "Nota" in *Il castello dei destini incrociati* (Torino: Einaudi, 1973), pp. 123–28.

3. August Caimmi-Lamoureux discusses the literary relationship of Calvino and Vittorini in her "Calvino e Vittorini: 'Modo di rifare la nuova realtà,'" *Canadian Journal of Italian Studies* 3 (1979): 8–13, as the two worked on the journal *Il Menabò.* Of the six essays by the two men, she deals with Calvino's "Il mare dell'oggettività," "Il midollo del leone," and "La sfida al labirinto."

4. *Eremita a Parigi* (Lugano: Pantarei, 1974); the translations that follow are mine. The original text here follows:

   La mia scrivania è un po' come un'isola: potrebbe essere qui come in un altro paese. E d'altronde le città si stanno trasformando in un'unica città, in una città ininterrotta in cui si perdono le differenze che un tempo caratterizzavano ognuna. Questa idea, che percorre tutto il mio libro *Le città invisibili,* mi viene dal modo di vivere che è ormai di molti di noi: un continuo passare da un aeroporto all'altro, per fare una vita pressoché uguale in qualsiasi città ci si trovi.

5. Sergio Pacifici cites this passage from a lecture given by Calvino at Yale, unpublished as far as I know, in *A Guide to Contemporary Italian Literature* (Cleveland: World Pub. Co., 1962), p. 148.

6. Donald Heiney, "Calvino and Borges: Some Implications of Fantasy," *Mundus Artium* 2 (1968–69): 66–76.

7. Italo Calvino, "Le cosmicomiche," *Il Caffè,* 12.4 (1964): 40.

8. That is, "un'opera narrativa fruibile e significante su molti piani che si intersecano," "Domande sul romanzo," *Nuovi Argomenti* 38–39 (maggio-agosto 1959): 7–12; these pages are Calvino's responses to the nine questions posed to him and other authors.

9. *Libri Nuovi* (agosto 1969): 5.

10. Besides Falaschi's overview mentioned in note 1 above, there has been increasing commentary on Calvino's work (see bibliography for a listing of his works and those of critics). Longer studies include monographs and dissertations: Germana Pescio Bottino, *Calvino* (Firenze: La Nuova Italia, 1967), Giuseppe Bonura, *Invito alla lettura di Italo Calvino* (Milano: U. Mursia, 1972), and Contardo Calligaris, *Italo Calvino* (Milano: U. Mursia, 1972). These earlier studies are complemented by Francesca Bernardini Napoletano's *I segni nuovi di Italo Calvino: Da "Le cosmicomiche" a "Le città invisibili"* (Roma: Bulzone Editore, 1977). Three other studies have more specific themes: J. R. Woodhouse, *Italo Calvino: A Reappraisal and an Appreciation of the Trilogy,* Occasional Papers in Modern Literature, No. 5 (Hull: University of Hull, 1968), Susanne Eversmann, *Poetik und Erzählstruktur in den Romanen Italo Calvinos: Zum Verhältnis von literarischer Theorie und narrativer Praxis,* Romanica Monacensia, 15 (München: Fink, 1979), and Martin Paul Sommer, *Die Stadt bei Italo Calvino: Versuch einer thematischen Interpretation* (Zürich: Juris, 1979).

    Franco di Carlo has studied the trilogy in his *Come leggere I nostri antenati di Italo Calvino* (Milano: U. Mursia, 1978), which has one of the best listings of Calvino's essays through that date. In her *Calvino: The Writer as Fablemaker* (Potomac, Md.: José Porrúa Turanzas, 1979), Sara Maria Adler studies various literary devices and themes. Chapter 2, "A Predilection for Fantasy," sketches fantasy in some of the early war stories, the trilogy, and the later works such as *The Castle,* without going into much detail. The latest and in many ways most mature criticism comes from I. T. Olken, in her *With Pleated Eye and Garnet Wing: Symmetries of Italo Calvino* (Ann Arbor: Univ. of Michigan Press, 1984), in which she analyzes structural and thematic symmetries. Both in book-length studies and in articles and essays (reviewed in the chapters below), many of Calvino's critics (and many of the most insightful) have been women.

11. Gore Vidal, "Fabulous Calvino," *New York Review of Books* 21.9 (30 May 1974): 13–21.

12. John Updike, "Readers and Writers," *The New Yorker* 57.24 (August 3, 1981): 90–93.

13. "Visiting Italo Calvino," an interview by Francine du Plessix Gray, *New York Times Book Review* 86.25 (21 June 1981): 1, 22–23.

14. "Notizie su Italo Calvino," in *I tarocchi: Il mazzo visconteo di Bergamo e New York,* I segni dell'uomo, No. 6 (Parma: Ricci, 1969), pp. 161–62. This material is not in the English edition; the translation is mine. The original runs as follows:

> Sono nato nel 1923 sotto un cielo in cui il Sole raggiante e il cupo Saturno erano ospiti dell'armoniosa Bilancia. Passai i primi venticinque anni della mia vita nell'a quei tempi ancora verdeggiante San Remo, che univa apporti cosmopoliti ed eccentrici alla chiusura scontrosa della sua rustica concretezza; dagli uni e dagli altri aspetti restai segnato per la vita. Poi mi tenne Torino operosa e razionale, dove il rischio d'impazzire (come già il Nietzsche) non è minore che altrove. . . . Sparsamente conobbi altre inclite metropoli, atlantiche e pacifiche, di tutte innamorandomi a prima vista, d'alcune illudendomi di averle comprese e possedute, altre restandomi inafferrabili e straniere. . . . Alla fine elessi stabilmente spose e dimora a Parigi, città circondata da foreste di faggi e carpini e betulle, in cui passeggio con mia figlia Abigail, e circondante a sua volta la Bibliothèque Nationale, dove mi reco a consultare testi rari, usufruendo della Carte de Lecteur n. 2516. Così, preparato al Peggio, sempre più incontentabile riguardo al Meglio, già pregusto le gioie incomparabili dell'invecchiare.

15. Letter from Calvino to Carter, 23 ottobre 1981. "Le notizie biografiche non corrispondono mai alla verità, soprattutto se sono prese dai giornali." "Perchè anche quando è l'autore stesso che fornisce le notizie, si tratta sempre di *fiction,* di notizie inventate. Solo quando un autore è morto si può intraprendere un lavoro di storico cercando documenti, confrontando testimonianze, etc. E allora si scopre che tutto quello che è stato scritto prima era falso."

Chapter 3

1. *Il sentiero dei nidi di ragno* (Torino: Einaudi, 1947) was Calvino's first book. He wrote a preface for a reissue of the novella, which appeared in 1964, again from Einaudi. The English translation *The Path to the Nest of Spiders,* by Archibald Colquhoun, appeared in 1957 (Boston: Beacon).

   "Ultimo viene il corvo" ("Last Comes the Crow"), finished in 1946, was first published in 1949 in a collection of 13 war stories with the same name: *Ultimo viene il corvo* (Torino: Einaudi); it also appears in the collected stories *I racconti* (Torino: Einaudi, 1958) in the section "Gli idilli difficili" ("The Difficult Idylls"), pp. 60–64. My citations are to the latter source, the more available text. Of all the 52 stories in *I racconti,* only one other, "Andato al comando" ("Gone to Headquarters") has an earlier date (1945): Calvino started his literary career on a high note.

   There is an English translation, "The Crow Comes Last," in Italo Calvino, *Adam, One Afternoon and Other Stories,* trans. Archibald Colquhoun and Peggy Wright (London: Collins, 1957), pp. 57–68. There is also another English version, "Last Comes the Raven," in Ben Johnson's *Stories of Modern Italy* (New York: Random House, 1960). For the purposes of this chapter, however, I prefer my own translations.

   This chapter is an expanded version of my "Calvino's 'Ultimo viene il corvo': Riflery as Realistic AND Fantastic," *Italian Quarterly* 22.84 (Spring 1981): 61–67, in which I discuss only "The Crow," not *The Path.*

2. See Giovanni Grazzini, "Lettura dei 'Racconti' di Calvino," *La Letteratura Moderna* 9 (1959): 621–37. *The Path* and "The Crow" have attracted a fair amount of critical commentary, even from Calvino himself, who was usually reticent to discuss his own work. In his preface to a reissue of *The Path* he discussed the relationship of his war experiences and his work; we shall take this up later in the chapter.

Pier Raimondo Baldini picks up on one of the phrases of Calvino's preface, "il più povero degli uomini" ("the poorest of men"), which refers to the impoverishment of an author
who has exhausted his store of memory by creating narratives; Baldini sees this dilemma
throughout Calvino's corpus, all the way up to *The Castle* in his "Calvino: 'Il più povero
degli uomini,'" *Forum Italicum* 10 (1976): 198–202.

3. Carlo Annoni discusses realism and the fabulous in several of Calvino's war stories, finding
Calvino to be divided between realism and an urge to comment essayistically, in "Italo Calvino: La resistenza tra realtà e favola," in *Vita e Pensiero* 51.11 (novembre 1968): 968–75.
Similarly, Claudia Patuzzi finds Calvino divided between the neorealistic, mimetic, "en-
gaged" Italian of *The Path* and the fabulous, allegorical, escapist European of *The Cloven
Viscount*, and *The Baron in the Trees*, in her "Italo Calvino: Un intellettuale tra poesia e impegno," *Nuova Antologia* 527 (1976): 140–47. She speaks of Calvino as going through
periods, such as his "periodo 'utopistico,'" but I believe that he is not so much a writer of
differing aesthetics or themes at different times as an evolving author who seeks literary freedom where he can find or create it; thus I think of his development as something more organic, more incremental.

Another approach stressing Calvino somehow divided between two imperatives is
Giovanni Falaschi's "Calvino fra realismo e razionalismo," *Belfagor* 26 (1971): 373–91.

Other critics have found dual aesthetics in Calvino's early work, but in more of a unity
of effect. Especially useful is Giovanna Finocchiaro Chimirri's "Realtà e favola in Italo Calvino" in *Teoresi* 21 (1966): 296–313. She finds that *Il sentiero dei nidi di ragno* shows a
coalescence of Calvino's early talent on the way toward his aesthetic of the trilogy (*The Cloven Viscount*, *The Baron in the Trees*, and *The Nonexistent Knight*), so that realism and the
fabulous are convincingly mixed. Nicholas A. DeMara emphasizes the two literary back-
grounds of neorealism and Ernest Hemingway in his "Pathway to Calvino: Fantasy and Reality in 'Il sentiero dei nidi di ragno,'" *Italian Quarterly* 14.55 (Winter 1971): 25–49. Finally, Antonia Mazza stresses irony in "The Crow" as a way toward a poetics of the negative
in her "Italo Calvino: Uno scrittore dimezzato?" *Letture* 26 (1971): 3–14. Most recently,
Claudio Milanini has studied the existentialist qualities of the setting in time and space of *Il
sentiero* in his "Natura e storia nel 'Sentiero' di Italo Calvino," *Belfagor* 40.5 (settembre
1985): 529–46.

4. "Narrative Discourse in Calvino: Praxis or Poiesis?" *PMLA* 90 (May 1975): 414–25, p. 414.

5. Ibid., pp. 414–15.

6. Philip Wheelwright, *The Burning Fountain: A Study in the Language of Symbolism*, rev. ed.
(Bloomington: Indiana Univ. Press, 1968), pp. 172–73.

7. Mircea Eliade, *Myth and Reality*, trans. Willard R. Trask (New York: Harper & Row, 1963),
chapters 1–3.

Chapter 4

1. *Il visconte dimezzato* (Torino: Einaudi, 1952). My citations will give the English first, from
Archibald Colquhoun's translation, *The Nonexistent Knight and The Cloven Viscount* (New
York: Random House, 1962), followed by parentheses with the page number for the English,
then the original Italian, followed by its page number.

2. Italo Calvino, note to "I giovani del Po," *Officina* 3, 4 (1957–58), p. 331.

3. J. R. Woodhouse, *Italo Calvino: A Reappraisal and an Appreciation of the Trilogy*, Occasional Papers in Modern Languages, No. 5 (Hull: University of Hull, 1968). There has not
been much commentary on *The Cloven Viscount*. JoAnn Cannon sees it, and the other two

novels of the trilogy, as a clear indication of Calvino's direction beyond realism, into an "inverisimilar" world that is both still related to social concerns and, self-reflexively, interested in "the nature of literature and literary language." See her "Literary Signification: An Analysis of Calvino's Trilogy," *Symposium* 34 (1980), 3–12.

4. In my interview with Calvino in Paris, 21 November 1969, he spoke of the need for openness in critical readings; in a letter, 24 January 1970, he affirmed that he had abolished the preface because he had tired of it.

5. Wolfgang Kayser, *The Grotesque in Art and Literature,* trans. Ulrich Weisstein (New York: McGraw-Hill, 1966).

Chapter 5

1. Italo Calvino, *Il barone rampante* (Torino: Einaudi, 1957). The standard English version is *The Baron in the Trees,* translated by Archibald Colquhoun (New York: Random House, 1959). There is another edition, still from Einaudi (1965) which is slightly abridged and expurgated by, presumably, Calvino himself, under the pseudonym of Tonio Cavilla. This name puns on the word "cavillare" and literally reads, in Italian "Tonio cavils" or "quibbles," a fine phrase for an editor. A somewhat sly note on the back of the title page offers an exercise in double meanings:

> Editor's note. Between himself and this very book, Italo Calvino has wished to introduce the personage of a meticulous scholar and educationist, Tonio Cavilla, who has analyzed and commented on the text with all the critical detachment and gravity which, to the author, appear necessary. (My translation)

> *Nota dell'editore.* Tra sè e il proprio libro Italo Calvino ha voluto introdurre il personaggio di un meticoloso docente e pedagogista, Tonio Cavilla, il quale ha analizzato e commentato il testo col distacco critico e la serietà che all'autore parevano necessari.

I am grateful to Professor Florindo Cerreta for pointing out that "Tonio Cavilla" is also an anagram for "Italo Calvino."

It is humorous in itself to consider expurgating Calvino's work, which is either chaste or intellectual (or both) to the extent that it is not likely to be consulted for matters of sex or filth. Indeed, in this case, the expurgation is of such light matters that it can only be for the protection of the most tender ears of the *scuola media.*

2. *Mircea Eliade, Myth and Reality,* trans. by Willard R. Trask (New York: Harper & Row, 1963).

3. Woodhouse, chapter 4 "The Role of the Naive Narrator and Other Ingenuous Characters." More recently, Woodhouse has produced an edition of *Il barone rampante* (Manchester: The University Press, 1970); this edition, with its 22-page introduction is reviewed favorably by Joy Hambuechen Potter in *Italica* 48.2 (Summer 1971): 278–80. Jill Margo Carlton observes that Biagio (among other devices) is a means by which Calvino can draw attention to the importance of storytelling within the novel in her "The Genesis of *Il barone rampante,*" *Italica* 61.3 (Autumn 1984): 195–206. Norbert Jonard studies the Enlightenment setting of the novel in his "Calvino et le siècle des lumières," *Forum Italicum* 18.1 (Spring 1984): 93–116.

4. The English rendering "Fauchelefleur" changes the gender of flower from the Italian original "Fauchelafleur"; in either case, the name means, roughly, "Sickle-the-flower," or "Bloomcutter."

5. Predictably enough, the entire paragraph regarding Cosimo's bathroom needs has been deleted from the school edition.

Chapter 6

1. Jean Baudrillard has some helpful remarks about the *beylisme* of the character of this book in his article, "Les Romans d'Italo Calvino," *Temps Modernes* 192 (mai 1962): 1728–34:

   > Finalement la plus grande sincerité et justesse de style se retrouve chez Calvino dans les personnages proprement romanesques, qui sont chez lui passionnés héroïques, très stendhaliens dans leur fougue et leur exigence. . . . En admiration d'abord devant le Chevalier Absent, Agilulf, elle évoluera normalement vers l'amour du Chevalier Vivant, Raimbaut. C'est cette évolution que semble la plus proche du sens du livre, et de la "verité" de Calvino: dépassement de l'absence et de la volonté vers un bonheur realisé. Donc, un art de vivre. (P. 1733)

   I do not agree, however, that Bradamante is the mouthpiece for Calvino, as Baudrillard concludes (p. 1733).

   The English translation of Calvino's *Il cavaliere inesistente* (Torino: Einaudi, 1959) is *The Nonexistent Knight* by Archibald Colquhoun; it is bound with *The Cloven Viscount* (New York: Random House, 1962). The story is the last of the trilogy.

   There is a cartoon version of this story, which I have not seen, by Pino Zac. Two stills from the animated film are reproduced in Antonia Mazza's article "Italo Calvino: Uno scrittore dimezzato?" *Letture* 26 (1971): 3–14.

2. Italo Calvino, "Presentazione," in Ludovico Ariosto, *Orlando furioso,* terza ed. (Milano: Einaudi, 1970), p. xxiv, my translation.

3. Woodhouse, following Calvino's preface, gives a limited view of the novel, especially the role of Bradamante/Theodora. Calvino reports that the equation of the two figures came to him late in composition, and Woodhouse feels that our response should be so governed. I should think that Calvino's sequence of composition, however interesting as creative process, is independent of our experience as we read the book.

4. Woodhouse, p. 67.

5. In 1977, Calvino published an essay on Saul Steinberg, later translated, by William Weaver as "The Pen in the First Person (For the Drawings of Saul Steinberg)" (New York: Pace Gallery, 1982), unpaged. In this essay Calvino picks up the idea of the implements of drawing as part of the reality of artists and thinkers such as Cavalcanti, Mallarmé, Galileo, and, of course, Steinberg.

6. Calvino describes the novel as "un'opera narrativa fruibile e significante su molti piani che si intersecano" ("a narrative work, enjoyable and significant on many intersecting planes") in "Domande sul romanzo," *Nuovi Argomenti* 38–39 (maggio-agosto 1959): 6–12, p. 12. Calvino is one of several novelists replying to the editors' questions.

7. Italo Calvino, "Presentazione," in *Orlando furioso,* pp. xxv–xxvi, my translation.

Chapter 7

1. "La formica argentina" first appeared in *Botteghe Oscure* (1952). It appeared in a 1958 edition (Venezia: Sodalizio del libro), and with "La nuvola di smog" in *La nuvola di smog e La formica argentina* (Torino: Einaudi, 1965), to which my page numbers refer. It also appears in *I racconti* (Torino: Einaudi, 1958), pp. 407–40.

   "La nuvola di smog" is in the edition just mentioned (to which, again, my citations refer): it is also available in *I racconti,* pp. 521–67.

Both "La formica argentina" and "La nuvola di smog" are included in *Gli amori difficili,* Gli Struzzi 5 (Torino: Einaudi, 1970). Calvino was skilled in presenting through a variety of formats!

La giornata d'uno scrutatore (Torino: Einaudi, 1963) has been translated, with the other two stories, by William Weaver as *The Watcher and Other Stories* (New York: Harcourt Brace Jovanovich, 1971). My English quotations come from this volume. "The Argentine Ant" is also translated by Archibald Colquhoun and Peggy Wright in *Adam, One Afternoon, and Other Stories* (London: Collins, 1957), pp. 151–90.

2. JoAnn Cannon, in her article "The Image of the City in the Novels of Italo Calvino," *Modern Fiction Studies* 24 (1977): 83–90, discusses the city in some of the *Marcovaldo* stories and in "Smog." She finds the city in "Smog" to be virtually any city, and the protagonist one who rationalizes his choice of being trapped in the city; the laundry cart scene, "however, calls this solution into question" (p. 89). Although Cannon is using the Harcourt Brace Jovanovich edition of *The Watcher and Other Stories,* she does not discuss the city at the end of "The Watcher," nor does she treat the concept in *Invisible Cities.*

     Martin Paul Sommer, in his *Die Stadt bei Italo Calvino: Versuch einer thematischen Interpretation* (Zürich: Juris, 1979), treats *The Path, Marcovaldo,* "Smog," the trilogy, and *Invisible Cities,* but not the ending of "The Watcher."

Chapter 8

1. Italo Calvino, *Le cosmicomiche* (Torino: Einaudi, 1965). The English translation, which won the National Book Award for 1968, is *Cosmicomics,* trans. William Weaver (New York: Harcourt, Brace, 1968). D. S. Carne-Ross, however, has been critical of this translation in his review of it and the French version in his "Writing between the Lines," *Delos* 3 (1969): 198–207.

     Besides the *t zero* (*Ti con zero,* 1967), which continues the Qfwfq tales for part of its length (see chapter 9), there is another volume *La memoria del mondo e altre storie cosmicomiche* (Torino: Einaudi, 1968) by Calvino which contains many of the *Cosmicomics* tales and the following: "La luna come un fungo," "Le figlie della Luna," "I meteoriti," "Il cielo di pietra," "Fina a che dura il Sole," "Tempesta solare," "Le conchiglie e il tempo," and "La memoria del mondo." All of these except the last follow the usual format of a scientific citation and an introductory mention of Qfwfq as the speaker; these have not, to my knowledge, been translated into English; there has been virtually no commentary or even mention of them: the *Cosmicomics* and *t zero* volumes, justly or unjustly, have received all the attention.

     Antonio Illiano discusses various intellectual sources of *Cosmicomics* and *t zero,* attempting to establish a "cosmogonic vein" in his "Per una definizione della vena cosmogonica di Calvino: Appunti su *Le cosmicomiche e Ti con zero,*" *Italica* 49 (1972): 291–301. Ernest L. Fontana finds Qfwfq to be an "undifferentiated Protean urge that endures as long as matter endures. Like Proteus, none of his transformations is final, none of them exhaustible of his creative plenitude" in his "Metamorphoses of Proteus: Calvino's *Cosmicomics,*" *Perspectives on Contemporary Literature* 5 (1979): 147–55, p. 147.

     For a philosophical approach, discussing subject, object, and mode of being, see Sandro Briosi, "La differenza, l'identità, l'inizio (saggio sull'ultimo Calvino)," in *Il Lettore di Provincia* 25–26 (1976): 19–27. Briosi finds a Sartrean circularity in the dilemmas of Qfwfq and Priscilla. Some of the most intelligent writing on the Calvino of *Cosmicomics* and *t zero* is by Mario Boselli and Gian-Paolo Biasin; I discuss both of these in chapter 9. For an excellent piece of research on Calvino from *Cosmicomics* to *Invisible Cities,* see Francesca Bernardini Napoletano's monograph, *I segni nuovi di Italo Calvino: Da "Le cosmicomiche" a "Le città invisibili"* (Roma: Bulzone Editore, 1977). While providing a full list of commentary and reviews and an excellent list of Calvino's essays, introductions, interviews, lectures, and fiction from 1965 to 1976 (some 88 items!), she discusses humor in *Cosmicomics* (pp. 20ff).

Of recent commentary on *Cosmicomics,* Kathryn Hume has contributed two useful articles: "Science and Imagination in Calvino's *Cosmicomics,"* *Mosaic* 15.4 (1982): 47–58, in which she points out that Calvino's imagination both challenges science and subsumes it into a search for wholeness, and "Italo Calvino's Cosmic Comedy: Mythography for the Scientific Age," *Papers on Language and Literature* 20.1 (Winter 1984): 80–95, in which she studies the etiological qualities of the tales and their lack of social acceptance and ritual reenactment. She also defends Calvino against an attack by John Gatt-Rutter; see my discussion in chapter 14.

In "Signs and Science in Italo Calvino's *Cosmicomiche:* 'Fantascienza' as Satire," *Forum Italicum* 17.1 (Spring 1983): 29–40, Gregory L. Lucente argues that such devices as irony and humor keep any overarching system (myth, science, cosmic awe) at bay. By contrast, Anca Vlasopolos finds a pervasive love as prime mover and first agent throughout the stories, although humans have perceptual difficulties that can lead to various kinds of extinction; see "Love and the Two Discourses in *Le cosmicomiche,"* *Stanford Italian Review* 4.1 (Spring 1984): 123–35.

Antonella Catalano discusses stories from both *Cosmicomics* and *t zero* in counterpoint with the work of Borges in her "Il viaggio, la parola, la morte: Sulle favole *Cosmicomiche* di Italo Calvino," *Il Lettore di Provincia* 15.56 (1984): 85–97.

2. A. N. Whitehead, *Science and the Modern World* (1926) (Cambridge, Eng.: Cambridge Univ. Press, 1953).

3. J. Bronowski, *Science and Human Values,* rev. ed. (New York: Harper Torchbook, 1965).

4. After eight stories there is a variation of Qfwfq's opening agreement. In "I dinosauri," he corrects the scientific version. In "La forma della spazio" and "Gli anni-luce" he does not give a specific recognition to the scientific view, proceeding instead to his narrative. In "La spirale" he questions (conversationally, not argumentatively) whether the scientific description applied to him. Once established, the device can stand variation; indeed we are probably anxious for change after eight stories.

5. Michael Feingold, "Doing the Universe Wrong," *The New Republic,* 2 November 1968: 34–36.

6. Unpublished lecture, delivered by Calvino in England and France in 1968–69; Calvino was kind enough to give me a copy of his notes.

7. David Hayman and Eric S. Rabkin include William Weaver's translation, "All at One Point," as an example of fantasy in their *Form in Fiction: An Introduction to the Analysis of Narrative Prose* (New York: St. Martin's Press, 1974), pp. 226–29, followed by a discussion of the story, pp. 229–33.

Chapter 9

1. Italo Calvino, *Ti con zero* (Torino: Einaudi, 1967). The English version, *t zero,* is translated by William Weaver (New York: Harcourt, Brace, 1969).

Without pursuing the matter in depth, Francesco Grisi has touched on the use of formulas in the thought of the characters of *Ti con zero* in his "Italo Calvino e le formule matematiche," *Idea* 24.1–2 (gennaio-febbraio 1968): 36–37.

Mario Boselli has written two fine articles on Calvino. The first, *"Ti con zero* o la precarietà del progetto," appeared in *Nuova Corrente* 49 (1969): 129–50. In this article Boselli weighs the relationship of Calvino's imagination, reason, and use of language, especially his gift to project hypotheses with such weight, vividness, or linguistic inevitability that we follow them willingly. In this ability to project alternative realities (Steiner comes to mind again) there is an affirmation of being and a vision of the world.

Boselli's second article is "Italo Calvino: L'immaginazione logica," *Nuova Corrente* 78 (1979): 137–50. Boselli opens with a discussion of Calvino's "Dall'Opaco," a short story printed in *Adelphiana* (1971), according to Boselli; I have not been able to locate this text. Boselli finds this story and others of the same epoch, including the *t zero* stories, to show an existential void ("vuoto") between reality and the images, apparently logical, carefully developed in the narrative, in a combination of abstraction and concreteness. This gap is partially healed in *Invisible Cities* as logic gives way to emotion and as language is seen as gesture, a behavior more than an external sign-system, but the Calvino of this era avoids, argues Boselli, anything like a Joycean epiphany in which truth is revealed and connections are found.

Gian-Paolo Biasin proposes a spatial approach to the metaphorical literary spaces of *Cosmicomics* and *t zero*, using the concepts of Jurij Lotman. Biasin finds a "linguistic sphericity" through "chaotic enumeration" and, more important, "artistic use of numerous, specialized and scientific languages, together with others taken from common speech" (p. 180). Biasin concludes: "By mythologizing and fabulizing the paradigms of science Calvino has taken up geological eras and millennia in the spatial form of his art, in the force of a geometrical writing which is continually renewed in an unexhausted combinatory process" (p. 187). I agree that the scientific formulas have been mythologized, but the terminology of "sphericity" and "hypersphericity" seems to me so abstract as to be no longer spatial but rather, in Biasin's other terms, pertaining to "metanarrative." I do not think that the opposition of temporal, linear, referential narrative to spatial, spherical, abstract metanarrative is the only way to understand new searches for mythologies. Calvino is rather abstract, but he also uses a mixture of linear narration with his self-reflexive effects, a combination referenced to lived, mundane reality as well as to cosmic and fantastic realms, and a texture that reads at once on the simple level of a tale as well as on a polyvalent, semiotic level of high abstraction. Biasin's inquiry into literary space helped push me in another direction in my chapter 11 on *Invisible Cities*. See his "$4/3\pi r^3$: Scientific vs. Literary Space" in *Versus* 19–20 (gennaio-agosto 1978): 173–88.

2.   Richmond Lattimore's introduction to his translation of Homer's *Iliad* (Chicago: The Univ. of Chicago Press, 1951) follows the work of Milman Parry in discussing the Homeric formula.

3.   My discussion here owes to Edward Kasner and James Newman, *Mathematics and the Imagination* (New York: Simon and Schuster, 1940), to M. Evans Munroe, *The Language of Mathematics* (Ann Arbor: Univ. of Michigan Press, 1963), and to George Gamow, *One Two Three . . . Infinity* (1947; rpt. New York: Bantam, 1965).

4.   Besides the humor of the sound of the word, there is meaning, since in English "vug" is actually a geological term. I am grateful to Professor Alan Nagel for calling this arcanum to my attention, since Calvino is obviously playing on the word. "Vug" means a cavity, a hollow in rock, lined with minerals, often well crystallized. See *Gems and Gem Materials* by Edward Henry Kraus and Chester Baker Slawson, 5th ed. (New York: McGraw-Hill, 1947), p. 93.

5.   "The Immortal," translated by James E. Irby, is included in *Labyrinths: Selected Stories & Other Writings*, rev. ed., eds. Donald A. Yates and James E. Irby (New York: New Directions, 1964), pp. 105–18.

6.   Paul Valéry, *Monsieur Teste* (Paris: Gallimard, 1946), p. 140.

Chapter 10

1. *The Castle of Crossed Destinies,* trans. William Weaver (New York: Harcourt Brace Jovanovich, 1977), from the original *Il castello dei destini incrociati* in the volume *I tarocchi: Il mazzo viconteo di Bergamo e New York* (Parma: Franco Maria Ricci, 1969). Ricci's original sumptuous version has also been done by him in English as *Tarots: The Visconti Pack in Bergamo and New York* (1976). The Harcourt Brace Jovanovich version is simplified, with line cuts instead of the printed cards; it faithfully follows the simplified Italian version *Il castello dei destini incrociati* (Torino: Einaudi, 1973), with *La taverna dei destini incrociati* as well as *Il castello;* I do not know of any separate publication of *La taverna.* Because the page number for the English and the Italian is usually the same, I will generally give just one number; when the page numbers differ, I will give both.

2. Calvino's "Nota" at the end of the Einaudi edition is of interest, since he discusses some of the intellectual sources of the book (pp. 123–28); the Harcourt Brace Jovanovich "Note" is, unfortunately, an inexact version, deleting some paragraphs, combining others. Thus, in my citations, I shall give the English version of HBJ when it exists, and, when it is lacking, my own.

3. Gertrude Moakley, *The Tarot Cards Painted by Bonifacio Bembo for the Visconti-Sforza Family: An Iconographic and Historical Study* (New York: The New York Public Library, 1966).

4. Mouni Sadhu, *Tarot: A Contemporary Course of the Quintessence of Hermetic Occultism* (London: George Allen and Unwin, 1962).

5. Calvino's "Nota" (my translation: "potevano ben rappresentare il mondo visuale nel quale la fantasia ariostesca s'era formata," p. 125). Calvino has also edited a shortened version of the *Orlando furioso* (Torino: Einaudi, 1970).

6. The Russian work is available in *I sistemi di segni e lo strutturalismo sovietico,* eds. Remo Faccani and Umberto Eco, *Idee nuove,* Vol. 1 (Milano: Bompiani, 1969).

7. *Twentieth Century Studies* 3 (1970): 93–101.

8. A good introductory article is JoAnn Cannon's, "Literature as Combinatory Game: Italo Calvino's *The Castle of Crossed Destinies,*" *Critique* 21.1 (August 1979): 83–91. One of the most common objections is to the elaborate rules which become, in *The Tavern,* increasingly abridged. Thus Francesca Bernardini Napoletano complains about the lax structure of the second book, but finally finds an affirmation of freedom through the "atteggiamento ludico" ("playful posture" or "ludic attitude") in her *I segni nuovi di Italo Calvino: Da "Le cosmicomiche" a "Le città invisibili"* (Roma: Bulzone Editore, 1977), p. 150, pp. 167–68.

     Five discussions illustrate the diversity of academic approaches that *The Castle* has invited: Gaetano Cipolla finds analogues, both ancient and modern, to the device of telling stories by the use of a square diagram, including moderns Mallarmé and Borges. He concludes that Calvino is mannerist in an ancient tradition of creating the world through primal material (words) and the basic shape of the magic square. See "Un Calvino manierista," *La Parola del Popolo* 146 (settembre-ottobre 1978): 32–34. Maria Corti takes a semiological tack in her "Il gioco dei tarocchi come creazione d'intrecci," *La Battana* 26 (1971): 5–20, referring to the ideas of Lekomceva, Uspenskij, and Egorov mentioned by Calvino and to terms from Greimas and Kristeva. Corti finds a "pluridimensional vision" in the stories including two levels, "a discursivity of problematic nature" and "a lyricity of fantastic nature" (p. 18). Gérard Genot also takes a semiological approach in his "Le Destin des récits entrecroisés," *Critique* 303/4.4 (1972): 788–809, but with a graphic emphasis, in the style of Cipolla and with an emphasis of *lecture* and *écriture* to illuminate the highly interpretive nature of the stories.

Marilyn Schneider advances the thesis that Calvino is at the center of this book: "Calvino figuratively declares himself as metanarrative subject of *Il castello*. If this point is granted, then the entire book may be viewed as an authorial 'identification card,' in keeping with each storyteller's explicit selection of a tarot for that purpose," "Calvino at a Crossroads: *Il castello dei destini incrociati, PMLA* 95.1 (January 1980): 73–90, p. 74. Pursuing several motifs (crosses, abandoned women, mythical figures), Schneider views the book as a flux of constructed then destroyed stories so that: "Clearly, Faust is a figure of Calvino; and Calvino, in writing *Il castello*, is attempting to discover himself within his textual universe" (p. 82), an aim at which he shall fail. I agree to the parallel between author and Faust, but hesitate to ascribe a purpose to Calvino either as author, implied author, or metanarrative subject, any more than any writer or reader is somehow reflected in the text (see May Ann Caws, *The Eye in the Text: Essays on Perception, Mannerist to Modern* [Princeton, N.J.: Princeton Univ. Press, 1981]). Constance Daryl Markey, in her dissertation "The Role of the Narrator in Italo Calvino's Fiction" (University of Illinois at Urbana-Champaign, 1980) suggests that the similarities of narrators throughout Calvino's work merge into a single role. She concludes that "At times individual narrators such as Quinto, Amerigo, and Kublai Khan simply melt together into one persona" in "a common mentality" as Calvino's "storyteller" (pp. 194–95). I cannot agree, since I see various exploitations of the possibility of a narrator. In general, I agree with Markey's reading of the book as claustrophobic, devious, and fascinating.

Two literary artists, John Updike and the late John Gardner, have also written about Calvino. Writing in *The New Yorker* ("Card Tricks," 18 April 1977, pp. 149–56), Updike says that Calvino's books "can no longer be called novels; they are displays of mental elegance, bound illuminations" (p. 149). The "tale-teller's prestidigitation," he finds, however, has "an empty center" (p. 149); he feels that the "magician has been bewitched" (p. 154). John Gardner is similarly respectful: "Although not yet as well known as he deserves to be, Italo Calvino is one of the world's best living fabulists, a writer in a class with Kobo Abe, Jorge Luis Borges and Gabriel García Márquez" (p. 15, *New York Times Book Review*, 10 April 1977, pp. 15, cols. a,b,c; 29, cols, a,b,c). Of *The Castle* Gardner says, "Like a true work of art, Calvino's *The Castle of Crossed Destinies* takes great risks—artificiality, eclecticism, self-absorption, ponderousness, triviality (what, yet another interpretation of the world's great myths?)—and, despite its risks, wins hands down" (p. 29).

The book continues to elicit commentary. Claudia J. Jannone undertakes the problem of meaning in the self-referentiality of *The Castle* in her "Plato's Fourth Bed: Italo Calvino," *New Orleans Review* 9.1 (Spring-Summer 1982): 37–40. Larry McCaffery, in seeing Calvino as a renewer for modern fiction (along with Coover and Borges), concludes that meaning is almost entirely contextual, so that new fictional patterns bring new ideas, new truths; see his "Form, Formula, and Fantasy: Generative Structures in Contemporary Fiction" in *Bridges to Fantasy*, ed. George E. Slusser, Eric S. Rabkin, and Robert Scholes (Carbondale: Southern Illinois Univ. Press, 1982), pp. 21–37.

Constance Markey has recently written two articles on the matter of choice in *The Castle*. In one, she writes on the satiric heroic quest, suggesting that there really is no choice, and the characters are crushed in a mournful existential chaos; see "The Hero's Quest in Calvino," *Quaderni d'Italianistica* 4.2 (1983): 154–66. In another article, Markey finds thematic roots for this conclusion in *The Baron;* see "Calvino and the Existential Dilemma: The Paradox of Choice," *Italica* 60.1 (Spring 1983): 55–70.

9. Marilyn Schneider proposes another set of terms for the oppositions in a second article by her treating, in part, *The Castle:*

> In *Il castello* Calvino expresses the male-female or arid-fertile binary posited throughout his fiction in terms of discontinuity-continuity. Like the others, this binary is an approach to the category of maleness-femaleness. The terms are not of *equality*

but of hierarchy. The (male) Simon and Garfunkel voice intones the lyric, "I'd rather be a forest than a street, yes I would, if I could." Female space is continuous ("mescolanza" on the forest floor; process) and is ruled by Cybele, while male space is discontinuous ("metallico," inorganic) and is ruled by Death, "il Principe della Discontinuità" (p. 44). (P. 117)

I do not know if I can buy this extreme version; there is a polarity, to be sure, and an abstract spirit, but I am not sure that it is only the male voice that is abstract, discontinuous, death itself. Faust, in particular, seems to have sympathy for both order and flux, both sterility and multiplicity. Schneider's article is of great interest in tracing sexual themes from *The Path* to *The Castle;* see her "Calvino's Erotic Metaphor and the Hermaphroditic Solution," *Stanford Italian Review* 2.1 (1981): 93–118.

Chapter 11

1. Italo Calvino, *Le città invisibili* (Torino: Einaudi, 1972), sensitively translated by William Weaver as *Invisible Cities* (New York: Harcourt Brace Jovanovich, 1974). As handsome as the typography of the Einaudi is, the HBJ volume goes another step beyond. The silver-paper dustjacket bears a magical photograph by Ryszard Horowitz; the text for each city has much more space between lines (roughly like double spacing, as opposed to the Italian single spacing), which is more appropriate to speculative, meditative reading. As Guido Almansi puts it, it is "a book to meditate more than to read" ("un libro da meditare piú che da leggere") in his "Le città illegibili," *Bimestre* 5.3–4 (1973): 28–31.

2. Various students of Calvino have come up with differing charts, all based around the groups of five. I do mine vertically, but Heinz Riedt does his horizontally in his "Ein fiktiver Marco Polo: Uber Italo Calvino," *Akzente* 24 (1977): 61–64. Aurore Frasson-Marin also does hers horizontally, but she proceeds further to propose a quite ingenious model, a spherical one, with spiral around an axis of an implied zero, which represents the conversations of Marco Polo and Kublai Khan. The groups of ones, twos, threes, fours, and fives line up parallel to this axis of zero. I think she goes too far, however, in asserting that there is a specific witness or commentary upon modern life. See her "Structures, signes et images dans *Les villes invisibles* d'Italo Calvino," *Revue des Etudes Italiennes* 22 (1977): 23–48. According to *Dissertation Abstracts International,* Ellen Joann Esrock demonstrates that a visual imagination as a reader response is crucial to *Invisible Cities* (as well as to specific works by Hawkes and Cortazar): "Reading and Visual Imagination," *DAI* 45 (1984): 1744A (New York University).

    Gian-Paolo Biasin draws on the concept of sphericity to discuss Calvino's spatial qualities, but with different assumptions, namely concepts from Jurij Lotman's *The Structure of the Poetic Text,* which he finds congruent with concepts of Gilbert Durand's *Les Structures anthropologiques.* While mentioning *The Castle of Crossed Destinies* and *Invisible Cities,* Biasin focuses on *Cosmicomics* and *t zero.* Biasin is particularly helpful with intellectual aspects of Calvino's writing (exploration of thought, in my terms), but his approach does not bring out much of the emotional or affective side of Calvino (manipulation of feelings: humor, surprise, melancholy). See his "4/3πr^3: Scientific vs. Literary Space," *Versus* 19–20 (gennaio-agosto 1978): 173–88.

    While semiotics and structuralist concepts have most certainly provided Calvino with points of departure for *Invisible Cities* and *The Castle,* and while those critical approaches may certainly yield insights in those books, I believe that those approaches are not the only, nor even the most suggestive way to explore the two books, which are richer than those theories and will outlive them. See Walter Pedullà's "Calvino alla corte di Lacan," *Il Caffè* 5–6 (1972): 77–85. Pedullà sees Calvino, projected as Polo and the Khan, as an adept of Claude Lévi-Strauss, Jacques Derrida, Michel Foucault, and Jacques Lacan.

Flavia Ravazolli's "Alla ricerca del lettore perduto in *Le città invisibili* di Italo Calvino," *Strumenti Critici* 12 (1978): 99–117, is a highly technical look at the stylistic-thematic dimension, macrostructures, semantic coherences, textualization, and "a web which is *metalinguistic* or generally metasemiotic" ("una trama *metalinguistica* o genericamente metasemiotica," p. 112). I must say that I find her work to be an overlay on Calvino's, possibly interesting to linguistic theorists and structural critics, but not particularly illuminating of his work. His work is complex enough to serve as a pole for her approach, but her approach does not bring about (for me) a discovery of the lost reader suggested by her title. I much prefer Angel Rama's use of structuralist terms in his "Italo Calvino: La semiologia del relato," in *Plural* 23 (1973): 8–12.

While I think that Francesca Bernardini Napoletano overstates the thematic control and the logical meanings of structure in *Invisible Cities*, I find suggestive her discussion of Calvino's unity of the Saussurean dichotomy of signifier and signified, or word and object, through the ironic level of deception and lie. Here we have another link with George Steiner's sense of lie, hypothesis, and fiction. Bernardini Napoletano finds metaphor fundamental to *Invisible Cities,* but she insists that Calvino is nonetheless faithful to his early commitment to literature as morally useful (p. 201). I agree on the question of metaphor but see *Invisible Cities* as detached from any literary duty. See her *I segni nuovi di Italo Calvino: Da "Le cosmiche" a "Le città invisibili"* (Roma: Bulzone Editore, 1977).

Philosophical and thematic approaches have also found fertile ground in *Invisible Cities.* M. Baker finds the coherence of the book on different lines: "The unity of the book offers at least four general levels of reality: physical, historical, symbol and literary. These all proceed from the same material which is organized or re-viewed to suggest through its layered allusions the amorphous, inconclusive, uniform, protean nature of all that is." "Some Notes on Calvino's *Città Invisibili*," *Proceedings and Papers, 16th Congress, Australian Universities, Language and Literature Association* (August 1974): 252–64, p. 256. For a more strictly philosophical approach (subject, object, existence), see Sandro Briosi, "La differenza, l'identità, l'inizio (saggio sull'ultimo Calvino)," in *Il Lettore di Provincia* 25–26 (1976): 19–27. In searching for a particular continuity of the use of the city in many of Calvino's works (although not, oddly enough, "The Watcher"), Martin Paul Sommer emphasizes thematic uses in *Invisible Cities,* touching on the concept of game as well. See *Die Stadt bei Italo Calvino: Versuch einer thematischen Interpretation* (Zürich: Juris, 1979), chapter 7. In her "Calvino's Invisible City," *Perspectives on Contemporary Literature* 3.1 (1977): 38–49, Angela M. Jeannet takes a slightly different tack, finding the city in dialectic with the country so that nature, as a concept, is a construction of city dwellers.

An interesting tribute to Calvino's imagination is the inclusion of 20 of his cities in *The Dictionary of Imaginary Places,* ed. Alberto Manguel and Gianni Guadalupi (New York: Macmillan Publishing Co., Inc., 1980). This rather extraordinary volume of over 400 pages has all sorts of strange entries, from writers such as François Rabelais, J. R. R. Tolkien, L. Frank Baum, Homer, Ursula LeGuin, Jules Verne, H. G. Wells, Arthur Conan Doyle, and so on. Of Calvino's 55 cities, here are the ones deemed by those editors as worthy of inclusion (*most* imaginary?): Aglaura, Anastasia, Argia, Baucis, Beersheba, Despina, Ersilia, Eudoxia, Eusapia, Isaura, Leonia, Moriana, Octavia, Perinthia, Phyllis, Thekla, Theodora, Valdrada, Zemrude, and Zenobia. For each there is generally a two- or three-paragraph entry, with the exception of Beersheba, Eudoxia, Eusapia, and Leonia, which rate entries almost as long as the original prose poems!

3. *Sewanee Review* 8 (1945): 221–40, 433–56, 636–53.

4. *Journal of Aesthetics and Art Criticism* 16 (1957): 112–23.

5. Gaston Bachelard, *The Right to Dream,* trans. J. A. Underwood (New York: Grossman, 1971), pp. 171–75.

6. In my citations I will give the name of the city, its group and number, then the English and, next, the Italian page numbers; for example, Despina (Cities and desire, 5; pp. 17–18; pp. 25–26), for the initial reference. Since the prose sections are so short, I will not give page numbers thereafter, as long as the city is clearly identified. If I am citing text independent of cities, I will give the English, then Italian page numbers, as usual.

Chapter 12

1. Italo Calvino, *If on a winter's night a traveller*, trans. William Weaver (New York: Harcourt Brace Jovanovich, 1983); originally, *Se una notte d'inverno un viaggiatore* (Torino: Einaudi, 1979). The novel was immediately popular in Italy, with more than 80,000 copies sold in the first month of publication, according to Russell Davies's review, "The Writer versus the Reader," *Times Literary Supplement*, 10 July 1981, pp. 773–74.

    In one of the earliest pieces of criticism, Cesare Segre cogently describes the numerous literary techniques Calvino works with as if they were games that Calvino enjoyed manipulating. See his "Se una notte d'inverno uno scrittore sognasse un aleph di dieci colori," *Strumenti Critici* 39–40 (1979): 177–214. Vittorio Stella feels none of this enjoyment but, rather, a certain coldness, even cruelty in the book in his article "Concezioni e poetica del più recente Calvino," *Veltro* 24 (1980): 119–21. (My emphasis is not on Calvino's aim, but on the structures of the book and possible reader reactions.) Stella finds a complexity in the moods of the book, nonetheless, that I see too. Robert Perroud also disagrees with Segre's cheerful reading, finding the humor ambiguous as well as complex; Perroud sees Lotaria as a satiric figure to be rejected and even a possible set of parodies in the novel fragments as parodies of Calvino's own books (a claim that I doubt); see "*Se una notte d'inverno un viaggiatore* d'Italo Calvino: Combinatoire et confession," *Revue des Etudes Italiennes* 27.2–3 (1982): 237–50. In two later articles we find the kind of polarity in critics' comments that Calvino's work seems to set off. On the one hand, Claudio Varese sees a continuity of Calvino's work reaching between *The Path to the Nest of Spiders* and *If on a winter's night a traveller*. On the other hand, Linda C. Badley finds that Calvino, in going through a series of stages in his career, has become a postmodernist who uses Roland Barthes's ideas as a conceptual base in *If on a winter's night*, but finally abandons, transcends, or corrects (in her word) Barthes by connecting readers and text through a dialectic of desire. I think both are correct, given their assumptions, and agree especially with Badley. See Varese, "Italo Calvino: Una complessa continuità," *Rassegna della Letteratura Italiana* 84.1–2 (1984): 252–56; and Badley, "Calvino *engagé*: Reading as Resistance in *If on a winter's night a traveller*," *Perspectives on Contemporary Literature* 10 (1984): 102–11. Miriam E. Friedman's dissertation on Calvino sees *If on a winter's night* as continuous with techniques and themes in Calvino's earlier work: "Love and Narrative Unity in Calvino," *DAI* 44 (1983): 3706A (Indiana University).

2. Cesare Garboli suggests that the novel is not so much about reading as about writing, and that Ludmilla is really a novelist, an aspect of Calvino. Garboli salutes this more feminine side of Calvino's art, preferring it to the somehow embittered masculine puzzling of, say, *The Castle*, in which he finds a sort of desperation. *If on a winter's night* seems more playful, festive. I like Garboli's comments on the festivity, but do not see Ludmilla as a novelist—an *anima* figure, surely, but still a reader, not a writer. Perhaps she relates to the reader *within* an author, the receptive critic who affirms the artistic transaction heartily enough to keep the artist going even when the odds seem unsurmountable. There is a sort of Beatrice quality about her. (Garboli closes with the observation that Calvino's aesthetic in the last book is reminiscent of Federico Fellini's movies *8½* and *Casanova;* someone should explore at length the parallels between these two visionary yet meticulous artists.) See Cesare Garboli, "Come sei, lettrice?" *Paragone*, 366 (1980), 63–71.

3. Reviewers have frequently seen the novel fragments (or "incipits" or "beginnings") as satirical. Calvino, however, denied that parody is actually the mode of writing. (See the interview with Alfredo Giuliani, "E il lettore grido: Fuori l'autore!" in *La Republica,* 6 febbraio 1979, p. 3, cols. 4–8.)

4. John Leonard, in his *New York Times* review (5 May 1981, Sec. C, p. 11, cols. a,b) observes that "Modernism, for Mr. Calvino, is too precious for its own good; it lacks a genital organ." Thus, Leonard sees it, "Literature, for Ludmilla, is sex."

   In discussing works previous to *If on a winter's night,* Marilyn Schneider accurately observes that:

   > Nothwithstanding its erotic element, Calvino's fiction is relatively inattentive to romantic love. Where he introduces a love element, it functions ultimately to elaborate a quest for wholeness rather than to develop a love story. The erotic relationships illustrate the tensions of desire as an internal psychic force and as a way of perceiving reality. They also allegorize the writer's relationship to his writing. In short, the sexual factor is broadly metaphoric and mythic.

   See her "Calvino's Erotic Metaphor and the Hermaphroditic Solution," *Stanford Italian Review,* 2.1 (1981), 93–118, p. 94. Thus we may argue Calvino develops a new use of romantic material and a decidedly nonhermaphroditic solution in *If on a winter's night.*

Chapter 13

1. *Mr. Palomar,* trans. William Weaver (San Diego: Harcourt Brace Jovanovich, 1985). *Palomar* (Torino: Einaudi, 1983). In discussing the stories, which are quite short, I will give the story name in English and Italian; for references scattered throughout the book, I will give page numbers, in the same order of languages.

2. I am indebted to Professor Pedro N. Trakas, Eckerd College, for help with Spanish meanings.

3. I have much admiration for Vidal's tribute "Remembering Italo Calvino," *New York Review of Books* 32.18 (21 November 1985), 3–10 (not to mention Vidal's important 1974 piece in the same pages), but I think it is a critical blind alley to make Palomar and Calvino into the same person. Likewise, Franco Ricci speaks of the "speculations of Calvino-Palomar" in his "*Palomar* by Italo Calvino: The (un)Covering of (un)Equivocal (un)Truth," *Quaderni d'Italianistica* 5.2 (1984): 236–46. I suppose that Palomar is a projection of some of Calvino's ideas, but this is a trivial point; it is too limiting of the novel (and Calvino's artistry) to equate the two figures, and the uses of irony against Palomar help separate him from any sort of implied author (in Booth's phrase) of the book. Thus I think JoAnn Cannon is correct when she clearly discriminates Palomar, the thinker who fails with thought, from Calvino, the artist who deploys Palomar: "Palomar represents not Calvino, but consciousness itself, swimming in a continuum of indeterminacy and uncertainty" (p. 198) in "Calvino's Latest Challenge to the Labyrinth," *Italica* 62.3 (Autumn 1985), 189–200.

Chapter 14

1. John Gatt-Rutter, "Calvino Ludens: Literary Play and its Political Implications," *Journal of European Studies* 5 (1975): 319–40. For another defense of fantasy as a resource to deal with the world see Richard Andrews's essay "Italo Calvino," in *Writers and Society in Contemporary Italy,* ed. Michael Caesar and Peter Hainsworth (New York: St. Martin's Press, 1984), pp. 259–81.

2. Teresa de Lauretis, "Narrative Discourse in Calvino: Praxis or Poesis?" *PMLA* 90.3 (1975): 414–25.

3. Italo Calvino, "The Written and the Unwritten Word," *New York Review of Books* 30 (12 May 1983): 38–39.

4. Olga Ragusa, "Italo Calvino: The Repeated Conquest of Contemporaneity," *World Literature Today* 57.2 (Spring 1983): 195–201.

5. Gore Vidal, "Remembering Italo Calvino," *New York Review of Books* 32.18 (21 November 1985): 3–10.

Bibliography

Works by Italo Calvino

This is a full listing of Calvino's major artistic works and a partial listing of his other works as essayist, editor, and translator; I give the Italian edition and, when available, the American translation (some British translations have still other titles). Through 1985, almost all of his work came out originally with Einaudi, but some of his work was then beginning to appear with Garzanti, which may have some of the future editions.

Creative Works

Il sentiero dei nidi di ragno. Torino: Einaudi, 1947. The 1964 edition (Einaudi) has a preface by Calvino. The English version is *The Path to the Nest of Spiders,* trans. Archibald Colquhoun. Boston: Beacon, 1957. Calvino's 1964 preface, translated by William Weaver, is in the Ecco Press edition (New York: 1976).

Ultimo viene il corvo. Torino: Einaudi, 1949. A collection of short stories; these, with "The Argentine Ant," are in *Adam, One Afternoon, and Other Stories,* trans. Archibald Colquhoun and Peggy Wright. London: Collins, 1957. Most of these stories are in *I racconti* (1958—see below).

Il visconte dimezzato. Torino: Einaudi, 1952. The English translation, by Archibald Colquhoun, is bound with the last of the trilogy in *The Nonexistent Knight and The Cloven Viscount.* New York: Random House, 1962. Also, New York: Appleton-Century-Crofts, 1968.

La formica argentina. Botteghe oscure, 10, 1952. This story is reprinted in *I racconti.* The English version, "The Argentine Ant," trans. by William Weaver, is in *The Watcher and Other Stories.* New York: Harcourt Brace Jovanovich, 1971. Also bound with *La nuvola di smog* (Torino: Einaudi, 1965).

L'entrata in guerra. Torino: Einaudi, 1954. These stories are also in *I racconti* (1958).

Fiabe italiane. Torino: Einaudi, 1956. There are two English versions: *Italian Fables,* trans. Louis Brigante. New York: Collier, 1961, and *Italian Folktales,* trans. George Martin. New York: Harcourt Brace Jovanovich, 1980. Also New York: Pantheon, 1980.

La Panchina: Opera in un atto di Italo Calvino; Musica di Sergio Liberovici. Torino: Tipografia Toso, n.d. (Probably 1956.).

Il barone rampante. Torino: Einaudi, 1957. There have been two school editions (Einaudi, 1959, 1965). The latter has a preface by Calvino. The English translation, by Archibald Colquhoun, is *The Baron in the Trees.* New York: Random House, 1959. There is also an Italian edition with English notes by J. R. Woodhouse, Manchester: Manchester Univ. Press, 1984.

Le speculazione edilizia. Torino: Einaudi, 1957. This story is also in *I racconti.*

I giovani del Po. Bologna: *Officina,* 9–12, 1957–58. This long story has not been translated into English to my knowledge.

I racconti. Torino: Einaudi, 1958. Some of these stories are translated in *Adam, One Afternoon, and Other Stories,* trans. Archibald Colquhoun and Peggy Wright. London: Collins. 1957.

Il cavaliere inesistente. Torino: Einaudi, 1959. The English version is by Archibald Colquhoun, published with the first tale of the trilogy as *The Nonexistent Knight and The Cloven Viscount.* New York: Random House, 1962.

I nostri antenati. Torino: Einaudi, 1960. This is the collected trilogy of *Il visconte dimezzato, Il barone rampante, Il cavaliere inesistente;* there is not an English version of the trilogy in one volume, but if there were, it should be translated as "Our Forefathers." The 1960 edition has a preface (later deleted) by Calvino.

La strada di San Giovanni, first published in *Questo e altro,* I (Milano, 1962). Republished in *I maestri del racconto italiano,* ed. E. Pagliarani and W. Pedullà. Milano: Rizzoli, 1963. This has not been translated into English to my knowledge.

La giornata d'uno scrutatore. Torino: Einaudi, 1963. The English version is in *The Watcher and Other Stories,* trans. William Weaver. New York: Harcourt Brace Jovanovich, 1971. The other stories are "The Argentine Ant" and "Smog."

Marcovaldo ovvero Le stagioni in città. Torino: Einaudi, 1965. This is a series of children's tales about the misadventures of Marcovaldo, an urban sad-sack. There are editions for Italian schools. The English version is *Marcovaldo,* trans. William Weaver. San Diego: Harcourt Brace Jovanovich, 1983.

La nuvola di smog e La formica argentina. Torino: Einaudi, 1965. Also included in *I racconti,* listed above. For the English translations, see the entry for *La giornata* above.

Le cosmicomiche. Torino: Einaudi, 1965. The English version is *Cosmicomics,* trans. William Weaver. New York: Harcourt Brace, 1968. An earlier Italian version was published in *Il Caffè* 12.4 (1964).

Ti con zero. Torino: Einaudi, 1967. The English version is *t zero,* trans. William Weaver. New York: Harcourt Brace, 1969.

"Il castello dei destini incrociati" in *I tarocchi: Il mazzo visconteo di Bergamo e New York.* Parma: Franco Maria Ricci, 1969. This is the coffee-table version, with fancy paper, photographed cards, silk binding, and box; Ricci also did an English version, *Tarots,* in 1976. Einaudi has a standard version, *Il castello dei destini incrociati* (1973), which has been faithfully copied as *The Castle of Crossed Destinies,* trans. William Weaver (New York: Harcourt Brace Jovanovich, 1977); both include *The Tavern of Crossed Destinies* and Calvino's "Nota" or "Note."

Gli amori difficili. Torino: Einaudi, 1970. This volume includes the nine stories of "Gli amori difficili" in *I racconti,* adding five others, one of which is "Il guidatore notturno" from *Ti con zero,* under a different title. Included also are "La formica argentina" and "La nuvola di smog." The "Nota introduttiva" is especially informative about Calvino's biography.

Le città invisibili. Torino: Einaudi, 1972. *Invisible Cities,* trans. William Weaver. New York: Harcourt Brace Jovanovich, 1974.

L'uccel belverde e altre fiabe italiane. Torino: Einaudi, 1972. This entry and the next are tales (illustrated) selected from the 1956 collection.

Il principe granchio e altre fiabe italiane. Torino: Einaudi, 1974.

Il gigante orripilante. Milano: Emme, 1975.

Se una notte d'inverno un viaggiatore. Torino: Einaudi, 1979. *If on a winter's night a traveller,* trans. William Weaver. New York: Harcourt Brace Jovanovich, 1983.

Palomar. Torino: Einaudi, 1983. *Mr. Palomar,* trans. William Weaver. San Diego: Harcourt Brace Jovanovich, 1985.

Prima che tu dica "Pronto." With *Before You Say "Hello,"* trans. William Weaver. (Verona and Cottondale, Ala.: Plain Wrapper Press, 1985).

Sotto il sole giaguaro. Milano: Garzanti, 1986. This posthumous volume contains three stories, "Il nome, il naso" (see below), the title story, "Sotto il sole giaguaro," and "Un re in ascolto" (see next entry).

Un re in ascolto. (I saw a notice at La Scala for the premier of this opera, libretto by Calvino, in May of 1986.)

There are also some short stories, for example the Palomar stories which appeared in two newspapers, *Corriere della Sera* and *La Repubblica* before they were collected as the volume *Palomar,* and some otherwise uncollected stories that have appeared in *Antaeus* (and perhaps other places) over the last decade:

"The Name, The Nose," trans. William Weaver, 20 (1976): 7ff.

"Glaciation," trans. William Weaver, 27 (1977): 46ff.

"Preface Story," trans. William Weaver, 32 (1979): 66ff.

"Dr. Spitzner's Waxworks," trans. William Weaver, 40–41 (1981): 526ff.

"Autobiography of a Spectator," trans. William Weaver, 45/46 (1982): 25ff.

"The Garden of the Stubborn Cats," trans. William Weaver, 51 (1983): 73ff. Also in *Marcovaldo.*

"The Birds of Paolo Uccelo," trans. Patrick Creagh, 54 (1985): 22ff.

"Man, the Sky, and the Elephant; Pliny's Natural History," forthcoming in Vol. 57.

Other Works by Italo Calvino

I list some of the most important essays, some of the editions, and some of the translations; my purpose is to show something of the considerable range of Calvino's interests. Some 42 of his essays appeared in the 1980 collection, *Una pietra sopra* (cited below); the single entries in that collection are marked "In *Ups.*" Fuller listings are in Bernardini Napoletano, Calligaris, Falaschi, and Markey, cited in the next section, "Works about Calvino."

"Ingegneri e demolitori." *Rinascita* II (novembre 1948), 400ff.

"Saremo come Omero!" *Rinascita* 12 (dicembre 1948): 448ff.

"Letteratura, città aperta?" *Rinascita* 14 (febbraio 1949): 168ff.

"Il realismo italiano nel cinema e nella narrativa." *Cinema Nuovo* 10 (1953): 292.

"Gli anni difficili dei romanzi coi film." *Cinema Nuovo* 43 (1954): 188–190.

"Hemingway e noi." *Il Contemporaneo,* 13 novembre 1954.

"Il midollo del leone." *Paragone* 66 (giungo 1955): 17–31. In *Ups.*

"Introduzione." In *Fiabe italiane,* 2 vols. (Torino: Einaudi, 1956), pp. xiii–xlii. The best English version is in *Italian Folktales,* trans. George Martin (New York: Harcourt Brace Jovanovich, 1980), pp. xv–xxxii (the Collier version is drastically cut).

"Domande sul romanzo." *Nuovi Argomenti* 38–39 (1959): 6–12.

"Il mare dell'oggettività." *Il Menabò* 2 (1960): 9–14. In *Ups.*

"Main Currents in Italian Fiction Today." *Italian Quarterly* 4.13–14 (Spring-Summer 1960): 3–14.

"L'erotismo in letteratura." *Nuovi Argomenti* 51–52 (1961): 21–24.

"La sfida al labirinto." *Il Menabò* 5 (1962): 85–99. In *Ups.*

"L'antitesi operaia." *Il Menabò* 7 (1964): 49–51. In *Ups.*

"L'italiano, una lingua tra le altre lingue." *Il Contemporaneo,* 30 gennaio 1965. In *Ups.*

"Cibernetica e fantasmi." *Le Conferenze dell'Associazione Culturale Italiana,* fascicolo xxi (1967–68): 9–23, and in other places and formats, see the *Ups* entry.

"Una cosa si può dirla in almeno due modi." *Il Caffè* I (1967): 57–58.

"Philosophy and Literature." *Times Literary Supplement,* 28 September 1967. In Italian in *Ups.*

I fiori blu, by Raymond Queneau. Trans. Italo Calvino. Torino: Einaudi, 1967.

La memoria del mondo e altre storie cosmicomiche. Torino: Einaudi, 1968. Contains many of the *Cosmicomics* tales and eight other stories (listed in ch. 8, n. 1).

"La letteratura come proiezione del desiderio" (review of an Italian translation of Northrop Frye's *Anatomy of Criticism*). *Libri Nuovi* 5 (agosto 1969): 5. In *Ups.*

Orlando furioso di Ludovico Ariosto, raccontato da I. Calvino. Torino: Einaudi, 1970.

"Lo squardo dell'archeologo," in *Ups* (not previously published, but dated 1972).

Eremita a Parigi. Lugano: Pantarei, 1974.

"Gli dèi della città" *Nuovasocietà* 67 (15 novembre 1975). In *Ups.*

"Il sigaro di Groucho." *Corriere della Sera,* 28 agosto 1977. In *Ups.*

"The Pen in the First Person (For the Drawings of Saul Steinberg)," introduction to *Saul Steinberg: Still Life and Architecture,* trans. William Weaver (New York: Pace Gallery, 1982), unpaged. Calvino's essay originally appeared in *Derrière le miroir* 224 (Paris: Maeght Editeur, 1977).

"I livelli della realtà in letteratura." Lecture from a 1978 conference in Florence, in *Ups.*

Una pietra sopra: Discorsi di letteratura e società. Gli Struzzi, 219. Torino: Einaudi, 1980. The forthcoming *The Uses of Literature* (San Diego: Harcourt Brace Jovanovich, 1986) is probably this same collection.

Racconti fantastici dell'ottocento. Ed. Italo Calvino, with an introduction. 2 vols. Milano: Mondadori, 1983.

"The Written and the Unwritten Word," *New York Review of Books* 30 (12 May 1983): 38–39.

"Readers, Writers and Literary Machines," *New York Times Book Review* (7 September 1986), 1, 30–31. A 1967 lecture, trans. Patrick Creagh, adapted from *The Uses of Literature.*

Works about Calvino

This is a selected listing of scholarly comment; I have listed only a few reviews. For fuller treatments, see Calligaris and Falaschi (cited below) for the early years and Bernardini Napoletano (cited below) for the years 1965 through 1976.

Adler, Sara Maria. *Calvino: The Writer as Fablemaker.* Potomac, Md.: José Porrúa Turanzas, 1979.

Almansi, Guido. "Le città illegibili." *Bimestre* 5.3–4 (1973): 28–31.

Andrews, Richard. "Italo Calvino." In Caesar, Michael and Peter Hainsworth, eds., *Writers and Society in Contemporary Italy.* New York: St. Martin's, 1984, pp. 259–81.

Annoni, Carlo. "Italo Calvino: La resistenza tra realtà e favola." *Vita e Pensiero* 51.11 (novembre 1968): 968–75.

Badley, Linda C. "Calvino *engagé:* Reading as Resistance in *If on a winter's night a traveller.*" *Perspectives on Contemporary Literature* 10 (1984): 102–11.

Baker, M. "Some Notes on Calvino's *Città invisibili.*" *Proceedings and Papers, 16th Congress, Australian Universities Language and Literature Association* (August 1974), pp. 252–64.

Baldini, Pier Raimondo. "Calvino: 'Il piú povero degli uomini.'" *Forum Italicum* 10 (1976): 198–202.

Barth, John. "The Replenishment of Literature: Postmodernist Fiction." *The Atlantic,* January 1980: 65–71. Translated as "La Littérature du renouvellement: La Fiction postmoderniste." *Poétique* 12.48 (November 1981): 395–405.

Baudrillard, Jean. "Les Romans d'Italo Calvino." *Les Temps Modernes,* 192 (mai 1962): 1728–34.

Bernardini Napoletano, Francesca. *I segni nuovi di Italo Calvino.* Roma: Bulzoni, 1977.

Biasin, Gian-Paolo. "4/3πr^3: Scientific vs. Literary Space." *Versus* 19–20 (gennaio-agosto 1978): 173–88.

Bonura, Giuseppe. *Invito alla lettura di Italo Calvino.* Milano: U. Mursia, 1972.

Boselli, Mario. "*Ti con zero* o la precarietà del progetto." *Nuova Corrente* 49 (1969): 129–50.

———. "Italo Calvino: L'immaginazione logica." *Nuova Corrente* 78 (1979): 137–50.

Briosi, Sandro. "La differenza, l'identità, l'inizio (saggio sull'ultimo Calvino)." In *Il Lettore di Provincia* 25–26 (1976): 19–27.

Bruscagli, Riccardo. "Autobiografia (perplessa) di Italo Calvino." *Paragone* 366 (1980): 82–87.

Caimmi-Lamoureux, August. "Calvino e Vittorini: 'Modo di rifare la nuova realtà!'" *Canadian Journal of Italian Studies* (1979): 8–13.

Calligaris, Contardo. *Italo Calvino.* Milano: U. Mursia, 1972.

Cannon, JoAnn. "The Image of the City in the Novels of Italo Calvino." *Modern Fiction Studies* 24 (1977): 83–90.

————. "Literature as Combinatory Game: Italo Calvino's *The Castle of Crossed Destinies*." *Critique* 21.1 (1979): 83–91.

————. "Literary Signification: An Analysis of Calvino's Trilogy." *Symposium* 34 (1980): 3–12.

————. *Italo Calvino: Writer and Critic*. Ravenna: Longo, 1981.

————. "Calvino's Latest Challenge to the Labyrinth." *Italica* 62.3 (Autumn 1985): 189–200.

Carlton, Jill Margo. "The Genesis of *Il barone rampante*." *Italica* 61.3 (1984): 195–206.

Carne-Ross, D. S. "Writing between the Lines." *Delos* 3 (1969): 198–207.

Carter, Albert Howard, III. "Calvino's 'Ultimo viene il corvo': Riflery as Realistic AND Fantastic." *Italian Quarterly* 22.84 (Spring 1981): 61–67.

Catalano, Antonella. "Il viaggio, la parola, la morte: Sulle favole *Cosmicomiche* di Italo Calvino." *Il Lettore di Provincia* 15.56 (1984): 85–97.

Cipolla, Gaetano. "Un Calvino manierista." *La Parola del Popolo* 146 (settembre-ottobre 1978): 32–34.

Corti, Maria. "Il gioco dei tarocchi come creazione d'intrecci." *La Battana* 26 (1971) 5–20. Collected, with two other essays on Calvino, in *Il viaggio testuale*. Torino: Einaudi, 1978.

Davies, Russell. "The Writer versus the Reader." *Times Literary Supplement*, 10 July 1981: 773–74.

de Lauretis, Teresa. "Narrative Discourse in Calvino: Praxis or Poiesis?" *PMLA* 90.3 (1975): 414–25.

————. "Calvino e la dialettica dei massimi sistemi." *Italica* 53 (1976): 75–89.

DeMara, Nicholas A. "Pathway to Calvino: Fantasy and Reality in 'Il sentiero dei nidi di ragno.'" *Italian Quarterly* 14.55 (Winter 1971): 25–49.

di Carlo, Franco. *Come leggere I nostri antenati di Italo Calvino*. (Milano: U. Mursia, 1978).

Dillard, Annie. "Is Art All There Is?" *Harper's*, August 1980: 61–66. Recast as "The Fiction of Possibility" in *Living in Fiction*, chapter 3. New York: Harper & Row, 1982, pp. 49–65.

Esrock, Ellen Joann. "Reading and Visual Imagination." *DAI* 45 (1984): 1744A. New York University.

Eversmann, Susanne. *Poetik und Erzählstruktur in den Romanen Italo Calvinos: Zum Verhältnis von literarischer Theorie und narrativer Praxis*. Romanica Monacensia, 15. München: Fink, 1979.

Falaschi, Giovanni. "Calvino fra realismo e razionalismo." *Belfagor* 26 (1971): 373–91.

————. "Italo Calvino." *Belfagor* 27 (1972): 530–58.

Feingold, Michael. "Doing the Universe Wrong." *The New Republic*, 2 November 1968: 34–36.

Finocchiaro Chimirri, Giovanna. "Realtà e favola in Italo Calvino." *Teorisi* 21 (1966): 296–313.

Fontana, Ernest L. "Metamorphoses of Proteus: Calvino's *Cosmicomics*." *Perspectives on Contemporary Literature* 5 (1979): 147–55.

Frasson-Marin, Aurore. "Structure, signes et images dans *Les villes invisibles* d'Italo Calvino." *Revue des Etudes Italiennes* 22 (1977): 23–48.

Friedman, Miriam E. "Love and Narrative Unity in Calvino." *DAI* 44 (1983): 3706A. Indiana University.

Fusco, Mario. "Il castello di carte di Italo Calvino." *Sigma* 14.1 (1981): 45–55.

Garboli, Cesare. "Come sei, lettrice?" *Paragone* 366 (1980): 63–71.

Gatt-Rutter, John. "Calvino Ludens: Literary Play and its Political Implications." *Journal of European Studies* 5 (1975): 319–40.

Genot, Gérard. "Le Destin des récits entrecroisés." *Critique* 303/4.4 (1972): 788–809.

Giuliani, Alfredo. "E il lettore gridò: Fuori l'autore!" *La Repubblica*, 6 febbraio 1979, p. 3, cols. 4–8.

Grazzini, Giovanni. "Lettura dei 'Racconti' di Calvino." *La Letteratura Moderna* 9 (1959): 621–37.

Grisi, Francesco. "Italo Calvino e le formule matematiche." *Idea* 24.1–2 (1968): 36–37.

Hayman, David and Eric Rabkin. *Form in Fiction: An Introduction to the Analysis of Narrative Prose*. New York: St. Martin's Press, 1974.

Heiney, Donald. "Calvino and Borges: Some Implications of Fantasy." *Mundus Artium* 2 (1968–69): 66–76.

Hume, Kathryn. "Science and Imagination in Calvino's *Cosmicomics.*" *Mosaic* 15.4 (December 1982): 47–58.

————. "Italo Calvino's Cosmic Comedy: Mythography for the Scientific Age." *Papers on Language and Literature* 20.1 (Winter 1984): 80–95.

Illiano, Antonio. "Per una definizione della vena cosmogonica di Calvino: Appunti su *Le cosmicomiche* e *Ti con zero.*" *Italica* 49 (1972): 291–301.

James, Carol P. "Seriality and Narrativity in Calvino's *Le città invisibili.*" *MLN* 97 (1982): 144–61.

Jannone, Claudia J. "Plato's Fourth Bed: Italo Calvino." *New Orleans Review* 9.1 (Spring-Summer 1982): 37–40.

Jeannet, Angela M. "Calvino's Invisible City." *Perspectives on Contemporary Literature* 3.1 (1977): 38–49.

Jonard, Norbert. "Calvino et le siècle des lumières." *Forum Italicum* 18.1 (Spring 1984): 93–116.

Junker, Hedwig. *Die Kongruenz von Inhaltsstruktur und Textstruktur bei Alain Robbe-Grillet und Italo Calvino.* Gottingen: Vandenhoeck und Ruprecht, 1978.

Lavagetto, Mario. "Per l'identità di uno scrittore di apocrifi." *Paragone* 366 (1980): 71–81.

Lucente, Gregory L. "Signs and Science in Italo Calvino's *Cosmicomiche:* 'Fantascienza' as Satire." *Forum Italicum* 17.1 (Spring 1983): 29—40.

McCaffery, Larry. "Form, Formula, and Fantasy: Generative Structures in Contemporary Fiction." In George E. Slusser, Eric S. Rabkin, and Robert Scholes, eds., *Bridges to Fantasy.* Carbondale: Southern Illinois Univ. Press, 1982, pp. 21–37.

McLaughlin, Martin. "Continuity and Innovation in Calvino's *Palomar.*" *Bulletin of the Society for Italian Studies* 17 (1984): 43–49.

Manguel, Alberto and Gianni Guadalupi. *The Dictionary of Imaginary Places.* New York: Macmillan, 1980.

Markey, Constance. "Calvino and the Existential Dilemma: The Paradox of Choice." *Italica* 60.1 (Spring 1983): 55–70.

————. "The Hero's Quest in Calvino." *Quaderni d'Italianistica* 4.2 (1983): 154–66.

————. "The Role of the Narrator in Italo Calvino's Fiction." *DAI* 41 (1980): 2631A. Univ. of Illinois at Urbana-Champaign.

Mazza, Antonia. "Italo Calvino: Uno scrittore dimezzato?" *Letture* 26 (1971): 3–14.

Milanini, Claudio. "Natura e storie nel 'Sentiero' di Italo Calvino." *Belfagor* 40.5 (settembre 1985): 529–46.

Olken, I. T. *With Pleated Eye and Garnet Wing: Symmetries of Italo Calvino.* Ann Arbor: Univ. of Michigan Press, 1984.

Pacifici, Sergio. *A Guide to Contemporary Italian Literature.* Cleveland: World Pub. Co., 1962.

Patuzzi, Claudia. "Italo Calvino: Un intellettuale tra poesia e impegno." *Nuova Antologia* 527 (1976): 140—47.

Pedullà, Walter. "Calvino alla corte di Lacan." *Il Caffè* 5–6 (1972): 77–85.

Perroud, Robert. "*Se una notte d'inverno un viaggiatore* d'Italo Calvino: Combinatoire et confession." *Revue des Etudes Italiennes* 27.2–3 (avril–settembre 1982): 237–50.

Pescio Bottino, Germana. *Calvino.* Firenze: La Nuova Italia, 1967.

Ragusa, Olga. "Italo Calvino: The Repeated Conquest of Contemporaneity." *World Literature Today* 57.2 (1983): 195–201.

Rama, Angel. "Italo Calvino: La semiologia del relato." *Plural* 23 (1973): 8–12.

Ravazzolli, Flavia. "Alla ricerca del lettore perduto in *Le città invisibili* di Italo Calvino." *Strumenti Critici* 12 (1978): 99–117.

Ricci, Franco. "*Palomar* by Italo Calvino: The (un)Covering of (un)Equivocal (un)Truth." *Quaderni d'Italianistica* 5.2 (Autumn 1984): 236–46.

Riedt, Heinz. "Ein fiktiver Marco Polo: Uber Italo Calvino." *Akzente* 24 (1977): 61–64.

Sanguinetti Katz, Giuliana. "Le 'adolescenze difficili' di Italo Calvino." *Quaderni d'Italianistica* 5.2 (Autumn 1984): 247–61.

Schneider, Marilyn. "Calvino at a Crossroads: *Il castello dei destini incrociati.*" *PMLA* 95.1 (January 1980) 73–90.

———. "Calvino's Erotic Metaphor and the Hermaphroditic Solution." *Stanford Italian Review* 2.1 (Spring 1981): 93–118.

Segre, Cesare. "Se una notte d'inverno uno scrittore sognasse un aleph di dieci colori." *Strumenti Critici* 39–40 (ottobre 1979): 177–214.

Sommer, Martin Paul. *Die Stadt bei Italo Calvino: Versuch einer thematischen Interpretation.* Zürich: Juris, 1979.

Stella, Vittorio. "Concezioni e poetica del piú recente Calvino." *Veltro* 24 (1980): 119–21.

Updike, John. "Card Tricks." (Review of *The Castle.*) *The New Yorker,* 18 April 1977: 149–56.

———. "Readers and Writers." (Review of *If on a winter's night.*) *The New Yorker* 57.24 August 1981: 90–93.

Varese, Claudio. "Italo Calvino: Una complessa continuità." *Rassegna della letteratura italiana* 84.1–2 (gennaio-agosto 1984): 252–56.

Vidal, Gore. "Fabulous Calvino." *New York Review of Books* 21.9 (30 May 1974): 13–21.

———. "Remembering Italo Calvino." *New York Review of Books* 32.18 (21 November 1985): 3–10.

Vlasopolos, Anca. "Love and the Two Discourses in *Le cosmicomiche.*" *Stanford Italian Review.* 4.1 (Spring 1984): 123–35.

Woodhouse, J. R. *Italo Calvino: A Reappraisal and an Appreciation of the Trilogy.* Occasional Papers in Modern Literature, No. 5. Hull: Univ. of Hull, 1968).

Interviews

I list only interviews referred to in the text; there are others.

Carter, Albert Howard, III. Unpublished; 21 November 1969.

du Plessix Gray, Francine. "Visiting Italo Calvino." *New York Times Book Review* 86.25 (21 June 1981): 1, 22–23.

Stille, Alexander. "An Interview with Italo Calvino." *Saturday Review,* March–April 1985, pp. 36–39.

General References

Attebery, Brian. *The Fantasy Tradition in American Literature: From Irving to Le Guin.* Bloomington: Indiana Univ. Press, 1980.

Bachelard, Gaston. *The Right to Dream,* trans. J. A. Underwood. New York: Grossman, 1971.

Bailey, J. O. *Pilgrims through Space and Time: Trends and Patterns in Scientific and Utopian Fiction.* London: Argus, 1947.

Bessière, Irene. *Le Récit fantastique: La poétique de l'incertain.* Paris: Librairie Larousse, 1974.

Birkhead, Edith. *The Tale of Terror: A Study of Gothic Romances.* (1921) Rpt. New York: Russell, 1963.

Breton, André. "Manifeste du surréalisme" (1924) in *Manifestes du surréalisme.* Paris: Gallimard, 1967.

Brion, Marcel. *Art fantastique.* Paris: Michel Albin, 1961.

Bronowski, J. *Science and Human Values.* Rev. ed. New York: Harper Torchbook, 1965.

Caillois, Roger. *Au coeur du fantastique.* Paris: Gallimard, 1965.

Capra, Fritjof. *The Turning Point.* New York: Simon and Schuster, 1982.

Carter, Albert Howard. "Continuity and Particularity; or the Pleasures of Recognition and the Pleasures of Discovery." Rpt. from Nobel Symposium 6, *Problems of International Literary Understanding*. Ed. Karl Ragnar Gierow. Stockholm: Almqvist and Wiksell, 1968.

Cassirer, Ernst. *Language and Myth*. Trans. Suzanne Langer. New York: Harper, 1946.

Castex, Pierre-Georges. *Le Conte fantastique en France*. Paris: José Corti, 1951.

Caws, Mary Anne. *The Eye in the Text: Essays on Perception, Mannerist to Modern*. Princeton: Princeton Univ. Press, 1981.

Coleridge, Samuel Taylor. *Biographia Litteraria*. 2 vols. Ed. J. Shawcross. Oxford: Oxford Univ. Press, 1954.

de Solier, Reno. *L'Art fantastique*. Paris: Pauvert, 1961.

Eliade, Mircea. *Myth and Reality*. Trans. Willard R. Trask. New York: Harper & Row, 1963.

Frank, Joseph. "Spatial Form in Modern Literature." *Sewanee Review* 8 (1945): 221–40, 433–56, 636–53.

Frye, Northrop. *Anatomy of Criticism*. Princeton: Princeton Univ. Press, 1957.

Gamow, George. *One Two Three . . . Infinity*. (1947). Rpt. New York: Bantam, 1965.

Hathaway, Baxter. *Marvels and Commonplaces: Renaissance Literary Criticism*. New York: Random House, 1968.

Hayman, David and Eric S. Rabkin. *Form in Fiction: An Introduction to the Analysis of Narrative Prose*. New York: St. Martin's Press, 1974.

Irwin, W. R. *The Game of the Impossible: A Rhetoric of Fantasy*. Urbana: Univ. of Illinois Press, 1976.

Jackson, Rosemary. *Fantasy: The Literature of Subversion*. London: Methuen, 1981.

Kasner, Edward, and James Newman. *Mathematics and the Imagination*. New York: Simon and Schuster, 1940.

Kayser, Wolfgang. *The Grotesque in Art and Literature*. Trans. Ulrich Weisstein. New York: McGraw-Hill, 1966.

Kraus, Edward Henry and Chester Baker Slawson. *Gems and Gem Material*. 5th ed. New York: McGraw-Hill, 1947.

Levin, Harry. *The Gates of Horn*. New York: Oxford Univ. Press, 1966.

Mazzoni, Jacopo. "Discourse in Defense of the Comedy." In *Literary Criticism: Plato to Dryden*. Trans. and ed. Allan H. Gilbert. Detroit: Wayne State Univ. Press, 1962, pp. 358–403.

Moakley, Gertrude. *The Tarot Cards Painted by Bonifacio Bembo for the Visconti-Sforza Family: An Iconographic and Historical Study*. New York: The New York Public Library, 1966.

Montgomery, Robert L., Jr. "Allegory and the Incredible Fable: The Italian View from Dante to Tasso." *PMLA* 81 (1946), pp. 45–55.

Munroe, M. Evans. *The Language of Mathematics*. Ann Arbor: Univ. of Michigan Press, 1963.

Peckham, Morse. *Man's Rage for Chaos: Biology, Behavior and the Arts*. New York: Schocken, 1967.

Penzoldt, Peter. *The Supernatural in Fiction*. New York: Humanities, 1952.

Rabkin, Eric. S. *The Fantastic in Literature*. Princeton: Princeton Univ. Press, 1976.

Sadhu, Mouni. *Tarot: A Contemporary Course of the Quintessence of Hermetic Occultism*. London: George Allen and Unwin, 1962.

Scarborough, Dorothy. *The Supernatural in Modern English Fiction*. New York: G. P. Putnam's Sons, 1917.

Steiner, George. *After Babel: Aspects of Language and Translation*. London: Oxford Univ. Press, 1975.

Sutton, Walter. "The Literary Image and the Reader: A Consideration of the Theory of Spatial Form." *Journal of Aesthetics and Art Criticism* 16 (1957): 112–23.

Todorov, Tzvetan. *Introduction à la littérature fantastique*. Paris: Seuil, 1970.

Vaihinger, Hans. *Philosophy of As If*. Trans. C. K. Ogden. New York: Harcourt Brace, 1924.

Valéry, Paul. *Monsieur Teste*. Paris: Gallimard, 1946.

Varma, Devendra P. *The Gothic Flame*. New York: Russell, 1957.

Weinberg, Bernard. *History of Literary Criticism in the Italian Renaissance*. 2 vols. Chicago: Univ. of Chicago Press, 1961.

Wheelwright, Philip. *Metaphor and Reality*. Bloomington: Indiana Univ. Press, 1962.

———. *The Burning Fountain: A Study in the Language of Symbolism*. Rev. ed. Bloomington: Indiana Univ. Press, 1968.

Whitehead, Alfred North. *Science and the Modern World* (1962). Rpt. Cambridge, England: Cambridge Univ. Press, 1953.

Index